THE ART OF
Indian Cuisine

To
Ha
Day!
Usha
1980

THE ART OF
Indian Cuisine

Everyday Menus, Feasts, and Holiday Banquets

Pranati Sen Gupta

HAWTHORN BOOKS
A Division of Elsevier-Dutton
New York

Acknowledgments

The author is grateful to Mrs. Jenny Capes and Mrs. Nancy McGee for assistance in preparation of the manuscript. The author also wishes to thank her husband, Joy G. Sen Gupta, for preparation of the index and Mrs. Nandita Bhatnagar for her contribution.

THE ART OF INDIAN CUISINE

Library of Congress Catalog Card Number: 80-80301

ISBN: 0-8015-0366-3 (cloth)
ISBN: 0-8015-0367-1 (paper)

1 2 3 4 5 6 7 8 9 10

This book is dedicated to the fond memory of my father,
Mr. Hirendra Nath Gupta.

CONTENTS

Preface

India is a beautiful country. It is separated from Northeast Asia by the Himalayas, one of the longest and highest mountain ranges in the world, which stretch from Kashmir to Burma. India is the seventh largest country in the world, and in population, it is second only to China. Its customs, religions, art, architecture, and philosophy represent one of the oldest and richest civilizations. Fourteen major languages and 250 regional dialects are spoken. English was the official language at the time of independence in 1947; Hindi became the official language on January 26, 1965.

The population of India is roughly 80 percent Hindu and 15 percent Muslim, with Christians, Sikhs, Buddhists, Parsis, and Jews comprising other main religious groups. From one province to the next, languages, food habits, cooking methods, and even the style of wearing the *sari*, the traditional woman's garb, vary widely. These cultural and religious differences as well as the climatic variations greatly influence the cuisine of India. During the greater part of the year the temperature rises to over 115°. Due to limited refrigeration facilities, the people of India discovered that if foods were cooked in certain spices, they would not spoil so easily. Because curries are piquantly hot, their pungency promotes perspiration, one of nature's ways of cooling the body. Curries are also very healthy, because many of the spices and aromatics used in them are rich in vitamins; hot spices, like chili, are very rich in vitamin C. Both onion and garlic are rich in vitamin C, copper, iron, sulfur, manganese, and aluminum. Garlic also is rich in vitamins B and D.

This book is the result of many years spent away from India, during which I did my own cooking and entertaining without the assistance of either cook or servants. In America, this may not seem unusual, but in India the cooking process is very lengthy, mainly because modern facilities (ovens, stoves, refrigerators, blenders) are not available in every kitchen. Therefore, servants and a cook are a common part of the household. Westerners are also more involved in outside interests than Indians and have less time to spend in the kitchen.

I have experimented with the preparation of various Indian dishes in a modern kitchen. Because of this practical experience, each recipe in the book is formulated in such a way as to give the simplest and quickest method of achieving authentic results.

Since most Indian cooking is based on British measurements, an approximate conversion to British measurement is given in brackets following the standard North American measurement.

THE ART OF
Indian Cuisine

Introduction
to Indian Cuisine

Indian cuisine is tastefully unique and incredibly varied. It is a combination of the cooking of many nationalities and cultures. Perhaps the most elaborate dishes come from the North, where they were inherited from the Moghuls, who invaded India from Persia in the sixteenth century. Many Moghlai dishes, such as *pullaos* (pilafs) and *biryanis* (meat and rice creations) are very rich and lavish due to the ingredients used: an abundance of meat, *ghee* (clarified butter), nuts, and saffron. Other Indian specialties include *kabobs* (grilled meats), *qorma* curries in their savory sauces; *tandoori* dishes, including *tandoori* chicken and *naan*, which are cooked in a special clay oven; and *rasgullas* and *pantua*, delicious, Bengali milk-based sweets.

There are vast differences between North and South India, not only in culture, language, or climate but in cuisine. In the North, home-made wheat breads such as *chappatis, parathas,* and *naan* are the staple food. There are elaborate meat dishes, cooked in *ghee* (clarified butter) rather than oil. Hot spiced tea is the favorite drink in the cold North Indian winter, whereas in the South people enjoy freshly roasted, ground coffee with sugar and milk. In southern India rice is the main staple, and it is served throughout the meal. For the most part in the South people are vegetarians, and dishes are hotter than in the North. A large amount of coconut oil and coconut milk is used in cooking. *Idlis* (steamed rice cakes) and *dosas* (pancakes made with ground rice and lentils) with hot coconut chutney or *sambhar* (a lentil preparation) are very popular among the South

Indians. They also prefer steamed food, whereas in the North, *tan-doori food* (barbecued in the Indian-style) is very popular.

In Bengal, in the northeast, which was my home, the diet shows wide variety including rice, wheat, fish, meat, eggs, milk, vegetables, *dal* (lentils), with lots of *ghee* and mustard oil. The staple food is rice, but wheat is also used in the form of breads like *luchis* and *chappatis*.

A typical Bengali meal starts with *shukto* (page 81), a dish made with different vegetables, including a bitter vegetable called *karela*, which stimulates the appetite during hot weather. This is followed by *dal*, then a fish or meat dish eaten with rice or *luchis*. Chutney or relish is the next item, followed by fried *poppadums* (fried lentil crisps) with sweet yogurt, and the meal ends with a Bengali sweet dish, such as *rasgulla* or *pantua*.

PREPARING AND SERVING INDIAN FOODS

In a comfortable Indian home, every meal is an occasion, and Indian women are very popular as gracious hostesses and are known for their warm hospitality. Hospitality in an Indian home is a ceremony with many patterns but one purpose—to give pleasure to others. People invite their friends and relatives to their home either by sending a card or by visiting them personally at least six to eight days before an occasion. It gives them enough time to plan and prepare for the meal. A special knowledge and skill are needed for the correct planning, preparation, and serving of an Indian meal. When you prepare an Indian dish, remember that it should be pleasing to the eye as well as to the palate, and the aroma must be appealing and appetizing. That is why Indians are very particular about the combination of spices and the blending of colors in their meals.

Most elegant Indian meals include a staple rice preparation (*pullao* or *biryani*) or Indian bread (*chappati*, *poori*, or *luchi*) or sometimes both. Dal, two to three varieties of vegetable preparations, a fish curry, and a meat curry. There are often several side dishes such as fried *poppadums*, a kind of lentil bread of wafer thinness, very crisp like potato chips. They can be eaten without the accompaniment of any other food or crumbled and eaten with yogurt or with *dal* and boiled rice.

Several condiments would also be served: various chutnies, some sweet, some very hot; and pickles—mango, chili, lime, and fresh gingerroot are the common varieties. Fresh green chilies, chopped coriander leaves, and lemon slices are always served for individual tastes. Most of the time you will find a little bowl with a tiny spoon containing melted *ghee*, which you can serve over boiled rice, *dal*, or curries. Remember that this is a traditional way to serve Indian food; that does not mean everybody must eat everything. Indians like variety, and this way they have the liberty to select the right foods for themselves.

When serving an Indian meal, start with small portions of each dish. An Indian hostess will offer small portions of a variety of curries rather than large portions of one or two dishes. This means preparing many varieties, which makes it ideal for a buffet supper. Each individual dish extends the servings by making the menu more elaborate. A menu composed of a dozen different dishes is not unusual for a banquet. Even in the poorest home, there would be at least four dishes for company. Choose the dishes you plan to serve and add up the number of small portions each dish provides. The total number of servings should be twice the number of people you plan to cook for.

If you are planning an Indian buffet dinner, decide on the menu well in advance. Make sure that at least some of the food can be prepared beforehand. Preparation of food for a large number of people can be difficult. An advantage of Indian food is that it keeps well and lends itself to reheating. If freezer space is available, the preparation can be started a few days before the dinner, and the finished product can be stored in the refrigerator or freezer until needed. But allow time for defrosting and reheating before serving, and be sure that foods reach the table at the right temperature. Serve hot foods really hot; cold foods, really cold. No matter how simple or elegant the menu is, it is preferable to cook in several moderate-sized batches, rather than in one large quantity.

Indian foods such as breakfast dishes and snacks are usually served to each person on a *rekabi*, a small, beautifully carved brass plate about eight to nine inches in diameter. Lunch, which is the main meal, and dinner are served on a *thali*, a large, round metal dish about fourteen to sixteen inches in diameter. Most families use a brass *thali*, which is polished to reflect light. But it can be made of copper, stainless steel, or even silver. There are several small matching metal bowls, each containing vegetables, *dal*, fish, meat, yogurt, and chutney. Rice or bread and the main course are placed directly on the *thali*. But the small bowls are placed on the table or on the side of the main *thali* so that each individual can choose freely what he wishes to eat. Melted *ghee*, green chilies, pickles, and salt are also set out on the table.

The traditional Indian way to dine is not at a dinner table, but on a beautifully embroidered individual floormat or low wooden seat that is placed on the floor. The polished metal *thali* is placed in front of the mat, and the metal bowls are placed in a half circle on the outside of the *thali*. A matching tumbler for drinking water completes the setting. Though water is the only drink that is served with dinner, the meal can be followed by either tea or coffee. Tea is the common drink in India and is served with sugar and milk. In India alcoholic beverages should never be served with a meal.

In a large gathering, banana leaves are used instead of *thalis* and little earthenware bowls and tumblers are used, which are always thrown away after the feast or banquet. This pottery is not glazed and so is not hygienic for reuse. It is used in India much in the way paper cups and plates are used in the West.

It is hard for some people to believe that the everyday convenience of knife, fork, and spoon are not essential in India and that most people in India eat their food with the fingers of the right hand. Because Indian people prefer to mix the rice and curry and scoop it up with broken pieces of chappati, using fingers is practical and satisfying. But one has to know how to use his fingers—only the fingertips are used, not the whole palm. Children are taught at an early age to eat delicately and properly. In the fifteenth century, man ate with his fingers most of the time, not only in India but around the world.

After meals, Indians often chew *paan*, folded betel leaves stuffed with aromatic spices, calcium powder, and *khoyer*, to freshen their breath. *Paan*-making is considered a specific art. There are special utensils used only for the preparation of *paan*. One large, deep brass or silver bowl holds *paan* leaves moistened with perfumed water. A set of five or six small matching containers—brass or silver, round or heart-shaped with lids—contain a variety of aromatic spices, roasted nuts, silver leaf, and so forth. Sometimes according to their means, this *paan*-set may be hand-carved or hand-painted. A girl will often receive a set as a wedding gift from her parents, among other things. The juice of *paan* gives a reddish glow to the lips, and it is considered an aid to digestion.

INDIAN KITCHENS AND UTENSILS

Indian kitchens are very different from those of the West. At first sight an Indian kitchen might appear a bit primitive to a Westerner; it lacks appliances and flatware or china. But the beautiful brass cookware, canisters, and other kitchen equipment are well suited in India, not only for the average kitchen, but for the rich family who can afford to buy some modern appliances.

Although gas stoves are very popular in India, many people still use the traditional *chula*, the Indian stove made of clay or cement with a round opening, fueled with coal or wood. There is no oven; the stove is like an open fire similar to a charcoal fire. The top of the stove is not flat, but has three humps a few inches apart from each other to hold the *karahi* securely. The *karahi* is a traditional deep, round-bottomed frying pan with handles on either side and is very similar to a Chinese *wok*. The value of the sloping sides of the *karahi* is that the food can easily be tossed and turned. It is not suitable for flat ranges, but it can be used with a metal collar that fits over the burner and on which the *karahi* is held steady. The *tava*, the Indian baking pan, is a heavy iron sheet with a concave shape about ten to twelve inches in diameter. It is very similar to an iron frying pan. Most Indian cooking can be done in a heavy iron frying pan, Dutch oven, or Chinese *wok*.

India has a special kind of clay barbecuing oven called a *tandoor*. It is shaped rather like a large barrel and is usually buried in sand or soil. A charcoal fire on the flat bottom of the *tandoor* distributes the heat up to the top. This oven is used to roast meat and fish and to bake some breads (*tandoori roti, naan*). This roasting method is called *tandoori* and is still used by many in India for whom modern ovens are out of the question. *Tandoori* cooking can, however, be successfully duplicated in a modern oven. The original home of *tandoori* food is Peshawar (now in Pakistan). These people used to eat a lot of meat and wanted some variety; to avoid monotony, they tried roasting food over an open fire instead of preparing curries, and they discovered that this method gives its own special flavor. Spices and yogurt are used for marinating fish or meat; then the fish or meat is roasted until golden brown and crisp. This marinating technique makes the difference between ordinary barbecuing and *tandoori* cooking. Most people abroad like *tandoori* food, not only for the flavor, but also because the preparation is very easy in our modern ovens and grills.

A grinding stone is one of the most important pieces of equipment in every Indian kitchen. It is a flat piece of stone about 12 to 14 inches long, 8 to 10 inches wide, and 3 to 4 inches thick. It comes with a stone roller, like a rolling pin without handles. This is used every day as a grinder, blender, and mixer for the spices that have to be freshly ground, pastes for lentil preparations, and for pounding meat or vegetables. Fresh coconut, essential in many Indian curries, is easy to grate with a very simple instrument (*kuruni*) made of a circular piece of steel edged with sharp teeth pointed at one end and joined to a long piece of wood.

Preserving is still done in the old ways—by pickling, salting, and sun-drying. Due to lack of refrigeration, women in India dehydrate their vegetables when they are available during the winter months. The vegetables have to be chopped and dried completely in the sun. These vegetables are then used during the summer months when very few are available in the market. They also prepare their own pickles with green mangoes, chilies, olives, limes, carrots, gingerroot, and cauliflowers.

FEASTS AND BANQUETS

At present throughout most of India, the modern way of life has changed. Food is no longer abundant, prices are very high; most of the time both parents have to work to keep a family together. So time is more valuable, and there is not as much time for relaxation. The large, casual gathering has practically disappeared; in its place, formal Western-style entertaining, such as buffets, cocktail parties, and tea receptions are becoming increasingly popular in India today. The Western-style kitchen table and chair are taking the place of the hand-painted mat or low wooden seat of the Indian home. But most rich families still celebrate important social occasions such as weddings and religious festivals in the traditional grand manner. Relatives and friends arrive from all corners of India a few days before the actual celebration, and the eating and celebrating go on for days.

Each province has its own way of celebrating a wedding procession, and they are always colorful and magnificent. In some parts of India, men dress in long, red costumes and carry an enormous illuminated chandelier on a long pole. Others carry the wedding gifts. The lights, the sparkling wedding costumes, the music, and a week-long celebration are all parts of the wedding ceremony. A wedding shower takes an important part in that procession. The bride's and the groom's families send each other a traditional gift of clothing, jewelry, fish, fruit, yogurt, sweets, and so on.

A wedding feast is very special in India. From one hundred to one thousand guests, including relatives, friends, and in-laws, attend the elaborate dinner. The actual wedding goes on for three days in the home of the bride and then for two to three days in the home of the groom. There are two elegant feasts—one in the bride's house and another in the groom's. No kitchen or dining room is big enough for this special occasion. So in India people usually rent a huge tent, as big as the house itself. Sometimes it is fixed on the top of the flat roof or sometimes in the backyard. The host rents tables and chairs similar to garden or picnic tables here in North America. Normally from two to four cooks with a few servants are hired for this special occasion. The big difference between family meals and feasts is, of course, the variety and quantity of food. Even in the most humble home, a feast will include at least four basic dishes including *dal*, fried foods, a vegetable curry, and a fish or meat curry. Along with these, chutney and sweets will be served to finish the feast. The interesting thing about these dinners is that one is served many varieties, yet no taste is repeated. This, of course, is what is aimed at in planning the menus. The general idea in planning an Indian meal is to have a variety of dishes, especially when a large number of people are invited. Long, elaborate banquets are delightful, but are usually beyond the scope of any ordinary cook and are impossible for the person who has to be hostess as well as cook. In India a hostess does not eat with her guests. She serves the food or observes the way it is served to her guests. But in large gatherings, volunteers from among the relatives or friends will serve the food. In a big banquet such as this, the different dishes are served one at a time. The order of an elegant Indian banquet usually includes both fish and meat or several kinds of fish and different varieties of vegetables cooked in different ways. People from other nations are likely to think it is pointless cooking such a large number of dishes. But when you consider that sometimes a thousand people are invited for the occasion, it is easier to prepare several dishes in relatively small quantities than a few dishes in a very large amount. With so much variety people can select what they want and not be forced to eat what they don't like. After dinner, *paan*, wrapped in silver leaf and perfumed with essence water, is served as a refreshment.

Women in India prepare *payasam*, *pittha*, *burfi*, *gauja*, and so forth, which do not require any special skill. But there are also special cooks, called *haluikar*, who are hired by either family to make more difficult sweets. These special cooks prepare *rasgullas*, *cham-cham*, *khir kadambo*, *sandesh*, *gilipi*, *pantua*, and the like. The hostess may also do away with the *haluikar* and buy sweetmeats from the corner sweetshop, just as a North American cook bakes her own cakes but buys boxes of chocolates.

Preparations for the banquet begin early. The cook estimates the ingredients required and starts to prepare the sweets two to three days before the wedding. The servants grind the spices, chop the vegetables, and cut the fish or meat for marinating. The main cooking starts early in the morning of the day of the banquet. The dinner is served in the evening.

Though Indians take their main meal at midday, big banquets are always served at night. The second banquet, held at the groom's home, is more or less the same, according to their means. A flute band will be hired by rich parents for two to three days. There is a special kind of music for this particular occasion.

During these times, or any other festival time, the house guests share the labor, because most people do not own refrigerators, and daily shopping for fish, vegetables, meat, and poultry is absolutely necessary. One guest will go to pick up the vegetables, some will turn toward the fish market or butcher shop, and still others will go to a sweet shop, where orders have been placed previously for a variety of sweets and sweet yogurt. It is usually the men who do the shopping, and when they return the women take over. These celebrations are a very happy time for the women. Those who haven't seen each other for a long time exchange news and greetings. They work together, gathering in a large area to chop the vegetables, cut the meat, and slice the fish.

Generally at breakfast the people eat puffed rice, crispy and flattened rice, with grated fresh coconut or coconut balls (made with grated coconut, milk, sugar, etc.). Sometimes Indian breads such as *luchi* or *poori* will be served with some vegetable preparation. In some provinces boiled rice and vegetables will be served with *ghee* as a breakfash dish.

Next, lunch (the main meal of the day) will be served in the early afternoon. In almost every family there are some vegetarians, and because of them vegetarian food will be prepared in a separate kitchen. Though there may be some hired cooks who will cook fish, meat, and other things, the women will cook the *payasam*, the sweet-rice preparation (page 201). In some provinces it is a must for a big occasion—the family will buy their rich pure whole creamy milk from dairy farmers, where the order has been placed weeks ahead of time. The sweet aroma will fill the open air and make one's mouth water.

At about four o'clock people enjoy tea with some snacks such as *singara, nimkis* (salted crisps), and some light sweets. They can be homemade or bought from the corner foodstalls. The last meal, dinner, is always served in the late evening, due to the teatime. But it is light—rice or *chappatis* as a main item will follow a light vegetable and fish or meat curry.

Festivals

India is a land of festivals and holidays. Festivals have always been an integral part of India's customs. There is no set date for a religious festival; it depends on the position of the stars. A visit to India is not complete without seeing a festival celebration. Every region, every religion has something to offer. It may be the holy festivals, harvest festivals, or the Republic Day pageant in New Delhi. The *Durga puja* (the holy festival) generally in October, lasts for four days. Bengal celebrates many holidays, but none as important nor as religious as *Durga puja*. Because of the great love for custom and tradition, it remains an old-fashioned, sentimental occasion. Special songs are sung during these holidays. People try to forget their sorrows and feel happy and cheerful. They enjoy giving presents to each other (mainly new clothes) as Christian people do during Christmas. Married children visit their parents, and there are large family gatherings. People worship gods and goddesses in temporary temples built by individual groups of people in different areas. On the last day, images of the warrior-goddesses are taken out in procession and immersed in a river or in the sea. People enjoy talking about good food, they exchange food, and they prepare some exotic foods. There is no traditional menu for the holy festivals. Each family tries to serve an elegant dinner according to their means. The last and fourth day when the *puja* (prayer) is over, *Dassara* is celebrated with pomp and great festivity. The sight of the sweets being sold during the festivals of *Dassara* and *Diwali* is incredible. Colorful Indian sweets such as *rasgullas, pantua, gilipi, cham-cham, sandesh,* and *burfi* are piled in towers in an open market. Most Indians buy their sweets from professional sweet makers, because they require a lot of time and practice. The anticipation is great and much planning is involved. Nevertheless, the joy of the days can readily be felt. People visit friends and relatives to exchange greetings. It is a tradition for people to welcome guests and serve them different varieties of sweetmeats.

Every region observes the *Dassara* festival in a special way. In northern India, the celebrations have a different flavor. The *Dassara* is a festival lasting about ten days and consists of recitations, music, and plays recalling the memory of Rama, a legendary hero. Amateurs perform plays based on this epic story. In some parts of India, villagers dressed in their colorful costumes parade a number of local deities with pipes and drum music.

The most popular and the brightest of all Indian festivals is *Diwali,* the festival of lights; it is celebrated with great excitement and rejoicing in most parts of India in November. On this night *Lakshmi,* the goddess symbolizing prosperity, is worshipped in most parts of India; *Kali,* the goddess symbolizing strength, is worshipped in Bengal. This prayer is followed by an impressive fireworks display, which the whole family enjoys. In some parts, *Diwali* marks the start of the New Year. The houses, palaces, and government buildings are lighted up by thousands of flickering oil lamps and electric lights. Again, greetings and sweets are exchanged.

Holi is one of the most colorful and especially beautiful of all Hindu festivals. It is celebrated in early spring all over India. The most interesting celebration is the *Lathmar Holi* at Barsanar, twenty-six miles from Mathura, and the most elaborate celebration is held in Mathura between Delhi and Agra. On *Holi* day men, women, and especially children dress in old but clean clothes and go out into the streets carrying colored water and colored powder. They smear each other's clothes and faces by throwing and squirting the colors just for fun. Most people eat different varieties of popular snacks such as *burfi, mott* (a colored figure, two to four inches long, made of sugar candy), *gilipi, samosas,* and fritters during the *Holi* festival.

Onam, the harvest festival (very similar to Thanksgiving in North America) is celebrated with great enthusiasm. It lasts for ten days in the state of Kerala in southern India. This special festival calls for a vegetarian feast with a variety of entertainment. The menu includes *payasam*, a delicious sweet rice preparation, cooked with rich milk, nuts, aromatic spices, and saffron (page 17). Banana is another important part of the menu. Raw green banana, fried crisp and sweetened with palm juice, is very popular. *Chana dal halva* (page 209), a lentil dish, cooked with coconut milk, *ghee*, spices, and sugar, and many other varieties will be included in the menu. Men mark the occasion by showing their strength and skill through different sports and games. Many of the women wear their special *Onam* costumes (elaborate light-colored saris trimmed with gold or silver, usually worn with a red blouse) and decorate their hair with a lot of flowers and garlands. They dance around traditional brass lamps. The most colorful and exciting part of the festival is the snake-boat race.

Paush-parvan is another special and unique festival, which is observed in Bengal around November to December. This festival is a time of feasting and happiness. A variety of savories are prepared out of milk, rice, palm juice, and different kinds of nuts; fresh coconut is a must. The different types of Indian pancakes, including *pittha*, a sweetmeat made from sweet potato (*aloo pittha*), *payasam*, and the lovely aroma of milk preparations fill the air.

In the annual calendar of Indian events, one of the greatest national festivals is Republic Day. On January 26 each year the spectacular celebrations are held in the capital city of New Delhi. A magnificent parade and a president's salute, followed by a colorful folk dance and fireworks, mark the event.

BASIC SPICES AND SEASONINGS

Indians use spices generously in their food preparation. Contrary to popular misconception, that harsh yellow powder associated with anything curried in this country is not authentically Indian. In India curry merely means any dish with a richly spiced sauce that is cooked very carefully to blend all the spices together with the flavor of the fish, meat, or vegetables.

Curry powder is a combination of herbs and spices, mixed together in varying proportions. In India people do not use this curry powder; instead they use separate spices—either whole or ground to a paste—to give an individual flavor to each particular dish. A curry does not have to be cooked with water to make its own gravy; other enrichments include onion, garlic, ginger, tomatoes, coconut, nuts, yogurt, and mustard. According to the ingredients, the curry may be rich or fairly simple.

Supermarkets now carry most of the basic Indian spices—cumin, coriander, caramom, turmeric, and cayenne pepper. Some of the more unfamiliar spices, such as fresh gingerroot, asafetida (*hing*), black cumin seeds, and *garam masala*, may be found in Chinese markets or Oriental specialty shops. In India people grind their spices daily because ground spices tend to lose their flavor more quickly than whole ones. Most of the basic spices are used ground, but a few, such as fennel seed, cumin seed, fenugreek (*methi*), and black cumin seed, are essential as whole spices. They are added whole or broken in half just before cooking.

The delicacy of Indian cuisine depends on the art of spicing. Spices should never taste raw; they must initially be heated in oil or *ghee* to develop their full flavor and allow them to blend together. Spices should never retain their individual flavors in a cooked dish; each dish has its own unique combination of spices. Remember, though, cooking is a creative art. It not only involves collecting authentic, dependable recipes, but improvising those recipes to satisfy personal preferences. So although a particular dish requires certain spices, the *quantity* of those spices—particularly hot pepper—can always be altered to accommodate personal needs and tastes. Substitutes can even be made if necessary.

In India many people are vegetarians. They do not use onion or garlic, which they consider a part of nonvegetarian food. Raw gingerroot is the best way to bring out the real flavor of the vegetarian dishes and is also good for thickening the sauce. Fresh raw gingerroot can be used immediately or frozen for further use. When you need it, thaw partly and grate for your dish. An inch of the root will yield about one tablespoon of minced ginger. Powdered ginger may be substituted, but keep in mind that the taste will not be the same as the fresh.

Green chilies and coriander leaves also can be frozen for wintertime, when they are hard to get in the store. Wash gingerroot, chili, or coriander leaves well before freezing. Dry thoroughly with a paper towel. Wrap a few pieces in plastic wrap; freeze. Do not thaw chilies or coriander leaves but add directly to the hot oil or hot gravy.

Basic Herbs and Spices for Curry

1. *Ajawn seeds* are pleasantly sharp. They are very similar to but a little smaller than caraway seeds.

2. *Asafetida*, or *hing*, is dried olegum resin from the roots of *Ferula foetida*, found in Iran and eastern India. It is extremely pungent.

3. *Black cumin seeds* are called *kalojeera* or *kalonji* in India. They are used mainly as a whole spice and rarely need to be ground. They are used for a light thin type of fish or vegetable curry, pulses (lentils), pickles, etc. They are very close to onion seeds.

4. *Coriander* is one of the oldest known spices. It is an important ingredient of curries. Without ground coriander and ground cumin, vegetable dishes would become dull and tasteless.

5. *Coriander leaves*, also known as Chinese parsley or *cilantro*, are widely used throughout India in many food preparations and are also frequently served as a garnish. A few chopped leaves give a beautiful aroma in any kind of Indian dish. You may buy them from a Chinese grocery, or you can easily grow these leaves in your own backyard or in a window box from the whole dried spice. They should be planted about ½ inch under the soil and kept well watered so that the seeds do not dry out. After a few days, the seeds may show up on the top of the soil. If the seeds are sown during summer months, they sprout within a few weeks. When the tiny plants appear, let them grow for a week; then pick the leaves from the top leaving the root and stem in the earth. This will furnish a constant supply. Spread some new seeds every three weeks to maintain a continuous growth. These delicious leaves are used to add an unusual flavor to many dishes.

6. *Chilies*, or hot peppers, come in many varieties. A popular one in India is the *green chili*; it is very thin and long and very hot in flavor. It is used as a flavoring, as an appetizer, or simply as a garnish. Green chili adds considerable heat to Indian food preparations. The recipes in this book use one or two chilies. If you prefer, use green pepper as a substitute to get the flavor without the hotness. The other type is the *cayenne red pepper*. When green chilies ripen, they become wonderfully red in color just like ripe tomatoes. Then they are dried and preserved either whole, ground, or crushed. The hottest part of hot chilies is the seeds—that is why I suggest you wash them out. Be careful not to touch your face or eyes until you have washed your hands with cold water and soap after handling the chili.

7. *Fenugreek seed (methi)* is really a pulse, but is used as a spice because of its delicate aroma. It has a pleasant, bitter flavor. It is used in chutneys and curries.

8. *Fenugreek leaves* are used like coriander leaves, as flavoring, or they can be cooked like spinach. They are delicious when cooked with potatoes. Also, like coriander leaves, they are easy to grow.

9. *Garam masala* (roasted ground spice mixture) is a combination of six different varieties of spices. It is available in Oriental shops, or can be prepared at home. To make about 1¼ cups, take 5 to 6 pieces of cinnamon stick about 1 inch each, ½ cup whole cardamoms, ¼ cup whole black peppercorns, ¼ cup whole cloves, ¼ cup whole cumin seeds, and ¼ cup whole coriander seeds. Combine all the spices in a baking dish and roast them in a preheated 200° oven for 20 to 30 minutes, stirring frequently. Discard cardamom peels. Grind the spice mixture in a blender at high speed for a minute or two; then stir and blend again until it is completely ground. Stored in a jar with a tight-fitting lid, the ground spice mixture will keep its flavor for up to three months.

10. *Mustard seeds* of the Indian variety are deep purple in color, almost black. They can be used whole or ground and may be made into a paste by adding a little water. Vast quantities of mustard are grown in India, where mustard seed oil is used for cooking, particularly in Bengal. The wonderful flavor of a fish-mustard dish may be known only by tasting. To make *prepared mustard*, take ¼ cup black or white mustard seeds, 2 to 3 green chilies, a pinch of salt, and ½ cup water. Combine them in the jar of an electric blender and blend at high speed for 30 seconds. Turn off the machine, scrape down the sides of the jar with a rubber spatula, and blend again until the mixture is reduced to a thick puree. Or take any powdered mustard and make a paste by the addition of a little water; cover until ready to use. Allow to stand for half an hour before using. The mustard gets hotter the longer it stands.

11. *Punch-phoron* is a mixture of five spices mixed in equal proportions. It is a combination of cumin, black cumin, mustard, fenugreek, and fennel seeds, and never needs to be ground. It is only used for vegetable dishes and chutneys.

12. *Roasted cumin* and *coriander*—Take some cumin or coriander seeds and roast in a frying pan without any fat over medium heat; stir constantly until the color changes and smoke forms, taking care not to burn them. Cool and grind just before using in a recipe. Or use ground

cumin and ground coriander and roast in the same way, but be very careful not to burn them.

13. *Sambhar spice* is a combination of ground spices such as cayenne pepper, mustard, asafetida, turmeric, and fenugreek with salt and mustard oil. It comes from Madras. It is truly a hot spice. Commercial barbecue spice or seasoned salt may be used as a substitute to get the flavor without the hotness.

14. *Turmeric* is an underground root. Ground turmeric is used for coloring curries; its brilliant yellow color gives an appetizing look to a dish. It also preserves food for a certain time.

15. *White cumin* is called *cumin* or *jeera*. During the Middle Ages it was a well known spice for fowl. Cumin seeds are used as a whole spice, but it is essential as a ground spice for basic curry. It has a nice aroma. Roasted cumin adds a delicate flavor to certain dishes.

Besides these common spices that are basic to Indian foods, a few other sweet spices are also used. Most Western people are familiar with these very rich spices.

16. *Cardamom* is the little seed inside the fruit capsules, and it forms a highly aromatic spice. The seeds are widely used in India as a flavoring, particularly in *pullaos* and *biryanis* as well as in curries. Do not take the seeds out of the pod until they are ready for use; that way the seeds will retain their aromatic flavor.

17. *Cinnamon*, the inner bark of the cinnamon tree, seems to have been one of the earliest known spices, and is used either whole, as a stick, or ground.

18. *Cloves* are the unopened flower buds of the clove tree. They are sweet and hot at the same time and are used whole or ground. With too much of this spice, the flavor of the dish would be spoiled.

19. *Fennel seeds* are used whole or ground for curries and are very popular in India as an after-meal spice because they freshen the breath. Arrange fennel seeds, whole cloves, and a few cardamom seeds on a small, attractive plate and serve them in the same manner as after-dinner mints.

20. *Nutmeg* and *mace* both come from an oval, smooth, pale orange-yellow colored fruit from a bushy tree. Nutmeg is the seed, and mace closely wraps the seed like an outgrowth from the base. In India, nutmeg is used in sweets and in some curries. Mace is used in sweet dishes and for *pullao*.

21. *Saffron* is called *jaffron* or *keser* in India. It is the stigmas of the crocus flower, has a pleasant bitter flavor, and is used to flavor

and color a number of *pullaos* and *biryanis*. It grows only in India and Spain. Add a pinch of saffron threads to boiling water that will be used in the preparation of a recipe, and it will give the food a golden color and an Oriental flavor.

Other Ingredients

1. *Almonds* are called *badam* in India. They are used as an ingredient for sweets, *pullao*, and other curry dishes. Ground almonds are used for making rich curries, and in a delightful way they thicken the gravy and bring out the nutlike flavor.

2. *Pistachio nuts* are another important ingredient for *pullao* and sweet dishes. They are used whole, chopped, or crushed.

3. *Coconut* is a very important ingredient in Indian cooking. Coconut milk, freshly chopped coconut, and grated coconut are essential in many Indian preparations. To open a fresh coconut, preheat oven to 375°. Punch a hole in each eye of the coconut, drain off the liquid, and bake the empty coconut in the oven for 15 minutes. While the coconut is still hot, hit it with a hammer. The coconut flesh should come out of the shell.

Grated coconut—Peel the brown skin off the coconut meat. Grate the coconut meat, piece by piece, with a hand grater or in a blender.

Coconut milk—Combine 2 cups of fresh grated coconut with 2 cups milk in a pan. Bring to a boil and remove from heat. Let it steep for 20 minutes, place in a blender, and run on low speed for a few seconds. Strain liquid before using in a recipe. For thin coconut milk: Use 1 cup milk and 1 cup boiling water. Or use 1 ounce creamed coconut (available in most specialty shops) in 1 cup boiling water; stir and use as a coconut milk.

Toasted coconut—Peel fresh coconut. Shred with a grater or sharp knife. Toast in 350° oven, about 5 minutes, or until just lightly browned along the edges and crisp.

4. *Tamarind* is deep brown in color and sour and sweet to the taste. It is cultivated throughout the tropical world. Tamarind is a very important ingredient for chutney. The sun-dried variety is the only one available to the Oriental shop. When tamarind is soaked in a little water, a thick creamy gravy will appear. This gravy is used as a seasoning.

5. *Yogurt* is used for meat or fish curries to make them rich and

tasty. It is an essential ingredient for *dohi-bora* and *rayta*. It is also used in place of water to make curry gravy.

To make homemade yogurt, boil 1 quart of milk, stirring all the time. Remove from heat, let stand until temperature lowers to 105° to 115° or if tested on inside of wrist feels warm instead of hot. Spread 2½ tablespoons plain yogurt all over the inside of a large bowl. Pour in warm milk and stir gently with a fork. Cover the bowl and set aside in a warm place for 6 to 12 hours, or until thickened. Chill in the refrigerator.

6. *Silver leaf* is edible and is used for decoration in sweets. It is prepared by heating pure silver into a very thin leaf. Although a common garnish in India, few specialty shops carry silver leaf.

7. *Essences* are used in India to flavor sweets. The very popular rose and *kewra* essences make a heavenly difference in some of the sweet dishes. Orange, almond, vanilla, and coconut extracts can also be used.

8. *Ghee* (clarified butter)—To make *ghee,* heat sweet butter in a pan over moderate heat until it foams. Skim off and discard foam. Remove from heat and allow the solids to settle to the bottom. Leaving the deposit at the bottom, pour the clear yellow liquid carefully from the top through a fine cloth into another pan. Heat melted butter again and simmer for another 10 to 15 minutes. Stored in a covered jar in the refrigerator, it will keep for several months.

9. *Spiced onion*—For a rich curry, blend 2 medium yellow onions, 1 inch of fresh gingerroot, 4 to 5 cloves garlic, 1 large peeled tomato, and 2 green chilies in a blender. Add ¼ cup tomato juice, and about 1 tablespoon white vinegar if necessary. Blend again until the mixture becomes smooth and creamy. Pour it into a jar with a tight-fitting lid and store in the refrigerator until needed. It will stay fresh for about a week as long as the lid is kept tightly closed. Use as needed for each recipe.

10. *Channa* (Indian-style cottage cheese)—To prepare *channa,* heat the desired amount of homogenized milk required for the recipe in a large pan with a heavy bottom over high heat. Stir with a wooden spoon continuously to prevent the formation of scum on the top or sticking on the bottom. Bring the milk to a full boil, remove from heat, and gradually add a combination of citric acid or white vinegar and warm water to the hot milk. Add the solution slowly, about a tablespoonful at a time, and stir until the curd and whey separate. (Use only as much as you need of the acid solution to just separate

the curd. This is very important: too much vinegar or citric acid may harden the cheese.) Pour milk mixture into three layers of cheesecloth set over a bowl; tie the ends of the cloth together and let the mixture drain, squeezing the bag frequently to press out all the liquid. Take care that the *channa* or *paneer* does not dry completely; a moist, not watery, *channa* is the most important ingredient in the success of making sweets.

11. *Khoa*—This is another preparation from homogenized milk. It is dried fresh milk that is prepared by boiling and stirring whole milk until it dries. The quick process for making *khoa* requires the mixing of equal amounts of 2 cups (16 ounces) half-and-half or 1 can (16 ounces) light cream and evaporated milk, with 2 tablespoons sweet butter in a heavy pan (preferably teflon-coated to prevent sticking) over high heat, stirring gently with a wooden spoon. When the milk thickens, stir continuously and vigorously so that it does not stick to the bottom of the pan. Remove dry particles from the sides of the pan as they form and keep them well mixed with the liquid so that large lumps do not form. Continuous stirring is necessary until the milk becomes the consistency of stiff dough. It will be sticky. At this point add sugar to taste and continue cooking. Then gradually add 2 to 4 tablespoons *ghee* a spoonful at a time, stirring after each addition, until the mixture leaves the sides of the pan and forms a compact mass.

12. *Poppadums* are lentil breads that are usually marketed in small packages or boxes. They can be either toasted or fried quickly in hot fat until crispy. To prepare *poppadums*, heat vegetable oil in a skillet about 2 inches deep and fry *poppadums*, one at a time, for a few seconds, or until puffed and crisp. Drain on paper toweling. Serve with *dal* or curry or eat as a snack.

13. *Vadi* or *bori* is a dried lentil preparation, available in specialty shops. To prepare *vadi* or *bori*, heat vegetable oil until it smokes and remove from heat. Add *vadi* or *bori* and fry for a few seconds, or until golden brown on all sides. With a slotted spoon, transfer the fried *vadi* to paper toweling to drain. They may be cooked with curries or eaten as a snack.

14. *Bora* is also a lentil preparation. To make *bora*, soak ½ pound gram (*chana dal*) or yellow split peas in enough water to cover overnight. Drain and blend with very little water until creamy. Combine *dal*, a pinch of cumin seeds, ¼ inch finely minced gingerroot, 1 teaspoon ground roasted cumin, a pinch of garlic powder, a pinch of ground turmeric, 2 to 4 tablespoons *besan* (chick-pea flour) or all-

purpose flour, salt to taste, a pinch of sugar, cayenne red pepper to taste, and ¼ cup grated coconut (optional) in a bowl and mix well. Heat vegetable oil about 3 to 4 inches deep in a deep fat fryer over moderate heat. For each *bora*, drop about a teaspoonful of the lentil mixture into the hot oil. You can fry at least 10 to 15 *boras* at a time, but do not overcrowd them because they will puff a little as they cook. Fry the *boras* about 2 minutes, turning them with a slotted spoon until they are golden brown. As they brown, transfer them to paper toweling to drain. Use as many as you need for the recipe; freeze the rest of the *boras* for later use.

15. *Chicken stock*—Combine 4 to 5 pounds chicken bones (backs and necks); 1½ quarts of water; 1 medium yellow onion, chopped; a few celery leaves; 2 bay leaves; 1 small carrot, chopped; and 6 to 8 black peppercorns and bring to a rapid boil. Cover and cook gently for 3 to 3½ hours. Drain, reserving liquid. Chill overnight in the refrigerator. Remove fat from the top.

16. *Umchur* (sun-dried raw mango)—This is a very sour ingredient, but tasty in a chutney. It is available both sliced and ground.

A guide to substitutions

If an ingredient is not available, by all means use a substitute.

1. ¼ teaspoon [⅕ E.] powdered ginger may be substituted for 1 inch fresh gingerroot (1 tablespoon minced).

2. Hot banana pepper may be substituted for green chilies.

3. Fresh coriander leaves add a special unique flavor to a dish; but chopped parsley or chopped chives can be used as a substitute.

4. Tamarind liquid or ground *umchur* may be replaced by lemon juice.

5. If *vadi* is not available, use croutons. To prepare croutons, cut stale bread into half-inch squares or small cubes. Place in a shallow baking pan and sprinkle with melted butter. Bake in a preheated 350° oven for 10 to 15 minutes, or until golden brown.

6. *Garam masala* may be omitted from the recipe if not available.

7. Asafetida—some people do not like its strong flavor. Just omit from the recipe.

8. Caraway seeds may be substituted for *ajawa* seeds.

9. Cumin seeds may be substituted for black cumin seeds.

10. Mustard oil is available in specialty shops, but vegetable oil may be used for mustard oil.

11. Silver leaf is used just as a garnish. All garnishes are optional. They may be changed the way you like best.

12. Any other regular long grain rice may be replaced for *basmati* rice.

13. Sometimes lentils can be substituted, as for example split yellow peas may be substituted for *chana dal* or *tur dal*. But *moong dal* or *urad dal* is very special. Because they have special flavor and *urad dal* also is very light, they are necessary for *dohi-bora* and *dosa*. When the recipe calls for either of these lentils, it should not be replaced.

14. Desiccated coconut may be substituted for fresh grated coconut; other chopped nuts may be replaced for chopped coconut.

15. Chicken stock or beef broth may be substituted for coconut milk.

16. Melted butter or vegetable oil may be substituted for *ghee*.

NORTH AMERICAN TABLE OF WEIGHTS AND EQUIVALENTS

1 cup	16 tablespoons
1 cup	8 fluid ounces
2½ cups	1 imperial pint
5 cups	1 imperial quart
1 pound	16 ounces
1 fluid ounce	2 tablespoons
⅓ cup	5 and ⅓ tablespoons
¼ cup	4 tablespoons
1 tablespoon	3 teaspoons
1 pound all-purpose flour	3 to 3¼ cups
1 cup all-purpose flour	about 5½ ounces
1 cup whole wheat flour	about 4½ ounces
1 cup red lentils or other small lentils	8 ounces
1½ cups raisins	about 8 ounces
¾ cup almonds	about 4 ounces
1 ounce almonds	18 to 22 whole almonds
3½ cups shredded coconut	about 8 ounces
1 cup grated cheese	4 ounces
1¼ cups dates (seedless)	about 7 ounces
2 tablespoons oil	1 ounce
2 tablespoons melted *ghee*	1 ounce

1 tablespoon sour cream . . . . . . 1 ounce
4 tablespoons yogurt . . . . about 3 ounces
2 tablespoons rice flour or *besan* . . . about 1 ounce
½ cup *umchur* (sliced and dried) . . about 2 ounces
2 tablespoons biscuit mix . . . . . about 1 ounce
1½ tablespoons fresh grated coconut . 1 tablespoon dried
 grated coconut
1 pound potatoes . . . . 2 cups mashed potatoes
1 cup granulated sugar . . . . . . 6½ ounces

Comparative North American and British Measurements

1 English imperial gill (10 ounces) . 1¼ North American cups
1 English fluid ounce . . . . . . 1 North American fluid
 ounce
1 English pound . . . . 1 North American pound
4 English tablespoons . . . . . . 5 North American
 tablespoons
1 English ounce . . . . 1 North American ounce

MENUS

The Indians do not divide their meals as courses. But for a big banquet or feast the food will be served in the following fashion. The various foods in an Indian banquet are ordinarily served as a sit-down dinner.

General menu for an elegant banquet

First course: *Poori* or *luchi, paraval* and eggplant fritters, *shukto*
Second course: *Chana* or *moong dal,* sometimes both; fish fry, *dhoka* and *channa* curry, cabbage or cauliflower curry
Third course: *Pullao* or *biryani,* shrimp *malai,* fish *kalia, rayta*
Fourth course: Mutton or lamb curry
Fifth course: Tomato or mango chutney
Sixth course: Fried *poppadums,* yogurt
Seventh course: Sweets (4 to 6 varieties)

Suggested menus

SIMPLE DINNER

No. 1. Boiled rice, *shukto*, red lentils, eggplant fritters, fish *kalia* or smelt mustard, chicken curry, tomato chutney, *gulab-jamon*.

No. 2. *Chappati*, *chana dal*, cabbage or cauliflower curry, vegetable cutlet, fish *kofta* curry, eggplant *rayta*, baked *sandesh*.

No. 3. Boiled rice or *poori*, spinach, *ghoogni*, chicken with buttermilk, potato *rayta*, pineapple chutney, *rasgulla*.

AVERAGE DINNER

No. 1. Shrimp *pullao*, cauliflower fritters, eggplant with tomato, fish in yogurt sauce, lamb curry, fried *poppadums*, spinach *rayta*, *payasam*, almond *sandesh*.

No. 2. *Moti pullao*, baked *karela*, *moong dal*, *channa* curry, steamed shrimp, liver curry, plum chutney, mango yogurt, *channa gilipi*.

No. 3. Chicken *pullao*, shrimp cutlet, *chole*, eggplant *bharta*, *kheema* curry, apple chutney, *badam khir*, *cham-cham*.

ELEGANT DINNER

No. 1. Fish *biryani*, chicken cutlet, egg-*kabab* curry, curried vegetable, *poori*, eggplant with egg, tomato relish, mango yogurt, *pantua*, and *sandesh*.

No. 2. Lamb *biryani*, butterfly shrimp, *channa-kabab* curry, cauliflower curry, fish *korma*, kidney curry, *bundi rayta*, *umchur* chutney, *aloo pittha*, *malai chop*.

No. 3. *Kheema biryani*, *tandoori* chicken, okra curry, vegetable *kofta* curry, spiced haddock, *dahi bora*, date chutney, mango yogurt, *khir kadambo*, *gilipi*.

Vegetarian Dinner

No. 1. Boiled rice or *chappati*, *moong* or *chana dal*, *pakoras*, *karela* with eggplant, *channa kofta* curry, tomato chutney, *gulab-jamon*.

No. 2. *Poori*, bean *foogath*, eggplant *bharta*, vegetarian kidney beans, *channa-kabab* curry, cucumber *rayta*, *bundi*, *badam khir*.

No. 3. *Dhakai paratha*, or *channa pullao* (or both), cauliflower fritters, *chana dal*, eggplant with sour cream, vegetable *kofta* curry, vegetable *samosa*, spinach *rayta*, mango yogurt, *rasgulla*, *pantua*.

The suggested menus are not in any sense compulsory or fixed, but are merely the kinds of truly Indian meals as served in my home, consisting of dishes from every part of the country.

Appetizers

Most of these appetizers can be made well in advance and can be either frozen or refrigerated and reheated just before serving.

SAMOSAS
(*Vegetable and Meat Turnovers*)

Pastry:

1½ cups [½ pound] all-purpose flour

½ teaspoon [⅓ E.] salt

3 tablespoons [2⅓ E.] *ghee*

½ cup [⅖ E.] water

Vegetable oil for deep fat frying

---

1. Sift flour before measuring. Add salt and resift. Mix in *ghee*. Add a tablespoon of water at a time until flour mixture becomes a soft dough. Knead until the dough becomes satiny and smooth.

2. Divide dough evenly into 18 to 22 portions. Roll between palms of hands into balls. Place balls on a large plate and cover with plastic wrap; let stand in a warm place about 30 minutes.

3. Roll balls into thin circles, about 3½ inches in diameter, on a floured board. Cut each circle in half and form cones, moistening edges with water to seal. Hold a cone in your left hand and fill with a tablespoon of either vegetable or meat mixture. Moisten edges of top of cone and seal carefully to form a triangle. Repeat rolling and filling using up remaining dough and filling.

4. Heat vegetable oil to 365°. Deep fry pastries until golden brown and crisp. Serve hot with fresh coriander chutney.

Vegetable Filling:

1 cup [8 ounces] vegetable oil
1 medium potato, peeled and cut into very small cubes
1 medium cauliflower, chopped
¼ cup [⅕ E.] *ghee*
4 to 5 [3 to 4 E.] tablespoons fresh coconut, peeled and chopped
Pinch of cumin seeds
1¼ teaspoons [⅓ inch] finely minced gingerroot
2 green chilies, seeded and chopped (optional)
½ cup [3 ounces] green peas
¼ teaspoon [⅕ E.] ground cayenne pepper
¼ teaspoon [⅕ E.] ground turmeric
Pinch of sugar
½ teaspoon [⅖ E.] salt
2½ tablespoons [2 E.] raisins
1¼ teaspoons [1 E.] ground roasted cumin
¾ teaspoon [⅗ E.] ground roasted coriander
⅓ cup [1½ ounces] chopped blanched peanuts
2½ tablespoons [2 E.] chopped coriander leaves

1. Heat oil in a large skillet. Fry potato cubes until light brown; lift out and set aside. Add cauliflower pieces and fry until almost cooked. Drain on paper toweling.

2. In another large skillet, heat *ghee*; add coconut, cumin seeds, gingerroot, green chilies, and peas. Fry for one minute; then add fried potato and drained cauliflower pieces with cayenne pepper, turmeric, sugar, and salt. Fry for a few minutes over medium heat, add raisins, and cover. Simmer for 8 to 10 minutes, or until vegetables are tender. Uncover and cook slowly until all moisture is absorbed. Add ground roasted cumin and coriander. Stir in chopped peanuts and coriander leaves. Remove from heat and cool.

Meat Filling:

2½ tablespoons [2 E.] *ghee*
1 medium onion, finely chopped
¾ teaspoon (¼ inch) finely
    minced gingerroot
1 clove of garlic, minced
½ pound lean ground beef or
    lamb
½ teaspoon [⅓ E.] salt
    Pinch of paprika
¾ teaspoon [⅗ E.] ground
    coriander

¼ teaspoon [⅕ E.] ground
    turmeric
¼ teaspoon [½ E.] cayenne
    pepper
¾ teaspoon [⅗ E.] ground
    roasted cumin
½ teaspoon [⅓ E.] *sambhar* spice
    Pinch of ground cardamom
¼ cup [2 ounces] plain yogurt
1½ tablespoons [1¼ E.] freshly
    chopped coriander leaves
    (optional)

Heat *ghee* in a heavy skillet. Add onion, gingerroot, and garlic; fry, stirring, for 3 minutes. Add meat, salt, paprika, coriander, turmeric, cayenne pepper, cumin, *sambhar* spice, and cardamom. Cover and cook slowly over low heat about 10 minutes. Drain off excess fat. Stir in yogurt and coriander leaves and mix well. Set aside to cool.

NOTE: *Samosas* or tuna *ghugras* can be made ahead of time. Cool finished pastries and freeze in a covered plastic container. Thaw at room temperature. Just before serving, drop pastries into vegetable oil at least 2 inches deep, preheated to 375°. Fry only until reheated and crisp; drain and serve.

YIELD: 20 to 25 *samosas*

GHUGRA
(*Tuna or Chicken Pastry*)

Pastry:

2 cups [10 to 11 ounces]
    all-purpose flour
¾ teaspoon [⅗ E.] salt
¼ cup [2 ounces] butter, melted

5 tablespoons [4 E.] plain yogurt
⅓ cup [3 ounces] water
    Vegetable oil for deep fat frying

---

1. Sift flour before measuring. Add salt and resift. Combine flour and butter in a bowl. Add yogurt and enough water to make a soft dough. Knead until dough becomes satiny and smooth.

2. Break off small pieces of dough about the size of a walnut and roll each between the palms of your hands to form a ball. Place balls on large plate and cover for 15 minutes. On a lightly floured board, roll pastry into very thin circles, 2 to 2½ inches in diameter.

3. Place one tablespoonful of the filling in the center of a circle and fold over the dough, to form a semicircle; moisten edges of dough with water and pinch to seal. Repeat filling and rolling until remaining dough and filling are used up.

4. Heat vegetable oil to 375°. Fry pastries until golden brown and crisp. Serve hot.

Filling:

2 tablespoons [1 ounce] vegetable oil
Pinch of cumin seeds
¾ teaspoon [¼ inch] freshly minced gingerroot
2½ tablespoons [2 E.] frozen green peas
Pinch of garlic powder

⅓ teaspoon [¼ E.] *sambhar* spice
Big pinch of ground 'turmeric
Cayenne pepper to taste
Salt to taste
2½ teaspoons [2 E.] lemon juice
6½-ounce can tunafish or chicken, drained and flaked
1½ tablespoons [1¼ E.] mashed potatoes
1 egg

Heat oil in a large skillet. Add cumin seeds, gingerroot, peas, garlic powder, *sambhar* spice, turmeric, cayenne pepper, and salt and fry for 2 to 3 minutes. Add lemon juice, cover, and simmer for 3 to 5 minutes, or until peas are tender. Mash ingredients together with a potato masher or fork. Stir in tuna or chicken and cook for 3 to 4 minutes. Add mashed potatoes and egg and continue to cook, stirring gently, another 2 to 3 minutes. Remove from heat and set aside to cool.

YIELD: 25 to 30 *ghugra*

NIMKI
(*Deep Fried Pastry*)

1 cup [¼ pound] all-purpose
flour
¼ teaspoon [⅕ E.] salt
Pinch of *ajawn* seeds
Pinch of black cumin seeds
Pinch of white cumin seeds
¼ teaspoon [⅕ E.] *sambhar* spice

¼ teaspoon [⅕ E.] ground roasted
cumin
¼ teaspoon [⅕ E.] crushed red
chilies
2 tablespoons [1 ounce] butter,
melted
5 tablespoons [4 E.] water
Vegetable oil for deep fat frying

1. Sift flour before measuring. Combine flour, salt, *ajawn* seeds, black and white cumin seeds, *sambhar* spice, roasted cumin, and chilies. Add butter and enough water to make a soft dough. Knead dough for about 10 minutes, until satiny and smooth. Divide into 20 equal-sized portions. Roll each between the palms of your hands to form a ball. On a lightly floured board, roll out the balls into very thin circles, about 3 inches in diameter.

2. With a knife make 4 or 5 parallel cuts in the pastry approximately ½ inch apart just to the edge but without cutting through the edge of the circle. Fold the pastry along the cuts and pinch the ends together to seal.

3. Heat vegetable oil to 375°. Fry pastries until golden brown. Remove *nimkis* with a slotted spoon and drain on paper toweling.

NOTE: Finished pastries may be frozen. Before serving place frozen *nimkis* on baking sheet and bake in a preheated 350° oven for about 7 minutes, or until they are warm and crisp.

YIELD: 20 *nimkis*

ALOO BORA
(*Potato Croquettes*)

2 medium potatoes, boiled,
    peeled, and mashed
1 medium yellow onion, finely
    chopped
1 egg
2 green chilies, seeded and
    chopped (optional)
2½ tablespoons [2 E.] *besan*
    (chick-pea flour) or
    all-purpose flour
Cayenne pepper to taste

Pinch of cumin seeds
Pinch of garlic powder
Pinch of turmeric
Pinch of baking powder
1½ tablespoons [1¼ E.] chopped
    coriander leaves (optional)
⅓ teaspoon [¼ E.] *sambhar* spice
½ teaspoon [⅓ E.] salt
Vegetable oil for deep fat
    frying

1. Combine mashed potatoes, onion, egg, chilies, *besan,* cayenne pepper, cumin seeds, garlic powder, turmeric, baking powder, coriander leaves, and *sambhar* spice in a bowl and stir to blend well. Mixture will be sticky. Heat vegetable oil to 375°. For each *bora,* scoop up a tablespoon of the potato mixture and with a second spoon, scrape the mixture directly into the hot vegetable oil.

2. Fry, turning occasionally with a slotted spoon, for 5 to 8 minutes, or until golden brown. As *boras* brown, remove them with a slotted spoon and drain on paper toweling. Serve hot with chutney.

YIELD: 18 to 20 *boras*

SABZI BORA
(*Vegetable Croquettes*)

2 pounds carrots, cooked and mashed

2 cups [12 ounces] green peas, cooked and mashed

1½ tablespoons [1¼ E.] chopped coriander leaves

¼ cup [⅕ E.] evaporated milk

2 egg yolks

Pinch of monosodium glutamate

Pinch of cumin seeds

½ teaspoon [⅓ E.] *sambhar* spice

½ teaspoon [⅓ E.] ground roasted cumin

2 green chilies, seeded and finely chopped

1¼ cups [1 E.] crisp rice cereal, crushed into fine crumbs

1¼ teaspoon [1 E.] salt

3 tablespoons [1½ ounces] *ghee*

2 egg whites

1 packet [5 ounces] commercial chicken coating mix or seasoned bread crumbs

1. Combine carrots, peas, coriander leaves, milk, egg yolks, monosodium glutamate, cumin seeds, *sambhar* spice, ground roasted cumin, chilies, rice cereal, salt, and *ghee* in a large bowl. Mix well; cover, and chill about 2 hours. Whip egg whites until stiff and gently fold into the vegetable mixture.

2. Grease a shallow baking pan. Shape the mixture into one-inch balls. Place coating mix in a plastic bag. Add a few *boras* at a time and shake until balls are evenly coated. Place on greased pan and chill until ready to bake.

3. Heat oven to 400°. Bake *boras* for 12 to 16 minutes, or until lightly browned and hot. To deep fat fry drop chilled *boras* into 375° vegetable oil. Cook 5 to 8 minutes, or until golden and crisp. Remove with a slotted spoon and drain on paper toweling.

YIELD: 40 to 50 *boras*

GOBI PAKORAS
(*Cauliflower Fritters*)

1 cup [5 ounces] *besan*
(chick-pea flour)
½ cup [⅖ E.] rice flour
½ teaspoon [⅓ E.] baking powder
Pinch of cumin seeds
Pinch of paprika
Pinch of turmeric
Pinch of sugar

½ teaspoon [⅓ E.] crushed red
chili
½ teaspoon [⅓ E.] salt
1 cup [8 ounces] water
1 tablespoon [½ ounce] vegetable
oil
1 large head cauliflower
Vegetable oil for deep fat frying

1. *Batter*: Combine *besan*, rice flour, baking powder, cumin seeds, paprika, turmeric, sugar, chili, and salt in a bowl. Add enough water to make a smooth pastelike batter. Add 1 tablespoon oil and beat for 2 minutes.

2. Trim cauliflower neatly. Divide into flowerets; rinse in fresh cold water. Cook flowerets in boiling salted water for 5 minutes. Drain and cool.

3. Heat vegetable oil to 375°. With tongs or fork, dip one flower at a time into the batter and place in hot oil. Fry the cauliflower in batches of 4 to 5 pieces for 5 to 6 minutes, or until golden brown on all sides. As they brown, transfer to paper toweling to drain. Serve hot.

YIELD: 10 to 15 fritters

NOTE: Traditionally, cauliflower fritters are presented as a snack, but they may be served as a vegetable to accompany a meal. For eggplant fritters: Cut unpeeled eggplant into thin slices. Dip each slice into the batter until thoroughly coated and drop into the hot oil. Fry until brown and drain.

TIKKI CHANA DAL
(*Chick-pea Cutlets*)

1 cup [½ pound] dried
   chick-peas
4 cups [32 ounces] water
1 large yellow onion, minced
2 green chilies, seeded and
   chopped (optional)
1½ tablespoons [1¼ E.] chopped
   coriander leaves
¼ teaspoon [⅕ E.] ground
   turmeric

¼ teaspoon [⅕ E.] cayenne
   pepper
1¼ teaspoons [1 E.] ground
   roasted cumin
Pinch of sugar
Salt to taste
3 eggs
1 cup [⅘ E.] all-purpose flour
Bread crumbs
½ cup [⅖ E.] vegetable oil

1. Wash chick-peas, cover with cold water, and soak overnight. Bring to a boil the water in which the chick-peas soaked and cook slowly about 1 hour, or until they are tender. Drain thoroughly and grind in a food mill to make a thick paste.

2. Mix ground chick-peas with onion, chilies, coriander leaves, turmeric, cayenne pepper, cumin, sugar, salt, and one egg in a large bowl. Chill for one hour in the refrigerator. Form mixture into ½-inch-thick heart-shaped cutlets about 2 inches in diameter.

3. In a small bowl, beat 2 eggs well. Roll cutlets in flour, dip them in the beaten eggs, and roll them in bread crumbs. Heat vegetable oil in a large skillet and fry cutlets gently over moderate heat until golden brown, turning once. Remove cutlets and drain on paper toweling. Serve hot with tomato and cucumber slices and lemon juice.

YIELD: 15 to 20 cutlets

UNDAY KABAB
(*Egg Cutlets*)

2½ tablespoons [2 E.] *ghee*
1 cup [⅘ E.] all-purpose flour
½ cup [⅖ E.] milk
4 to 5 hard-cooked eggs
2½ tablespoons [2 E.] boiled
    mashed rice or bread crumbs
2½ tablespoons [2 E.] chopped
    coriander leaves
1 green chili, seeded and
    chopped

⅓ teaspoon [¼ E.] ground
    roasted coriander
⅓ teaspoon [¼ E.] ground
    roasted cumin
Pinch of ground turmeric
Pinch of garlic powder
¾ teaspoon [⅗ E.] salt
1½ tablespoons [1 E.] lemon juice
1 egg
1 cup bread crumbs
1 cup [⅘ E.] vegetable oil

1. Heat *ghee* in a small saucepan. Sprinkle 2½ tablespoons of flour into the *ghee* and stir with wire whisk until smooth, being careful not to burn the flour. Remove from heat and add the milk all at once. Stir to blend; return to moderate heat and stir until sauce is thickened and smooth.

2. Chop the eggs; add the coriander leaves, chili, ground roasted coriander and cumin, turmeric, garlic powder, salt, lemon juice, and mashed rice. Mix well. Stir in the white sauce and cook over moderate heat for 2 to 3 minutes. Remove from heat and let cool. Shape mixture into 6 to 8 ½-inch-thick cutlets. Chill in refrigerator. In a bowl, lightly beat egg. Roll each cutlet in flour, dip in lightly beaten egg, and roll in bread crumbs.

3. Heat oil in a skillet and fry cutlets in hot oil until golden brown, turning once. Drain and serve hot with relish or chutney.

YIELD: 6 to 8 cutlets

JHINGA KABAB
(*Shrimp Cutlets*)

2 pounds raw shrimp, shelled, deveined, and finely chopped (reserve tails)
1 tablespoon [1 inch] finely minced gingerroot
2 medium yellow onions, finely chopped
2 to 3 green chilies, seeded and finely chopped
2 tablespoons [1 ounce] *besan* (chick-pea flour)
2 tablespoons [1 ounce] rice flour
4 slices white bread, shredded and dried in warm oven

2½ tablespoons [2 E.] chopped coriander leaves
Pinch of monosodium glutamate
Pinch of garlic powder
¾ teaspoon [⅗ E.] salt
2 teaspoons [1⅗ E.] ground roasted cumin
2½ tablespoons [2 E.] lemon juice
3 eggs
1 cup bread crumbs
Vegetable oil for deep fat frying

1. Combine chopped shrimp, gingerroot, onions, chilies, *besan*, rice flour, dried bread, coriander leaves, monosodium glutamate, garlic powder, salt, cumin, lemon juice, and 2 eggs in a bowl. Knead until the mixture is smooth. Cover and refrigerate for 30 minutes. Take one tablespoon of the mixture and with floured palms shape into a crescent (like a shrimp). Press a tail at the end of each "shrimp." Chill several hours, or until completely cold. In a small bowl, lightly beat one egg. Dip each shrimp cutlet into egg and roll in bread crumbs to coat well. Chill again until firm.

2. Heat vegetable oil to 375°. Fry cutlets until crisp and golden. Lift out with a slotted spoon; drain well. Keep in a warm oven until all cutlets are cooked. Serve with chutney.

YIELD: 20 to 25 cutlets

MACHI KOFTA
(*Fish Balls*)

1 pound fish fillet (lemon or grey
    sole, cod, perch, or bluefish)
Pinch of ground turmeric
Pinch of garlic powder
Pinch of sugar
Pinch of cumin seeds
¾ teaspoon [⅗ E.] salt
¾ teaspoon [⅗ E.] seasoned salt
¾ teaspoon [¼ inch] gingerroot,
    freshly minced
2½ tablespoons [2 E.] rice flour
2 eggs, one separated

1 medium yellow onion, minced
¼ teaspoon [⅕ E.] cayenne
    pepper
1½ tablespoons [1¼ E.] plain
    yogurt
1½ tablespoons [1¼ E.] lemon
    juice
1 cup crisp rice cereal or corn
    flakes, crumbed
Vegetable oil for deep fat
    frying

1. Bake fish fillet in preheated 400° oven for 10 to 15 minutes. Remove bones and drain the juice from the fish. Flake fish with a fork. Combine cooked fish with turmeric, garlic powder, sugar, cumin seeds, salt, seasoned salt, gingerroot, rice flour, egg yolk (discard white), onion, cayenne pepper, yogurt, and lemon juice. Cover and set aside for ½ hour. Shape mixture into balls the size of a walnut.

2. In a bowl, lightly beat one egg. Heat vegetable oil to 375°. Dip fish balls in egg, roll in crumbs, and fry about 3 to 5 minutes or until dark, golden brown. Drain and serve hot with toothpicks.

YIELD: 30 *koftas*

MOTRI
(*Crunchies*)

1¼ cups [1 E.] biscuit or pancake
    mix
Big pinch of salt
Dash of cumin seeds
Dash of cayenne pepper

⅓ teaspoon [¼ E.] *sambhar* spice
5 to 6 tablespoons white vinegar
Vegetable oil for deep fat
    frying

1. Combine biscuit mix, salt, cumin seeds, cayenne pepper, and *sambhar* spice in a bowl. Gradually add vinegar to form a soft dough. Knead to blend well. Divide in half and form 2 balls.

2. On a lightly floured board, roll out each ball until about ¼ inch thick. Cut into very small (½ inch long) diamond shapes. Heat vegetable oil to 375°. Fry *motri* in oil until golden brown. Drain. Serve warm.

NOTE: *Motri* may be frozen. To serve, place frozen *motri* on baking sheet and bake in preheated 400° oven for 8 to 10 minutes, or until hot.

SERVES 4 to 6

KAKRA or JHINGA KHASTA
(*Crab or Shrimp Roll*)

Pastry:

1½ cups [½ pound] all-purpose
    flour
½ teaspoon [⅓ E.] salt
¼ pound butter

2 to 3 tablespoons [1 to 1½
    ounces] cold milk
1 egg, separated
1 tablespoon [⅘ E.] *sambhar*
    spice

Filling:

1 5-ounce can small shrimp or
    crab meat, drained
2 tablespoons [1 ounce] butter,
    softened

Pinch of ground cayenne
    pepper
Pinch of salt
½ teaspoon [⅓ E.] *sambhar* spice
1½ tablespoons [1¼ E.] chopped
    coriander leaves

1. *Pastry:* Sift flour before measuring. Mix butter, salt, and sifted flour with a fork then with the tips of the fingers until crumbly. Add just enough milk so dough will hold together when pressed lightly with fingers. On a lightly floured board, roll dough into a circle about ⅛ inch thickness. Cut into circles using a 2½-inch cookie cutter and brush edges with lightly beaten egg white.

2. *Filling:* With a fork, mash shrimp or crab meat in a bowl. Add butter, cayenne pepper, salt, *sambhar* spice, and coriander leaves and blend well.

3. Heat oven to 425°. Place about one teaspoon of filling in the center of each round and roll to make filled tubes. Place rolls on

ungreased cookie sheet. Refrigerate until ready to bake. Sprinkle rolls lightly with *sambhar* spice. Bake in preheated oven for 10 to 12 minutes, or until crisp.

YIELD: 20 rolls

VADAS
(*Tiny Cashew Doughnuts*)

1¼ cups [1 E.] farina (*suji*)
1 cup [⅘ E.] water
1 medium yellow onion, finely chopped
1 or 2 green chilies, drained and chopped
½ teaspoon [⅓ E.] salt
1½ tablespoons [1¼ E.] chopped coriander leaves

¼ cup [⅕ E.] cashew nuts, chopped
2 tablespoons [1 ounce] plain yogurt
¾ teaspoon [¼ inch] freshly minced gingerroot
Vegetable oil for deep fat frying

1. Bring water to a boil. Place farina in a bowl and add water, stirring, to make a dough. Add onion, chilies, salt, coriander leaves, cashew nuts, yogurt, and gingerroot and mix well.

2. Take 2 tablespoons of dough mixture and make a thick, round patty. Cut with a doughnut cutter or use your fingers to make a hole in the center of the patty. Repeat with remaining dough. Heat vegetable oil to 375°. Fry about 3 to 4 *vadas* at a time for 8 to 10 minutes, turning as necessary, until light brown. Drain on paper toweling. Serve hot with chutney.

YIELD: 10 to 12 *vadas*

PANEER PAKORAS
(*Cheese Tidbits*)

4½ ounces mild cheddar cheese, grated
2½ tablespoons [2 E.] all-purpose flour
1½ tablespoons [1¼ E.] rice flour
½ teaspoon [⅓ E.] paprika
2½ tablespoons [2 E.] chopped coriander leaves

2 green chilies, seeded and chopped
¼ teaspoon [⅕ E.] salt
Pinch of cumin seeds
3 large egg whites
½ cup [⅖ E.] crisp rice cereal, crumbed
Vegetable oil for deep fat frying

1. Combine cheese, all-purpose flour, rice flour, paprika, coriander leaves, chilies, salt, and cumin seeds in a large bowl. In another bowl, beat egg whites until stiff and fold into the cheese mixture. Chill in the refrigerator for 5 to 8 minutes. Take a teaspoon of the mixture and lightly roll in crumbs until evenly coated.

2. Heat vegetable oil to 375° and fry *pakoras* a few at a time until golden. Remove with a slotted spoon and drain on paper toweling.

NOTE: *Pakoras* can be made the day before and refrigerated overnight. Reheat in a preheated 350° oven for 8 to 10 minutes until hot.

YIELD: 20 to 25 *pakoras*

SIKAMPURI KABAB
(*Lamb Kabob*)

2 tablespoons [1 ounce] *ghee*
½ pound lean lamb, minced
2 medium yellow onions, finely chopped
1 large clove of garlic, minced
½ teaspoon [⅓ E.] salt
½ teaspoon [⅓ E.] cayenne pepper
½ teaspoon [⅓ E.] ground roasted cumin

2 to 3 tablespoons *besan* (chick-pea flour) or yellow split peas, boiled and mashed
1¼ tablespoons [1 E.] minced coriander leaves
2 green chilies, seeded and chopped
1½ teaspoons [½ inch] freshly grated gingerroot
1 egg

1. In a large skillet, heat *ghee*, and add lamb, one-half of the chopped onion, garlic, salt, cayenne pepper, and cumin; fry for 2 to 3 minutes. Cover and cook slowly for 10 minutes. Remove from heat and allow mixture to cool. Add *besan*, coriander leaves, chilies, remaining onion, gingerroot, and egg to the lamb mixture and mix well. Form into flat walnut-sized balls.

2. Broil balls over slow-burning charcoal fire, under broiler, or deep fat fry in 375° vegetable oil until brown. Drain on paper toweling and serve hot.

YIELD: 15 to 20 *kababs*

Pullaos and Biryanis

PREPARATION OF RICE

For half the world's population rice is the staple food. It is the most important food crop for the people of India, and India is one of the largest rice-growing countries in the world. There are hundreds of varieties of rice available in India. An Indian recognizes the variety of rice by its fragrance, shape, and color. Indians do wonderful culinary feats with rice; *pullaos* and *biryanis* are among the most superb rice dishes in the world. For *pullao*, the special *basmati* rice is fried in *ghee* and then steamed with stock and nuts. It can be prepared with shrimp, chicken, *channa*, lamb, or simply with nuts and vegetables.

Biryanis are the most elaborate of the rice dishes, with a variety of flavors produced by pistachio nuts, shredded almonds, raisins, and chopped fresh coconut. They are made by arranging steamed rice in layers with poultry, meat, fish, saffron, nuts, and lots of *ghee*. The dish is baked to blend all the seasonings. It is served in India for special formal occasions, garnished with fried onion rings, eggs, nuts, and sometimes with rose water.

In India raw rice is used as an important ingredient during our *puja* (holy festival) and also for Hindu weddings. It signifies wealth and prosperity. *Basmati* rice (which is available in specialty shops), has a delicate aroma and sweet nutlike flavor and is suitable for making *pullao* or *biryani*. But *patna* rice or any other long grain rice may be used.

MURGH PULLAO
(*Chicken with Seasoned Rice*)

Spice paste:

2 medium yellow onions,
   chopped
4 cloves of garlic
1¼ teaspoons [1 E.] cumin seeds
2½ tablespoons [2 E.] lemon juice
1 tablespoon [1 inch] freshly
   grated gingerroot
1¼ teaspoons [1 E.] coriander
   seeds

2 cardamoms
2 cinnamon sticks
2 peppercorns
½ teaspoon [⅓ E.] ground
   turmeric
2 red chilies
2 cloves
1 medium tomato, peeled and
   seeded

Pullao:

1½ cups [12 ounces] plain yogurt
2 tablespoons [1 ounce]
   vegetable oil
2 teaspoons [1⅗ E.] salt
10 pieces dark-meat chicken, legs
   and thighs
½ cup [⅖ E.] *ghee*
4 large yellow onions, thinly
   sliced
2 bay leaves
4 cardamoms, crushed
2 small [1 inch] pieces of
   cinnamon stick
½ cup [3 ounces] almonds,
   blanched
2 green chilies, seeded

1 cup [6 ounces] fresh green peas
2 cups [1 pound] *basmati* rice,
   washed and drained
¼ teaspoon [⅕ E.] saffron
   threads, soaked in 1 tablespoon warm water
1¼ teaspoons [1 E.] ground
   nutmeg
¾ teaspoon [⅗ E.] ground mace
½ teaspoon [⅓ E.] ground
   cinnamon
¼ teaspoon [⅕ E.] ground cloves
1¼ teaspoons [1 E.] sugar
3 cups [24 ounces] chicken
   stock
5 tablespoons [4 E.] raisins

1. In a blender, or with a mortar and pestle, blend onions, garlic, cumin seeds, lemon juice, gingerroot, coriander seeds, cardamoms, cinnamon sticks, peppercorns, turmeric, chilies, cloves, and tomato to make a smooth, creamy paste.

2. Combine 1 cup of the yogurt, the spice paste, vegetable oil, and ½ teaspoon of the salt in a bowl. Add chicken pieces and mix thoroughly. Cover and set aside to marinate for 4 to 6 hours in a cool place.

3. Heat ¼ cup [⅕ E.] of the *ghee* in a large skillet. Add half of the sliced onions and fry until soft. Remove chicken pieces from spice mixture and add to onions in skillet; brown chicken 5 to 8 minutes adding more *ghee* if necessary. Stir often to prevent chicken from burning or sticking to the bottom of the pan. Reduce heat, pour spice mixture over chicken, and cover and cook gently about 20 minutes, or until chicken pieces are well browned and thoroughly cooked. Uncover and cook slowly until most of the liquid evaporates. Remove pan from heat.

4. Preheat oven to 350°. Heat remaining *ghee* in a large heavy casserole with a tight-fitting lid. When *ghee* begins to smoke, add the rest of the sliced onions and cook until pale brown. Lift out and set aside. Add bay leaves, cardamoms, cinnamon sticks, almonds, chilies, and peas to *ghee* left in pan. Cook for a few minutes. Sprinkle in rice, saffron with its soaking water, nutmeg, mace, cinnamon, cloves, sugar, and remaining salt. Cook, stirring, over medium heat about 2 minutes. Add chicken stock and raisins and mix well. Bring to a rapid boil. Boil for 3 to 4 minutes; top with cooked chicken pieces and cover.

5. Bake *pullao* in preheated oven for 30 to 35 minutes, or until the rice is tender and the water is absorbed. With a fork, lightly beat remaining ½ cup of yogurt. Fluff *pullao* with a fork and gently stir in yogurt, being careful not to break rice grains. The rice should not be sticky; every grain should stand apart. Garnish *pullao* with sliced eggs and fried onions. Serve hot on a warm platter.

SERVES 8

MOTI PULLAO
(*Meatballs with Seasoned Rice*)

Meatballs:

1½ pounds lean lamb, beef, or
uncooked turkey, finely
minced
1 medium yellow onion, minced
½ cup [⅖ E.] yogurt or sour
cream
¼ cup [⅕ E.] ground almonds
½ teaspoon [⅓ E.] salt

¼ teaspoon [⅕ E.] garlic powder
¼ teaspoon [⅕ E.] cayenne
pepper
¼ teaspoon [⅕ E.] *garam masala*
1¼ teaspoons [1 E.] ground roasted
cumin seeds
1 egg yolk
¼ cup [⅕ E.] *ghee*

Pullao:

½ cup [⅖ E.] *ghee*
2 green peppers, seeded and cut
into rings
½ cup [⅖ E.] whole blanched
almonds
2 bay leaves
2 to 3 1-inch cinnamon sticks
6 cardamoms, crushed
2 medium yellow onions, finely
chopped
1¼ cups [1 E.] frozen mixed
vegetables
2 cups [1 pound] *basmati* or long
grain rice, washed and
drained
¼ teaspoon [⅕ E.] saffron
threads, soaked in 1 tablespoon warm water

1¼ teaspoons [1 E.] ground
nutmeg
¾ teaspoon [⅗ E.] ground mace
⅓ teaspoon [¼ E.] ground cloves
½ teaspoon [⅓ E.] ground
cinnamon
2 teaspoons [1⅗ E.] salt
2 teaspoons [1⅗ E.] sugar
2½ tablespoons [2 E.] pistachio
nuts
½ cup [⅖ E.] raisins
3 cups [24 ounces] beef broth or
chicken stock
½ cup [⅖ E.] plain yogurt, lightly
beaten with a fork

1. Combine minced meat, onion, yogurt, ground almonds, salt, garlic powder, cayenne pepper, *garam masala*, cumin seeds, and egg yolk and mix well. Set aside, covered, for ½ hour. Lightly shape meat mixture into 20 meatballs. Heat ¼ cup [⅕ E.] *ghee* in a large skillet. Add meatballs and cook over medium-high heat, turning occasionally, until lightly browned. Set aside.

2. Preheat oven to 300°. In a large skillet, heat ½ cup *ghee*, fry green peppers for one minute; remove with a slotted spoon and set

aside. Add almonds, bay leaves, cinnamon sticks, cardamoms, and chopped onions to *ghee* left in pan and cook on medium-high heat for 2 minutes. Add frozen vegetables and cook until the moisture evaporates. Add rice and saffron with its soaking water and cook for 2 to 3 minutes more. Add nutmeg, mace, cloves, cinnamon, salt, and sugar. Stirring, add pistachio nuts, and raisins. Transfer mixture to a casserole, add broth or stock, and boil for 2 to 3 minutes. Add meatballs, cover, and bake in preheated oven for 40 minutes.

3. Remove casserole from oven and add green pepper and yogurt. Stir lightly with a fork and remove pieces of cinnamon stick. Cover again and bake another 10 minutes, or until rice is tender and liquid is absorbed. Remove *pullao* from oven and keep covered for another 5 minutes; fluff with a fork. Serve hot. Garnish with coriander leaves.

SERVES 8 to 10

YAKHNI PULLAO
(*Lamb with Seasoned Rice*)

2 pounds boned leg of lamb or lamb shoulder, cut into ½-inch cubes
2½ tablespoons [2 E.] spiced onion
½ cup [⅖ E.] plain yogurt
½ teaspoon [⅓ E.] salt
1¼ teaspoons [1 E.] ground cumin
1¼ teaspoons [1 E.] ground coriander
¼ teaspoon [⅕ E.] ground turmeric
¼ teaspoon [⅕ E.] cayenne pepper
½ cup [⅖ E.] *ghee*
¼ teaspoon [⅕ E.] paprika
2 medium yellow onions, finely chopped
2 bay leaves
6 cardamoms, crushed
4 whole cloves
2 green chilies, seeded (optional)
2 cups [1 pound] *basmati* rice, washed and drained
⅓ cup [2 ounces] sliced blanched almonds
¼ cup [⅕ E.] cashew nuts
1¼ teaspoons [1 E.] ground nutmeg
¾ teaspoon [⅗ E.] ground mace
¼ teaspoon [⅕ E.] ground black pepper
¼ teaspoon [⅕ E.] ground cinnamon
¼ teaspoon [⅕ E.] ground cloves
2 teaspoons [1⅗ E.] salt
2 teaspoons [1⅗ E.] sugar
¼ teaspoon [⅕ E.] saffron threads soaked in 1 tablespoon warm water
3 cups [24 ounces] beef broth or chicken stock

1. Combine lamb, spiced onion, yogurt, salt, cumin, coriander, turmeric, cayenne pepper, ¼ cup *ghee*, and paprika and marinate for 2 hours, covered. Cook the mixture over medium heat, stirring, about 6 minutes. Cover and simmer 40 minutes, or until meat is tender. Remove from heat and set aside.

2. Heat remaining *ghee* in a large casserole with a tight-fitting lid. Fry onions, bay leaves, cardamoms, cloves, and chilies for 2 minutes. Stir in rice, almonds, cashew nuts, nutmeg, mace, black pepper, cinnamon, and cloves. Stirring and cooking over medium heat, add salt, sugar, saffron with its soaking water, and broth. Boil mixture for 3 to 4 minutes. Mix in the meat and gravy and cover tightly.

3. Preheat oven to 350°. Bake *pullao* for 45 to 55 minutes, or until rice is cooked and liquid is absorbed. Fluff *pullao* with a fork; if the mixture seems too dry, sprinkle with rose water, one tablespoonful at a time. Serve hot. Garnish with chopped coriander leaves, sliced hard-cooked eggs, and some green chilies.

SERVES 8 to 10

CHANNAR PULLAO
(*Homemade Cottage Cheese Cubes with Seasoned Rice*)

10 cups [80 ounces] homogenized milk
¼ cup [2 ounces] white vinegar
½ cup [⅖ E.] *ghee*
½ cup [⅖ E.] warm water
2 ounces (about 40) almonds, blanched
2 bay leaves
6 cardamoms, crushed
2 small (one-inch) pieces cinnamon stick
4 whole cloves

1 large yellow onion, chopped
1¼ cups [1 E.] fresh green peas
1½ cups [12 ounces] *basmati* rice, washed and drained
1½ teaspoons [1⅕ E.] salt
1½ teaspoons [1⅕ E.] sugar
1¼ teaspoons [1 E.] ground nutmeg
½ teaspoon [⅓ E.] ground mace
Pinch of saffron threads
2½ cups [20 ounces] thin coconut milk (page 18)

1. Prepare *channa* (see page 19). Put bag containing *channa* on a flat wooden board and press with a weight to extract any remaining liquid. Chill. Cut into small ½-inch cubes. Brown them in ¼ cup [⅕ E.] *ghee* and set aside.

2. Heat remaining *ghee* in a skillet and fry almonds, bay leaves,

cardamoms, cinnamon sticks, cloves, and onion for 2 minutes. Add peas and cook, stirring, until moisture evaporates. Stir in rice, salt, sugar, nutmeg, mace, and saffron. Add coconut milk and boil for 3 minutes. Top with fried *channa* cubes. Cover and simmer about 15 minutes, or until rice is cooked. Keep covered another 10 minutes. Toss very lightly with some chopped coriander leaves. If it is too dry, sprinkle with rose water, one tablespoonful at a time. Garnish with pitted cherries and fried crushed *vadi* (optional).

SERVES 6 to 8

BADAM PULLAO
(*Coconuts and Nuts with Seasoned Rice*)

½ cup [⅖ E.] *ghee*

2 ounces (about 40) almonds, blanched

¼ cup [⅕ E.] fresh coconut, finely chopped

¼ cup [⅕ E.] pistachio nuts

¼ cup [⅕ E.] raisins

¾ teaspoon [¼ inch] gingerroot, freshly minced

2 bay leaves

6 cardamoms, crushed

4 whole cloves

¼ teaspoon [⅕ E.] saffron threads soaked in 1 tablespoon warm water

1¼ teaspoons [1 E.] ground nutmeg

¾ teaspoon [⅗ E.] ground mace

2 green chilies, seeded

2½ tablespoons [2 E.] chopped coriander leaves

2 cups [1 pound] *basmati* rice, washed and drained

2 teaspoons [1⅗ E.] salt

2 teaspoons [1⅗ E.] sugar

3 cups [24 ounces] thin coconut milk

½ cup [⅖ E.] *vadi*, fried and crushed (optional)

Heat *ghee* in a large skillet and fry almonds, coconut, and pistachio nuts for one minute. Add raisins, gingerroot, bay leaves, cardamoms, cloves, saffron with its soaking water, nutmeg, mace, chilies, and coriander leaves and cook for a few seconds, stirring. Add rice, salt, sugar, and coconut milk and boil for 3 minutes over medium heat. Cover and simmer for 15 minutes, or until rice is cooked. Remove from heat; let stand, covered, 10 more minutes. Fluff rice and toss with fried crushed *vadi*. Serve warm on a heated platter. Garnish with more nuts, coriander leaves, green chilies, and tomato slices.

SERVES 6 to 8

JHINGA PULLAO
(*Shrimp with Seasoned Rice*)

Pinch of salt
Pinch of ground turmeric
Pinch of monosodium
    glutamate
1½ teaspoons [½ inch] fresh
    gingerroot, finely minced
1½ pounds shrimp, shelled and
    deveined
½ cup [⅖ E.] *ghee*
2 medium yellow onions, thinly
    sliced
2 green peppers, cut into rings
½ cup [3 ounces] almonds,
    blanched
3 small [1 inch] cinnamon sticks
6 cardamoms, crushed
2 bay leaves
2 cups [12 ounces] frozen green
    peas

2 cups [1 pound] *basmati* or long
    grain rice, washed and
    drained
¼ teaspoon [⅕ E.] saffron
    threads soaked in 1 table-
    spoon warm water
¼ cup [⅕ E.] raisins
1¼ teaspoons [1 E.] ground
    nutmeg
¾ teaspoon [⅗ E.] ground mace
¼ teaspoon [⅕ E.] ground cloves
½ teaspoon [⅓ E.] ground
    cinnamon
2 teaspoons [1⅗ E.] salt
1¼ teaspoons [1 E.] sugar
3 cups [24 ounces] coconut milk
4 eggs, prepared as omelets
½ cup [⅖ E.] pitted red cherries,
    canned or bottled

1. Add pinch of salt, turmeric, monosodium glutamate, and ginger-root to the shrimp and mix well. Heat ¼ cup of the *ghee* in a large heavy saucepan or Dutch oven. Fry onions over medium heat until light brown; remove from pan and set aside. Repeat with green peppers. Add shrimp to pan and fry for one minute until slightly firm; lift out and set aside.

2. Add rest of *ghee* to saucepan. When it begins to smoke remove pan from heat; add almonds, cinnamon sticks, cardamoms, bay leaves, and frozen peas. Return pan to heat and, stirring, sprinkle in rice and saffron with its soaking water. Cook for 2 minutes. Add raisins, nutmeg, mace, cloves, cinnamon, salt, sugar, and coconut milk and bring to a boil. Boil for 3 minutes. Top with fried shrimp, reduce heat, cover, and simmer for 12 minutes, or until liquid is absorbed. Remove from heat; let stand, covered, for another 10 minutes. Fluff *pullao* with a fork. Serve on a hot platter and garnish with omelets, fried onions, green peppers, and cherries.

SERVES 6 to 8

KHEEMA BIRYANI
(*Minced Meat with Rice*)

Saffron Rice:

⅓ teaspoon [¼ E.] black
  peppercorns
⅓ teaspoon [¼ E.] cumin seeds
⅓ teaspoon [¼ E.] coriander
  seeds
¼-inch fresh gingerroot, crushed
4 small pieces [1 inch] cinnamon
  sticks

8 cloves
8 cardamoms, crushed
2 bay leaves
2½ cups [2 E.] chicken stock or
  beef broth
2 teaspoons [1⅗ E.] salt
¼ teaspoon [⅕ E.] saffron threads
2 cups [1 pound] rice

---

1. Make a bouquet garni by placing peppercorns, cumin seeds, coriander seeds, gingerroot, cinnamon sticks, cloves, cardamoms, and bay leaves in a 4-inch square of cheesecloth and tie with white string.

2. In a large saucepan bring stock to a rapid boil. Add salt, bouquet garni, and saffron and sprinkle in rice. Boil over moderately high heat for 2 to 3 minutes. Reduce heat, cover, and simmer for 10 minutes. Remove from heat. Let stand for 5 minutes. Fluff rice with a fork and set aside until ready to use.

Kheema:

¼ cup [⅕ E.] *ghee*
2 medium yellow onions, finely
  chopped
3 cloves garlic, minced
1½ teaspoons [½ inch] freshly
  grated gingerroot
2 bay leaves
  Pinch of cumin seeds
2 pounds ground lamb or
  uncooked turkey
½ teaspoon [⅓ E.] ground
  turmeric

½ teaspoon [⅓ E.] ground
  nutmeg
½ teaspoon [⅓ E.] ground mace
½ teaspoon [⅓ E.] ground
  cardamom
½ teaspoon [⅓ E.] ground
  cinnamon
¾ teaspoon [⅗ E.] ground cumin
¾ teaspoon [⅗ E.] salt
1 cup [6 ounces] plain yogurt or
  sour cream
2 to 3 tablespoons [2 E.]
  chopped coriander leaves

Heat *ghee* in skillet. Add onions, garlic, gingerroot, bay leaves, and cumin seeds and cook over medium heat about 2 minutes. Stir in meat, turmeric, nutmeg, mace, cardamom, cinnamon, ground cumin, and salt. Cook gently about 8 to 10 minutes. Stir in yogurt and coriander leaves. Remove from heat and set aside.

Biryani:

6 tablespoons [3 ounces] *ghee*

1 large yellow onion, thinly sliced

2 green chilies, seeded and halved

2 ounces [about 40] blanched almonds

¼ cup [⅕ E.] cashew nuts

½ cup [⅖ E.] raisins

1¼ cups [1 E.] chicken stock or beef broth

2½ tablespoons [2 E.] rose water

---

1. Heat 3 tablespoons of the *ghee* in a large Dutch oven with a tight-fitting lid. Brown onion; then add chilies, almonds, cashews, raisins, and saffron rice. Stir for 1 or 2 minutes over medium heat.

2. Remove two-thirds of the rice mixture and spread the remaining rice evenly over the bottom of the pan. Spoon one-half of the meat mixture over the rice. Add another layer of rice using one-half of that remaining. Cover with remaining meat mixture and end with a layer of rice. Pour on the stock and remaining *ghee*; sprinkle with rose water.

3. Preheat oven to 375°. Cover pot with lid or foil and bake about 30 to 35 minutes, or until the rice has absorbed the liquid. Fluff *biryani* with a fork. Garnish with additional chopped coriander leaves, seeded green chilies, tomato wedges, and green pepper rings. *Biryani* may be removed to a hot platter or served directly from the pot.

SERVES 6 to 8

MOGHLAI BIRYANI
(*Spiced Lamb with Rice*)

4 pounds lean lamb, cut into
    1-inch cubes
1½ cups [12 ounces] plain yogurt
½ cup [⅖ E.] spiced onion
2½ teaspoons [2 E.] ground
    coriander
2½ teaspoons [2 E.] ground cumin
2½ teaspoons [2 E.] lemon juice
1¼ teaspoons [1 E.] salt
1¼ teaspoons [1 E.] nutmeg
⅓ teaspoon [¼ E.] mace
⅓ teaspoon [¼ E.] *garam masala*
⅓ teaspoon [¼ E.] cayenne
    pepper
⅓ teaspoon [¼ E.] turmeric
Pinch of sugar

Pinch of black pepper
Pinch of monosodium
    glutamate
5 to 6 tablespoons [3 ounces]
    ghee
1 large yellow onion, finely
    chopped
3 cloves of garlic, minced
1¼ teaspoons [1 E.] finely minced
    gingerroot
2 large tomatoes, peeled, seeded,
    and chopped
2 bay leaves
Saffron rice (page 51)
Biryani (see page 52)

1. Put lamb cubes in a large bowl. Combine yogurt, spiced onion, coriander, cumin, lemon juice, salt, nutmeg, mace, *garam masala*, cayenne pepper, turmeric, sugar, black pepper, and monosodium glutamate; pour over lamb. Cover and let marinate 2 to 4 hours at room temperature.

2. Heat *ghee* in an oven-proof pan; fry onion, garlic, and gingerroot over medium heat for 2 to 3 minutes. Add tomatoes, bay leaves, and lamb with its marinade. Cook, stirring, for 10 to 15 minutes.

3. Prepare saffron rice and *biryani* as explained in the previous recipe for *Kheema Biryani*, but use lamb cubes instead of *kheema* between the layers of rice. Cook as directed. Garnish with additional chopped nuts and silver leaf.

SERVES 6 to 8

MACHI BIRYANI
(*Fish and Rice*)

2 pounds fish fillet (carp, haddock, sole, or perch)
2 cups [16 ounces] coconut milk
¼ teaspoon [⅕ E.] salt
¼ cup [3 ounces] plus 2 table-spoons *ghee*
1 medium yellow onion, thinly sliced
2 cloves garlic, minced
2½ teaspoons [2 E.] spiced onion
4 medium tomatoes, seeded and chopped

1¼ teaspoons [1 E.] ground cumin
1¼ teaspoons [1 E.] ground coriander
½ teaspoon [⅓ E.] cayenne pepper
½ teaspoon [⅓ E.] *garam masala*
½ cup [3 ounces] almonds, sliced
1 bay leaf
¼ cup [⅕ E.] raisins
Saffron rice (see page 51)
1¼ cups [1 E.] coconut milk or fish stock

1. Cut fish into serving pieces and poach in coconut milk (chicken stock may be used) and salt for about 5 minutes, or until fish flakes easily with a fork. Remove fish with a slotted spoon and set aside.

2. Heat ¼ cup *ghee* in a small pan and brown onion. Add garlic, spiced onion, tomatoes, cumin, coriander, cayenne pepper, *garam masala*, almonds, and bay leaf. Cook, stirring, about 2 to 3 minutes. Add raisins and mix well. Remove from heat.

3. Preheat oven to 375°. Prepare saffron rice as directed on page 51. Spread one-third of the saffron rice on the bottom of a well-greased, large casserole, add a layer of fish, and sprinkle some of the almond-raisin mixture on top. Repeat layers until all rice, fish, and almond-raisin are used, ending with a layer of rice. Pour coconut milk and remaining *ghee* over rice. Cover with foil and bake about 20 minutes, or until the liquid has been absorbed. Garnish with green chilies, hard-cooked eggs, coriander leaves, and fried crushed *vadi*. Sprinkle with rose water before serving.

SERVES 6 to 8

QORMA CHAWAL
(*Hot Curried Rice*)

¼ cup [⅕ E.] *ghee*
2 medium yellow onions, thinly
   sliced
¾ teaspoon [¼ inch] finely
   minced gingerroot
3 green chilies, seeded and
   halved
1 bay leaf
2 cups [12 ounces] frozen mixed
   vegetables
2 cups [1 pound] long grain rice,
   washed and drained

½ teaspoon [⅓ E.] ground
   turmeric
½ teaspoon [⅓ E.] cayenne
   pepper
½ teaspoon [⅓ E.] *garam masala*
1¼ teaspoons [1 E.] ground cumin
1¼ teaspoons [1 E.] ground
   coriander
2 teaspoons [1⅗ E.] salt
3 cups [24 ounces] chicken stock
   or beef broth
1¼ cups [1 E.] fried crushed *vadi*
   (optional)

Heat *ghee* in a large saucepan and fry onions until light brown. Add gingerroot, chilies, bay leaf, and frozen vegetables and cook, stirring, about 2 minutes. Add rice, turmeric, cayenne pepper, *garam masala*, cumin, coriander, and salt. Add stock and boil for 2 to 3 minutes. Reduce heat to simmer; cover and cook gently for 12 to 15 minutes. Remove from heat and let stand another 10 minutes. Fluff rice with a fork, and stir in fried crushed *vadi*. Sprinkle with chopped coriander leaves and serve warm.

NOTE: Slight adjustments in the quantity of water used may be necessary depending on the quality of the rice. It is very important that in *pullao* or *biryani* every grain should be separate so the rice is fluffy, not sticky.

SERVES 4 to 5

Kitchuris

Kitchuri is another delicious rice preparation that is very popular in Bengal. It is a combination of rice and *dal* (lentils) cooked with vegetables and spices. *Kitchuri* is eaten with fried fish, omelets, fried potatoes, and vegetables. It is an ideal supper dish for a cold night. Care must be taken not to allow *kitchuri* to burn, which may be prevented by occasionally shaking the pot, or stirring its contents with a wooden spoon. *Kitchuri* often tastes better the day following preparation; just reheat before serving.

GEELA KITCHURI
(*Vegetables with Rice and Lentils*)

1½ cups [12 ounces] rice
¾ cup [5 to 6 ounces] red lentils
¾ cup [⅗ E.] yellow split peas,
   soaked in 1 cup water
7 to 8 cups [6 to 7 E.] boiling
   water
½ pound (about 4) carrots, sliced
   into 1½-inch lengths
1 small cauliflower, cut into
   flowerets
½ pound green beans, sliced into
   2-inch lengths
2 cups [12 ounces] fresh green
   peas
1½ tablespoons [1½ inches]
   freshly grated gingerroot
2 green chilies, seeded and
   chopped
2 bay leaves
¼ cup [⅕ E.] vegetable oil
⅓ teaspoon [¼ E.] ground
   turmeric

⅓ teaspoon [¼ E.] garlic powder
⅓ teaspoon [¼ E.] cayenne
   pepper
1½ tablespoons [1¼ E.] salt
¾ teaspoon [⅗ E.] sugar
2 to 3 tomatoes, seeded and cut
   into pieces
¼ cup [⅕ E.] *ghee* or vegetable
   oil
3 large yellow onions, thinly
   sliced
¼ cup [⅕ E.] freshly chopped
   coconut
1¼ teaspoons [1 E.] ground
   roasted cumin
1¼ teaspoons [1 E.] ground roasted
   coriander
1¼ teaspoons [1 E.] ground
   sambhar spice
2½ tablespoons [2 E.] chopped
   coriander leaves

1. Wash rice and red lentils together. Place in a large 5- to 6-quart pan and add boiling water. Cover and bring to a boil, removing scum as it forms. Add split peas, carrots, cauliflowerets, green beans, green peas, gingerroot, chilies, bay leaves, and vegetable oil. Stir in turmeric, garlic powder, cayenne pepper, salt, and sugar. Cover and cook slowly 30 to 40 minutes, or until vegetables are tender. Care must be taken not to allow the *kitchuri* to burn. This may be prevented by occasionally shaking the pot or stirring its contents with a wooden spoon. When cauliflowerets are cooked, remove them and set aside. Add tomatoes and continue cooking over low heat until *dal* and rice all blend together.

2. Heat *ghee* in a large skillet and brown onions. Stir in coconut and add the rice-and-bean mixture. Stir gently with a wooden spoon over low heat. Add cumin, coriander, *sambhar* spice, and coriander

leaves and return cauliflowerets to the mixture. Serve hot with additional *ghee* and fried fish, eggs, potatoes, or vegetables.

SERVES 6 to 8

BHOONEE KITCHURI
(*Rice and Lentil Curry*)

1 cup [about ½ pound] *moong dal*

¼ cup [2 ounces] *ghee*

¼ cup [2 ounces] vegetable oil

6 medium yellow onions, sliced

2 bay leaves

Pinch of cumin seeds

2 green chilies, seeded

1½ tablespoons [1½ inches] freshly minced gingerroot

1 cup [½ pound] long grain rice, washed and drained

½ cup [about 4 ounces] red lentils, washed and drained

1¼ teaspoons [1 E.] ground cumin

½ teaspoon [⅓ E.] ground turmeric

½ teaspoon [⅓ E.] cayenne pepper

½ teaspoon [⅓ E.] cinnamon

½ teaspoon [⅓ E.] sugar

1½ tablespoons [1¼ E.] salt

4 cardamoms, crushed

4 black peppercorns

1¼ cups [1 E.] fresh green peas

4½ to 5½ cups [3⅗ to 4⅖ E.] boiling water

5 tablespoons [4 E.] chopped coriander leaves

4 tomatoes, peeled, seeded, and chopped

1¼ teaspoons [1 E.] ground roasted cumin

½ teaspoon [⅓ E.] paprika

1. Roast *moong dal* on top of the stove in a pan without any fat over medium heat until golden brown. Stir continuously to prevent burning. Wash roasted *moong dal* and drain.

2. Heat *ghee* and vegetable oil in a large heavy saucepan or Dutch oven. Fry onions until light golden and soft; remove from the pan and set aside. Add bay leaves, cumin seeds, chilies, and gingerroot; fry, stirring, for a few seconds. Add rice and lentils. Cook a few more seconds and add ground cumin, turmeric, cayenne pepper, cinnamon, sugar, salt, cardamoms, and peppercorns. Stirring, add peas, and cook for 2 minutes over medium heat.

3. Add washed *moong dal* and boiling water. Boil over high heat for 3 to 5 minutes. Reduce heat, cover tightly, and cook gently about 30 minutes, or until soft and well cooked. Stir rice mixture up from the bottom occasionally. Uncover, add chopped coriander leaves and

tomatoes, and simmer a few more minutes. Sprinkle with ground roasted cumin and paprika. *Bhoonee kitchuri* will be more like *pullao*, but not as thin as *geela kitchuri*. Serve hot with fried onion on top, accompanied by other fried foods.

SERVES 6 to 8

SABZI KITCHURI
(*Baked Rice and Lentils*)

Baked *kitchuri* is delicious and very easy to make. It is a perfect dish for a holiday lunch.

1 cup [½ pound] long grain rice
½ cup [⅖ E.] red lentils
½ cup [⅖ E.] *moong dal*
1 cup [6 ounces] fresh green peas
2 to 3 celery stalks, cut diagonally into ½-inch pieces
3 to 4 carrots, cut into ½-inch pieces
3 to 4 broccoli stems, peeled and cut into ½-inch pieces
1 small cauliflower, cut into flowerets
2 tomatoes, peeled, seeded, and chopped
2 green peppers, cut into rings
2 green chilies, seeded and halved
2 medium yellow onions, coarsely chopped
2½ teaspoons [2 E.] salt
½ teaspoon [⅓ E.] cayenne pepper

½ teaspoon [⅓ E.] sugar
½ teaspoon [⅓ E.] ground turmeric
½ teaspoon [⅓ E.] ground cumin
1½ tablespoons [1¼ inches] freshly minced gingerroot
1 bay leaf
2 black peppercorns
4½ cups [36 ounces] water
½ cup [⅖ E.] *ghee* or vegetable oil
½ cup [⅖ E.] freshly grated coconut
2½ teaspoons [2 E.] roasted ground cumin
2½ teaspoons [2 E.] ground roasted coriander
1¼ teaspoons [1 E.] *sambhar* spice
⅓ teaspoon [¼ E.] *garam masala*
¼ cup [⅕ E.] tomato catsup
2 to 3 tablespoons [2 E.] chopped coriander leaves

Roast *moong dal* as directed in recipe for *Bhoonee Kitchuri* on page 58. Preheat oven to 350°. Wash rice and *dal*. Combine rice, lentils, roasted *moong dal*, peas, celery, carrots, broccoli stems, cauliflowerets, tomatoes, green peppers, chilies, onions, salt, cayenne pepper, sugar turmeric, cumin, gingerroot, bay leaf, and peppercorns in a Dutch oven or roasting pan. Add water and *ghee* and bake, covered, for 40 to 50 minutes. Uncover and, stirring with a fork, mix in coconut, roasted cumin and coriander, *sambhar* spice, *garam masala,* catsup, and coriander leaves. Cover and return to the oven for another 20 to 30 minutes, or until rice and *dal* are well cooked. Serve hot with omelets, fried fish, or any cutlets.

SERVES 6 to 8

MOGHLAI KITCHURI
(*Spicy Rice and Lentils*)

- 5 tablespoons [4 E.] *ghee* or vegetable oil
- 1 bay leaf
- 4 to 6 medium yellow onions, finely chopped
- 1 tablespoon [1 inch] freshly minced gingerroot
- 2 green chilies
- 1 large beet, peeled and cut into ¼-inch-thick slices
- 4 carrots, scraped and cut into 2-inch-long pieces
- ½ pound green beans, trimmed
- 1¼ cups [1 E.] fresh green peas
- 2 to 3 celery stalks, cut into 1-inch-long pieces
- ½ cup [4 ounces] yellow split peas, washed and soaked in ½ cup [4 ounces] water
- ¾ cup [⅗ E.] white split *moong dal*
- ½ cup [⅖ E.] whole green *moong dal,* washed and soaked in ½ cup [4 ounces] water for 1 hour
- 1¼ cups [1 E.] long grain rice, washed and drained
- 1¼ teaspoons [1 E.] ground cumin
- 1¼ teaspoons [1 E.] ground coriander
- ½ teaspoon [⅓ E.] ground turmeric
- ½ teaspoon [⅓ E.] cayenne pepper
- ½ teaspoon [⅓ E.] sugar
- 1½ tablespoons [1¼ E.] salt
- 1 7-ounce can tomato sauce or 2 large tomatoes, seeded and chopped
- 7 to 8 cups [56 to 64 ounces] chicken stock
- ¼ teaspoon [⅕ E.] *garam masala*
- ¼ cup [⅕ E.] chopped coriander leaves

1. Roast and wash white split *moong dal* as directed for *moong dal* in recipe for *Bhoonee Kitchuri* (see page 58).

2. Heat *ghee* or vegetable oil in a large 5- to 6-quart Dutch oven and add bay leaf, onions, gingerroot, and chilies. Cook for 2 minutes

over medium high heat, stirring often. Add beet, carrots, green beans, peas, and celery and stir to blend well. Cook about 5 minutes. Add yellow split peas, roasted split white *moong dal*, whole green *moong dal*, and rice. Stirring continuously, add cumin, coriander, turmeric, cayenne pepper, sugar, salt, tomato sauce, and chicken stock. Mix well. Boil for 2 to 3 minutes; reduce heat. Cover and cook gently for 40 to 50 minutes. Remove from heat and sprinkle with *garam masala* and chopped coriander leaves. Stir to blend well. Serve with warm *ghee* and fried fish, eggs, potatoes, or vegetables.

SERVES 6 to 8

Indian Breads

Indian breads are delicious and easy to prepare. They take less time to prepare than most other types of breads because they contain no yeast and so have no rising time; also they are quite flat and cook much faster than loaf-shaped breads. The most popular of the breads in Northern India is *chappati*, which is flat, about the size of a luncheon plate, and is made with whole wheat flour. However, Indian bread can be made of many different grains, including rice. Slight adjustments in the quantity of water used may be necessary depending on the fineness of the flour. The success of making Indian bread depends on kneading the dough to the right consistency. It should be kneaded soft and allowed to stand for about an hour before being shaped and cooked. Most Indian breads are cooked on a *tava*, which is very similar to an iron skillet except that it is concave in shape. Indian breads can be served on a *thali* or in a deep wooden bowl, covered with a piece of linen. They are eaten by tearing off a piece of the bread, wrapping the curry inside, and then eating it.

CHAPPATI
(*Baked Whole Wheat Bread*)

Chappati is more familiar to Westerners than other Indian breads. Hot *chappatis* can be served plain or with a little *ghee*. They can be kept soft and warm by wrapping them in a cloth and keeping them in a warm covered container. But they are best if served immediately after they have been cooked.

1½ cups [1⅕ E.] whole wheat
    flour
¾ cup [⅗ E.] all-purpose flour
¼ teaspoon [⅕ E.] salt

1¼ tablespoons [1 E.] *ghee* or
    vegetable oil
1 to 1¼ cups [8 to 10 ounces]
    water

---

1. Combine whole wheat flour, all-purpose flour, and salt in a bowl. Add *ghee* and mix well. Make a well in the center and gradually add enough water to make a soft dough. If the dough crumbles, add a little more water until the dough can be gathered into a compact ball. Stretch and knead well until dough is smooth and leaves the bowl clean. The more you knead, the lighter the bread will be. Cover bowl and allow dough to rest for at least 30 to 40 minutes at room temperature.

2. Divide the dough into 10 to 12 equal portions and form each one into a ball. On a lightly floured surface, roll out each ball to the thickness of a pancake. It should be about 6 inches in diameter and ⅛-inch thick. (*Chappatis* should be uniformly thick in order to puff properly.) Be sure not to let the *chappatis* dry out before baking.

3. Preheat oven to 450°. Place two or three ungreased baking sheets in the oven while the oven is being preheated. When oven reaches proper temperature, remove baking sheets and arrange breads side by side on baking sheets; bake in the center of the oven for 2 minutes, or until *chappatis* are firm to the touch. Increase heat to broil (550°) and sliding baking sheets under the broiler. Broil *chappatis* until they puff completely and are hollow in the middle. This will take about 2 minutes. Turn and broil *chappatis* a few seconds until they are set but not brown. Watch carefully to prevent *chappatis* from burning. A little *ghee* or butter may be brushed on one side. Serve immediately.

4. ALTERNATE COOKING METHOD: Heat an ungreased heavy frying pan; one at a time, place each *chappati* in the pan, and cook for one minute or less on each side (until it is firm to the touch). Then

place the *chappati* on a handled screen or open spatula, hold it over the flame of a gas burner (or an electric burner on high heat) for a few seconds on each side, until the bread puffs like a balloon.

YIELD: 10 to 12 *chappatis*

POORI
(*Fried Whole Wheat Bread*)

1 cup [⅘ E.] whole wheat flour
½ cup [⅖ E.] all-purpose flour
¼ teaspoon [⅕ E.] salt
2 tablespoons [1 ounce] *ghee* or
   vegetable oil

5 to 6 tablespoons [4 to 5 E.]
   water
Vegetable oil for deep fat
   frying

1. Combine whole wheat flour, all-purpose flour, and salt in a bowl. Add *ghee* and mix by hand. Add enough water to make a very stiff dough. Knead dough for 10 to 12 minutes. Cover bowl and set aside for 30 minutes. Break off small pieces of dough about the size of a walnut. Roll out like *chappati*, except smaller in size, about 2½ to 3 inches in diameter.

2. Heat 2 to 3 inches of vegetable oil to 425°. Drop the *poori* into the hot oil; press them lightly with the back of a spoon, to allow hot air to expand and the *poori* to puff completely. Fry breads only a few seconds, turning once; they should puff and set, but not brown. Drain on paper toweling and serve hot.

NOTE: *Poori* can be kept warm for 30 to 40 minutes by wrapping them completely in aluminum foil and placing them in a warm covered container until needed. *Poori* can also be reheated, still wrapped in foil, by placing them in a 300° oven for 15 to 25 minutes.

YIELD: 15 to 20 *pooris*

LUCHI
(*Crisp Puffed Bread*)

Luchi, a specialty made in Bengal, is tasty, very light, and crisp. It is made from all-purpose flour, a large amount of *ghee* or shortening, and very little water. The preparation is similar to *poori*.

1 cup [⅓ pound] sifted
   all-purpose flour
Big pinch of salt
2 tablespoons [1 ounce] *ghee* or
   melted butter

2 tablespoons [1 ounce] water
Vegetable oil for deep fat
   frying

1. Sift together flour and salt. Mix in *ghee* or melted butter. Add just enough water to make a stiff dough. Knead vigorously for 10 to 15 minutes. Divide evenly into 20 balls. Cover balls and set aside at room temperature for about 15 to 20 minutes. Roll out balls on an unfloured board into small, flat, thin circles. If the dough is too stiff grease the rolling pin. Roll each *luchi* as thin as possible; they should be thinner than *poori*.

2. Fry in deep fat as directed in recipe for *poori*. *Luchi* will puff to make a big bubble.

YIELD: 20 *luchis*

MATAR KOCHURI
(*Fried Bread Stuffed with Peas*)

2½ tablespoons [2 E.] *ghee*
Pinch of cumin seeds
Pinch of ground asafetida
   (optional)
¾ teaspoon [¼ inch] freshly
   minced gingerroot
1½ cups [8 to 9 ounces] green
   peas, boiled and mashed

¼ teaspoon [⅕ E.] salt
Pinch of ground turmeric
Pinch of sugar
Pinch of garlic powder
¼ teaspoon [⅕ E.] cayenne
   pepper
½ teaspoon [⅓ E.] ground
   roasted cumin
Luchi dough
Vegetable oil for deep fat
   frying

1. Heat *ghee*, fry cumin seeds, asafetida, and gingerroot for a few seconds. Add peas, salt, turmeric, sugar, and garlic powder and cook, stirring, 2 to 3 minutes over medium heat. Add cayenne pepper and roasted cumin and continue cooking about 5 to 8 minutes, or until all moisture evaporates. Remove from heat and allow to cool. Form little balls about the size of grapes.

2. Prepare *luchi* dough as directed on page 65. Divide the dough into 10 to 12 even-sized balls. Press a thumb into the center of each ball to form a cup. Fill cup with pea mixture. Reform ball so that pea mixture is enclosed in center. Flatten balls and roll very carefully, so that filling remains inside, into circles about 2 to 2½ inches in diameter. Heat vegetable oil to about 375° and fry until *kochuris* are light golden, crisp, and puffed. Drain and serve immediately.

YIELD: 10 to 12 *kochuris*

ASAFETIDA POORI
(*Spicy Lentil Bread*)

1 cup [8 ounce] *chana dal* (chick-pea *dal*), boiled for 30 minutes, or until tender, and drained
¼ cup [2 ounces] *ghee*
1¼ teaspoons [1 E.] freshly grated gingerroot
¼ teaspoon [⅕ E.] ground asafetida

½ teaspoon [⅓ E.] *garam masala*
½ teaspoon [⅓ E.] crushed red chili
¾ teaspoon [⅗ E.] salt
Poori dough
Vegetable oil for deep fat frying

1. Grind cooked lentils in a food mill. Heat *ghee* in a skillet and fry gingerroot and asafetida for a few seconds. Stirring, add *garam masala*, chili, and salt. Cook about 5 to 8 minutes; remove from heat and cool. Form little balls about the size of grapes.

2. Prepare *poori* dough as directed on page 64. Form pieces of the dough into balls the size of a walnut. Flatten balls in the palm of your hand and put a little lentil ball inside dough. Carefully reform *poori* balls so lentil balls are contained within. Roll into a flat circle ⅛ inch thick.

3. Heat vegetable oil to 375°. Fry *poori,* turning with a slotted spoon, until they are golden brown on both sides. As they puff and brown, transfer them to paper toweling to drain. Serve hot.

YIELD: 15 to 20 *pooris*

MOOLI POORI
(*Fried Bread Stuffed with Radish*)

2 tablespoons [1 ounce] *ghee*
Pinch of cumin seeds
1¼ teaspoons [1 E.] freshly grated gingerroot
1 bay leaf
1¼ cups [1 E.] grated horseradish or red radishes, drained
½ teaspoon [⅓ E.] salt
Crushed dried red pepper

½ teaspoon [⅓ E.] ground roasted cumin
1½ tablespoons [1¼ E.] finely grated fresh coconut
¼ teaspoon [⅕ E.] *garam masala*
Poori dough
Vegetable oil for deep fat frying

1. Heat *ghee* in a skillet. Add cumin seeds, gingerroot, and bay leaf and fry, stirring, for a few seconds. Add grated radishes, salt, red pepper, and ground roasted cumin and cook, stirring, over medium heat, about 5 to 8 minutes. Stir in coconut and *garam masala* and continue cooking until moisture evaporates. Remove bay leaf and set aside to cool. Form radish mixture into balls the size of grapes.

2. Prepare *poori* dough as directed on page 64. Break off pieces of dough about the size of a walnut and form into balls. Make a cup-shaped depression in the dough, insert a radish ball, and reform the dough ball so that the radish mixture is entirely contained within. Carefully roll each *poori* into a flat circle ⅛ inch thick.

3. Heat vegetable oil to 375°. Fry *pooris,* turning with a slotted spoon, until they are golden brown. As they puff and brown, transfer *pooris* to paper toweling to drain. Serve hot.

YIELD: 15 to 20 *pooris*

DHAKAI PARATHA
(*Flaky Fried Bread*)

1½ cups [½ pound] all-purpose flour
⅓ teaspoon [¼ E.] salt
¼ teaspoon [⅕ E.] baking powder
3½ tablespoons [2⅘ E.] soft butter or shortening
⅓ cup [2½ ounces] milk

1. Sift together dry ingredients. Mix in 2½ tablespoons butter or shortening. Add enough milk to make a soft dough. Cover bowl containing dough with a damp cloth and set aside for 30 minutes.

2. Knead dough well. Divide into 2 balls. Roll out each ball into a round about 6 inches in diameter and ⅙ inch thick. Brush each round with ½ tablespoon butter and sprinkle lightly with flour. Make a cut from the center of the round to the edge. Roll dough from one cut edge to the other to form a crescentlike roll. Cut each roll into 3 equal parts. Place cut side of each up, flatten, and roll out to the size of a pancake. Heat *ghee* in a shallow frying pan and fry *paratha*, turning, about 5 to 7 minutes, or until both sides are golden brown and crisp. Serve while hot.

YIELD: 6 *parathas*

GOBI or ALOO PARATHA
(*Bread Stuffed with Cauliflower or Potato Filling*)

Paratha:

3 cups [1 pound] all-purpose flour
1 cup [⅘ E.] whole wheat flour
1 teaspoon [⅘ E.] salt
1 cup [⅘ E.] *ghee*
¼ cup [2 ounces] plain yogurt
1 cup [⅘ E.] water

1. Combine all-purpose flour, whole wheat flour, salt, and ¼ cup of the *ghee* in a bowl. Mix thoroughly with hands. Add yogurt and enough water to make a stiff dough. Knead for 6 to 8 minutes. Cover bowl and set aside for 30 to 40 minutes.

2. Divide the dough into 14 to 16 equal portions. Roll portions into small, flat circles, 4 to 5 inches in diameter, on a lightly floured board. Place about 2 tablespoons of either of the following fillings

on one portion of dough circles, spreading it evenly over the surface. Cover with another dough circle, sealing edges with a little milk or water. Flatten each *paratha* with your hands, and gently roll out being careful that stuffing does not ooze out.

3. Heat an ungreased heavy skillet or griddle and place one of the filled *parathas* in the pan; cook for about a minute. With a wide spatula, turn the *paratha* over and add about one tablespoon *ghee*. Cook slowly for 2 minutes, turn *paratha* over again, add a little more *ghee*, and fry a few more minutes. Fry *paratha* until it is crisp and brown on both sides. Fry remaining *parathas* in same manner. Serve with *rayta* or chutney.

Cauliflower Filling:

3 to 4 tablespoons [3 E.] *ghee* or vegetable oil
1 medium yellow onion, finely chopped
1 large clove of garlic, finely minced
2½ teaspoons [2 E.] freshly minced gingerroot
Pinch of cumin seeds

1 green chili, seeded and chopped
1 medium cauliflower, trimmed and chopped
1¼ teaspoons [1 E.] salt
1¼ teaspoons [1 E.] ground cumin
¼ teaspoon [⅕ E.] ground turmeric
⅓ teaspoon [¼ E.] *garam masala*

Heat *ghee* in a skillet. Add onion, garlic, gingerroot, cumin seeds, and chili and fry until onion is soft. Add cauliflower, salt, cumin, turmeric, and *garam masala*. Fry for 2 more minutes; cover and cook gently until cauliflower is tender but not mushy, 6 to 8 minutes. Uncover and cook until the moisture evaporates.

Potato Filling:

3 to 4 tablespoons [3 E.] *ghee* or vegetable oil
1 medium yellow onion, finely chopped
1 to 2 cloves of garlic, finely minced
½-inch piece of finely minced gingerroot
2 to 3 large potatoes, peeled, boiled, and mashed

2 green chilies, seeded and finely chopped
1¼ teaspoons [1 E.] salt
1¼ teaspoons [1 E.] ground cumin
1¼ teaspoons [1 E.] chopped coriander leaves
⅓ teaspoon [¼ E.] turmeric
⅓ teaspoon [¼ E.] *garam masala*

Heat *ghee* or vegetable oil in a frying pan. Add onion, garlic, and gingerroot, and fry until onion is soft. Add mashed potatoes, chilies, salt, cumin, coriander leaves, turmeric, and *garam masala* and fry for 8 minutes, or until moisture evaporates.

NAAN
(*Roasted Bread*)

1¼ cups [1 E.] sifted all-purpose flour
¾ teaspoon [⅜ E.] sugar
¼ teaspoon [⅕ E.] salt
Pinch of baking soda
Pinch of baking powder
1 egg, lightly beaten

2 tablespoons [1 ounce] plain yogurt
½ cup [⅖ E.] milk (approximately)
1½ tablespoons [1¼ E.] *ghee*
Poppy seeds

1. In a large bowl, sift together flour, sugar, salt, baking soda, and baking powder. Add egg and yogurt and mix with hands. Gradually add enough milk to make a soft dough. Moisten your hands with *ghee* and knead well. Cover the bowl and set aside in a warm place for 2 to 4 hours.

2. Divide the dough into 6 to 8 equal portions. Moistening your palms with *ghee* as necessary to keep dough from sticking to your hands, flatten each portion and form it into the shape of a leaf, wide at the base and narrowed at the top. It should be about 6 inches long, 4 inches wide, and ¼ inch thick. Brush tops of leaves with *ghee* and sprinkle with a few poppy seeds.

3. Preheat oven containing two to three baking sheets to 450°. Arrange breads side by side on baking sheets and bake in the middle of the oven for 6 to 8 minutes. Slip baking sheets under the broiler for a few seconds, or until *naan* are lightly browned.

YIELD: 6 to 8 *naan*

KHASTA MOGHLAI PARATHA
(*Flaky Meat Pastry*)

2 tablespoons [1 ounce] *ghee* or vegetable oil

1 medium yellow onion, finely chopped

1 pound lean beef or lamb, minced

¾ teaspoon [⅗ E.] ground cumin

¾ teaspoon [⅗ E.] ground coriander

¼ teaspoon [⅕ E.] turmeric

¼ teaspoon [⅕ E.] ground dried red pepper

¼ teaspoon [⅕ E.] *garam masala*

2½ tablespoons [2 E.] chopped coriander leaves

2½ tablespoons [2 E.] sour cream

¼ teaspoon [⅕ E.] salt

Paratha dough (page 68)

¼ cup [⅕ E.] *ghee*

1. Heat *ghee* in a frying pan and fry onion, beef, cumin, coriander, turmeric, red pepper, and *garam masala* for 8 to 10 minutes over medium heat. Stirring, add coriander leaves, sour cream, and salt. Remove from heat, drain excess fat, and cool.

2. Prepare *paratha* dough as directed on page 68. Divide dough into 16 equal balls. Roll out each ball into a flat round about 6 inches in diameter and ⅛ inch thick. Sprinkle the surface of one circle with a little water and spread with a very thin layer of meat mixture. Cover with another thin circle and another thin layer of meat mixture until you have 3 layers of meat and 4 layers of thin pastry. Crimp edges with a fork, being sure they are well sealed.

3. Heat an ungreased skillet. Place a pastry in the pan and cook over medium heat 5 to 8 minutes on each side, or until evenly cooked. Add one tablespoon of *ghee* at a time and fry gently another 4 to 5 minutes, turning a few times, until *paratha* is crisp.

YIELD: 4 *parathas*

Dal or Lentils

Lentils are very popular in India and available in a number of varieties—red lentils, split yellow peas, and so on. *Dal* is served with boiled rice or *chappatis* or as a regular main dish. In India a large number of people are vegetarians. Lentils are highly nutritious, rich in vitamins B1 and B2, and are the major source of protein in vegetarian diets.

Cooking *dal* is usually a quick and easy procedure, although some beans—like chick-peas and dried beans—may require several hours of soaking followed by 2 to 2½ hours of simmering. (Note that lentils should always be cooked in the water in which they are soaked.) After *dal* becomes tender, it is mixed, over low heat, with onions that have been previously sauteed with spices in *ghee.*

MOONG DAL
(*Lentil Curry*)

1¼ cups [1 E.] *moong dal*, roasted
1½ to 2 cups [12 to 16 ounces]
    water
1¼ teaspoons [1 E.] salt
¼ teaspoon [⅕ E.] ground
    turmeric
3 tablespoons [1½ ounces] *ghee*
Pinch of cumin seeds
2 small bay leaves
2 red chilies
2 medium yellow onions, thinly
    sliced (optional)

1¼ teaspoons [1 E.] freshly grated
    gingerroot
2½ tablespoons [2 E.] raisins
¼ cup [⅕ E.] finely chopped
    fresh coconut
¼ teaspoon [⅕ E.] ground
    cardamom
¼ teaspoon [⅕ E.] *garam masala*
¼ teaspoon [⅕ E.] sugar
2 to 4 tablespoons [1½ to 3 E.]
    chopped coriander leaves

1. Wash roasted *dal* and bring to a boil. Add salt, and turmeric. While boiling, remove scum. Cover and simmer about 20 to 30 minutes, or until tender. Be careful not to disturb *dal* during the simmering process since stirring may break the grains.

2. Heat *ghee* in a large saucepan. Add cumin seeds, bay leaves, chilies, onions, and gingerroot. Fry about 2 minutes, stirring. Add raisins and coconut and mix in prepared boiled *dal*. Add cardamom, *garam masala*, sugar, coriander leaves and mix well. Simmer over low heat, uncovered, for 16 to 20 minutes. If *dal* is too thick, add a little warm water. It should be creamy and thick, like pea soup.

SERVES 4 to 6

JHINGA MASOOR
(*Red Lentils with Shrimp*)

1¼ cups [1 E.] red lentils
2½ cups [2 E.] water
1 medium yellow onion, chopped
1¼ teaspoons [1 E.] salt
⅓ teaspoon [¼ E.] turmeric
¼ cup [2 ounces] *ghee*
Pinch of black cumin seeds
2 whole red or green chilies

2 medium yellow onions, finely
    chopped
1 pound shrimp, peeled and
    deveined
Pinch of salt
Pinch of ground turmeric
2 to 4 tablespons [1½ to 3 E.]
    chopped coriander leaves

1. Wash lentils and bring to a boil. Add onion, salt, and turmeric. Skim foam from the top during boiling. Cover and simmer until the lentils are creamy, about 20 minutes.

2. Heat *ghee* in a saucepan. Add black cumin seeds, whole chilies, and onions and fry gently until onions are soft. Add shrimp, salt, and turmeric. Cook, stirring, about one minute. Add lentils and boil for 2 to 3 minutes. Add coriander leaves and mix well. Remove from heat. Serve with boiled rice.

NOTE: For a creamier *dal*, beat boiled lentils with an egg beater.

SERVES 4 to 6

GRAM DAL
(*Chick-pea Lentil Curry*)

½ pound (about 1 cup) *gram dal*
2½ to 3 cups [20 to 25 ounces] water
1¼ teaspoons [1 E.] salt
¼ teaspoon [⅕ E.] ground turmeric
¼ cup [2 ounces] *ghee*
Pinch of cumin seeds
Pinch of ground asafetida (hing)

1¼ teaspoons [1 E.] freshly grated gingerroot
1 bay leaf
2½ tablespoons [2 E.] freshly chopped coconut
2½ tablespoons [2 E.] raisins
1¼ cups [1 E.] frozen green peas
¼ teaspoon [⅕ E.] sugar
¼ teaspoon [⅕ E.] paprika
¼ teaspoon [⅕ E.] *garam masala*

1. Soak *gram dal* in water for 2 hours. Bring lentils to a boil in their soaking water. Add salt and turmeric and continue to boil for 2 or 3 minutes. Remove scum during boiling. Cover and cook slowly about 30 to 40 minutes, or until lentils are tender. Remove from heat.

2. Heat *ghee* in a saucepan; add cumin seeds, asafetida, gingerroot, and bay leaf. Fry for a few seconds, stirring. Add coconut, raisins, and peas. Cook over medium heat for 2 minutes. Stir in boiled lentils. Add sugar, paprika, and *garam masala* and mix well. Simmer for 15 minutes. Serve with Indian bread.

SERVES 4 to 6

MATAR DAL
(*Yellow Split-pea Curry*)

½ pound (about 1 cup) yellow split peas
2½ cups [2 E.] water
1¼ teaspoons [1 E.] salt
Big pinch of ground turmeric
1¼ teaspoons [1 E.] ground cumin
2½ tablespoons [2 E.] lemon juice
1¼ teaspoons [1 E.] ground coriander
¼ teaspoon [⅕ E.] cayenne pepper
Pinch of garlic powder
Pinch of sugar
¼ cup [2 ounces] *ghee*

Pinch of cumin seeds
2 red or green chilies
2 medium yellow onions, finely chopped
¾ teaspoon [⅗ E.] freshly grated gingerroot
1 bay leaf
½-pound slab of bacon or chicken livers, chopped
2½ tablespoons [2 E.] tomato paste
Pinch of monosodium glutamate
Pinch of seasoned salt
Pinch of paprika

---

1. Wash split peas and soak in water for 20 minutes. Boil split peas in their soaking water. Add salt and turmeric and boil for 2 minutes, removing scum. Cover and cook gently 15 to 20 minutes, or until tender. Remove from heat. Add ground cumin, lemon juice, coriander, cayenne pepper, garlic powder, and sugar to boiled split peas.

2. Heat *ghee* in a large saucepan and cook cumin seeds, chilies, onions, gingerroot, bay leaf, and bacon or chicken livers for 3 to 4 minutes. Add tomato paste, monosodium glutamate, and seasoned salt. Stirring, add boiled peas mixture. Sprinkle with paprika and mix well. Cook slowly for 15 to 20 minutes. If mixture is too thick, add a little warm water.

SERVES 4 to 6

SAMBHAR
(*Peas with Fresh Vegetables*)

1 cup (½ pound) *tur dal*
4 cups [32 ounces] water
1¾ to 2 teaspoons [1½ E.] salt
¼ teaspoon [⅕ E.] ground
  turmeric
2 tablespoons [1 ounce]
  vegetable oil
1 eggplant (about 1 pound),
  washed but not peeled, and
  cut into 2-inch cubes
  Big pinch of salt
2 to 3 tablespoons [2 to 3 ounces]
  dried tamarind or ⅓ to ½
  cup lemon juice may be used
1 cup boiling water

¼ cup [⅕ E.] vegetable oil
  Pinch of fenugreek seeds
  Pinch of black mustard seeds
¼ pound green beans, cut into
  2-inch pieces
1 green pepper, roughly chopped
4 to 6 small white onions, peeled
6 to 8 small radishes, halved
1 or 2 green or red chilies
1 bay leaf
1¼ teaspoons [1 E.] *sambhar* spice
¼ cup [⅕ E.] chopped coriander
  leaves
1 large tomato, seeded and
  roughly chopped
¼ cup [⅕ E.] freshly chopped
  coconut

1. Wash *tur dal* and soak for 15 minutes. Add salt, turmeric, and 2 tablespoons vegetable oil to soaking water. Boil 30 to 40 minutes or until tender. Remove from heat.

2. Place eggplant pieces in a bowl and sprinkle with salt. Mix well and set aside for 30 to 40 minutes. Place tamarind in another bowl, add boiling water, and set aside to soak for 15 minutes. Strain the tamarind mixture through a strainer set over a bowl and keep the liquid, discarding tamarind remains. (Or use lemon juice to taste.)

3. Drain eggplant pieces on a paper towel. Heat vegetable oil in a large pan over moderate heat. Fry fenugreek seeds and black mustard seeds until they crack open. Add green beans, green pepper, onions, radishes, chilies, and bay leaf and cook for 2 to 3 minutes, or until the vegetables are lightly brown. Add eggplant pieces and continue cooking and stirring about 5 more minutes. Stir in *sambhar* spice, coriander leaves, tomato, and coconut and cook gently for another 2 minutes. Cover and cook gently until the vegetables are tender but not mushy. Mix in tamarind liquid (or lemon juice) and boiled lentil mixture. Stir to blend well. Simmer uncovered for 10

to 15 minutes. Sprinkle with some more chopped coriander leaves. Serve with boiled rice or Indian bread.

SERVES 4 to 6

PIAZA SAMBHAR
(*Onion Sambhar*)

1 pound small white onions, peeled
⅓ teaspoon [¼ E.] ground turmeric
1¼ teaspoons [1 E.] salt
2 cups [16 ounces] water
1½ tablespoons [1¼ E.] dried tamarind
½ cup [⅖ E.] red lentils, boiled with 2 cups [16 ounces] water

2 tablespoons [1 ounce] *ghee* or vegetable oil
Big pinch of mustard seeds
1 red chili
Pinch of ground asafetida (*hing*), (optional)
1¼ teaspoons [1 E.] *sambhar* spice
2½ tablespoons [2 E.] finely chopped coconut
2½ tablespoons [2 E.] chopped coriander leaves

1. Boil onions with turmeric, salt and 1½ cups water for 3 to 4 minutes. Place tamarind in a bowl, add ½ cup of boiling water, and set aside for 15 minutes. Strain the tamarind mixture through a strainer set over a bowl and keep the liquid, discarding tamarind remains. Add tamarind liquid to the onions and liquid, cover, and cook gently until the onions are tender, about 10 minutes. Mix in boiled lentils. Remove from heat.

2. Heat *ghee* in a saucepan and add mustard seeds, chili, and asafetida and fry for a few seconds. Add lentil mixture, *sambhar* spice, coconut, and coriander leaves. Simmer for 20 minutes. Onion *sambhar* should not be too thick; if necessary add a little warm water.

SERVES 4 to 6

MASSALEDARH SAMBHAR
(*Tomato Rasam*)

½ cup [⅖ E.] yellow split peas, boiled with 4 cups [32 ounces] water until tender
Big pinch of ground turmeric
Big pinch of black pepper
Big pinch of ground asafetida (*hing*)
⅓ teaspoon [¼ E.] ground cumin
⅓ teaspoon [¼ E.] cayenne pepper
2½ tablespoons [2 E.] lemon juice
1¼ teaspoons [1 E.] salt

2 tablespoons [1 ounce] vegetable oil
¼ teaspoon [⅕ E.] mustard seeds
1 bay leaf
1 small yellow onion, finely chopped
1 green pepper, finely chopped
4 large tomatoes, peeled and chopped
¼ cup [⅕ E.] chopped coriander leaves

1. Grind the lentil mixture in a food mill until creamy. Mix in turmeric, black pepper, asafetida, cumin, cayenne pepper, lemon juice, and salt.

2. Heat vegetable oil in a large skillet. Fry mustard seeds until they crack open; add bay leaf, onion, green pepper, and tomatoes. Cook, stirring, for 2 to 3 minutes. Mix in lentil mixture. Stir in coriander leaves. Simmer for 10 to 15 minutes.

SERVES 4 to 5

MOGHLAI URAD DAL
(*Spiced Kidney Beans*)

½ pound kidney beans
6 to 7 cups [5 to 6 E.] water
½ pound black *dal* (whole *urad*)
¼ pound split *urad* lentils
2 teaspoons [1⅗ E.] salt
2 small bay leaves
¾ teaspoon [⅗ E.] ground
 turmeric
2 green chilies, seeded and
 chopped
3 tomatoes, peeled, seeded, and
 chopped
3 to 4 cups [24 to 32 ounces]
 chicken stock
½ pint [8 ounces] sour cream
¼ cup [⅕ E.] *ghee*
2 medium yellow onions, finely
 chopped

Pinch of cumin seeds
Pinch of ground asafetida
 (*hing*)
1 tablespoon [1 inch] freshly
 grated gingerroot
4 cardamoms, crushed
Pinch of ground nutmeg
Pinch of ground cloves
Pinch of sugar
½ teaspoon [⅓ E.] cayenne
 pepper
½ teaspoon [⅓ E.] *garam masala*
2½ tablespoons [2 E.] ground
 roasted cumin
2½ tablespoons [2 E.] chopped
 coriander leaves
¼ cup [⅕ E.] lemon juice

1. Wash kidney beans, black *urad dal* and split *urad* lentils. Cover with 6 to 7 cups water and soak for 4 to 5 hours. Boil beans, *dal*, and lentils in their soaking water with salt, bay leaves, turmeric, and chilies over medium heat 1 to 1½ hours, or until beans and lentils are very tender. Stir lentils with a wooden spoon while boiling as they stick to the pan easily. Add chopped tomatoes and chicken stock and continue cooking another 10 to 15 minutes. Mix in sour cream. Remove from heat.

2. Heat *ghee* in a large saucepan. Add onions, cumin seeds, and asafetida. Cook until onion is soft. Stir in gingerroot, cardamoms, nutmeg, cloves, sugar, cayenne pepper, and *garam masala*. Mix in boiled bean, *dal*, and lentil mixture. Add roasted cumin and coriander leaves and mix thoroughly. Simmer for 30 minutes, uncovered, stirring often. Remove from heat and mix in lemon juice before serving. If the gravy is too thick, add in additional chicken stock. The flavor of *Moghlai Urad Dal* improves a day or two after preparation. Serve with Indian bread.

SERVES 8 to 10

Vegetables

Most people in the world enjoy curries, and India is noted for her curry dishes. All curries are not made in the same way; each province has its own way of preparing different dishes. There are different types of curries such as vegetable curry, egg curry, fish curry, meat curry, or liver curry. But it is very important to remember that in India people do not use curry powder. Instead they use several individual spices. Each recipe uses its own special combination of spices, and that makes the difference.

Vegetable curries are prepared from one or more vegetables combined with various combinations of spices. It's sad that so many people do not enjoy vegetables. Perhaps they've never had a well-prepared vegetable dish. Vegetable curry is very simple to make, but when cooked properly, it is delicious and as satisfying as meat. Because such a large number of Indians are vegetarians, Indians are expert in the art of cooking vegetables. Vegetables can be cooked with or without gravy. Leafy vegetables such as spinach and cabbage always taste better without gravy, while others (cauliflower, potatoes, beans, eggplant, peas, etc.), are very good for gravy curries. In India there is a tremendous variety of vegetables, but not all are available in North America. Some North American vegetables, however, are very close to those grown in India and may be used as a substitute. Zucchini, for example, is very similar to our Indian white gourd, *kuddoo* or *laou*. Bean sprouts can be substituted for the Indian vegetable banana flower (*mocha*). *Karela*, bitter-gourd or bitter melon, is a very popular vegetable in India. This vegetable and *paraval* (sometimes called *patol*) are available in a can. Occasionally fresh *karela* is available at Chinese or special markets. For cooking, always cut fresh *karela* without peeling. Add canned *karela* in a recipe when the other vegetables are almost cooked.

SHUKTO
(*Karela Curry*)

4 to 6 tablespoons [2 to 3
  ounces] *ghee*
Pinch of *punch-phoron* seeds
1½ teaspoons [½ inch] freshly
  minced gingerroot
1 bay leaf
2 carrots, scraped and cut into
  1-inch pieces
1 sweet potato, scraped and cut
  into 1-inch cubes
2 to 3 broccoli stems, peeled and
  cut into 1-inch lengths
¼ pound green beans, cut into
  2-inch lengths

2 to 3 celery stalks, cut into
  1-inch lengths
1¼ cups [1 cup E.] *karela*, roughly
  chopped
10 to 15 small radishes, halved
½ cup [⅖ E.] fresh green peas
½ teaspoon [⅓ E.] ground
  turmeric
1¼ teaspoons [1 E.] salt
Pinch of sugar
½ cup [⅖ E.] freshly grated
  coconut
2½ teaspoons [2 E.] dry mustard
2 tablespoons water

Heat *ghee* in a large pan and fry *punch-phoron* seeds, gingerroot, and bay leaf for a few seconds. Add carrots, sweet potato, broccoli stems, green beans, celery, *karela*, radishes, and peas. Cook over high heat, stirring quickly and constantly, about 5 minutes. Stir in turmeric, salt, and sugar. Cover tightly and cook over medium heat about 10 to 15 minutes, or until the vegetables are tender yet firm. Uncover, stir with a fork, and continue cooking gently until excess liquid boils away. Prepare mustard paste as directed on page 16. Add coconut and mustard paste and mix well. Serve with boiled rice.

NOTE: ¼ cup [⅕ E.] poppy seeds, blended in a blender with a little water until smooth, may be used instead of mustard paste. Also ¼ cup [⅕ E.] fried and crushed *vadi* may be used if desired (page 20). Mix *vadi* into the vegetables with mustard paste or poppy seed paste.

SERVES 4 to 6

KARELA DOLMA
(Stuffed Karela)

1 19-ounce can *karela*
Pinch of salt
¼ cup [2 ounces] *ghee* or
vegetable oil
Pinch of cumin seeds
1 green chili, seeded and
chopped
1 tablespoon [1 inch] finely
minced gingerroot
1 medium yellow onion, finely
chopped
2 large potatoes, peeled, boiled,
and mashed

1¼ teaspoons [1 E.] ground
roasted cumin
1¼ teaspoons [1 E.] ground roasted
coriander
¼ teaspoon [⅕ E.] turmeric
¼ teaspoon [⅕ E.] crushed dried
red pepper
¾ teaspoon [⅗ E.] salt
4 to 5 tablespoons [3 to 4 E.]
tamarind liquid or lemon
juice
¼ cup [⅕ E.] all-purpose flour
¼ cup [⅕ E.] bread crumbs
¾ cup [⅗ E.] vegetable oil

1. Strain *karela* into a pot reserving the liquid. Heat liquid to boiling and add *karela* and pinch of salt. Cover and cook gently for 3 minutes; drain the liquid and dry the *karela* pieces on paper toweling. Cool.

2. Heat *ghee* in a large skillet; fry cumin seeds, green chili, gingerroot, and onion for 2 minutes. Add mashed potatoes, cumin, and ground roasted coriander, turmeric, red pepper, and salt. Stirring, cook about 10 minutes over medium heat. Mix in tamarind or lemon juice and set aside to cool.

3. Cut *karela* into 2-inch pieces. Stuff with potato mixture and tie with a piece of thread to hold together. Roll in all-purpose flour, then carefully dip in well beaten egg and roll in bread crumbs; repeat egg and bread-crumb coatings. Place on wire rack and chill in the refrigerator for about one hour. Fry in preheated vegetable oil about 5 minutes, or until golden brown. Drain, remove thread, and serve hot with *dal* and boiled rice.

YIELD: 15 to 16 *karela*

KARELA BHUJJIA
(*Karela with Eggplant*)

- ¼ cup [⅕ E.] vegetable oil
- 1 fresh *karela* or ½ of a 19-ounce can *karela*, chopped
- ⅛ teaspoon [1/10 E.] turmeric
- 4 medium yellow onions, finely chopped
- 1 tablespoon [1 inch] freshly minced gingerroot
- 2 green chilies, seeded and chopped (optional)
- 1 medium eggplant, chopped but not peeled
- ¼ teaspoon [⅕ E.] salt
- Pinch of sugar

Heat vegetable oil in a large skillet. Fry onions until light golden brown. Remove from pan and set aside. Add fresh *karela*, pinch of salt, and pinch of turmeric and cook for about 5 minutes, or until all moisture evaporates. (Cook canned *karela* for about 3 minutes.) Remove and set aside. Fry gingerroot, chilies, eggplant, salt, big pinch of turmeric, and sugar for 2 to 4 minutes. Cover and simmer until eggplant is tender. Uncover; add *karela* and fried onion. Cook, stirring, for another 5 to 8 minutes. Serve with boiled rice.

SERVES 4 to 6

BHAPA KARELA CHOP
(*Baked Karela Chops*)

- 2 large potatoes, peeled, boiled, and mashed
- 1¼ teaspoons [1 E.] ground roasted cumin
- 1¼ teaspoons [1 E.] ground roasted coriander
- ¼ teaspoon [⅕ E.] ground turmeric
- ¼ teaspoon [⅕ E.] crushed red chili
- ½ teaspoon [⅓ E.] *sambhar* spice
- ¼ cup [2 ounces] vegetable oil
- 2 medium yellow onions, finely chopped
- 1½ teaspoons [½ inch] freshly grated gingerroot
- 1 19-ounce can *karela*, drained and chopped
- 1 large egg
- ¾ teaspoon [⅗ E.] salt
- 2 to 4 tablespoons [1½ to 3 E.] grated cheddar cheese

1. Combine mashed potatoes, cumin, coriander, turmeric, chili, and *sambhar* spice and mix well. Heat vegetable oil in a skillet and

fry onions and gingerroot for about 2 minutes. Add potato mixture and cook, stirring, about 5 minutes over medium heat. Remove from heat and mix in *karela*, egg, and salt.

2. Preheat oven to 350°. Grease an 8-inch-square baking pan. Spread the *karela* mixture evenly in the baking pan and bake for 20 minutes. Sprinkle cheese on top and slide under the broiler for one minute, or until cheese starts to melt. Cut into squares before serving. Serve with *dal* and boiled rice.

YIELD: 6 to 8 chops

SAIM FOOGATH
(*Green Beans with Coconut*)

2 tablespoons [1 ounce] vegetable oil
Pinch of mustard seeds
2 green chilies, seeded and chopped
1 pound green beans, chopped
⅛ teaspoon [1/10 E.] turmeric

½ teaspoon [⅓ E.] salt
Pinch of sugar
½ cup [⅖ E.] freshly grated coconut
2½ teaspoons [2 E.] dry mustard
2 tablespoons [1⅗ E.] water

Heat vegetable oil in a heavy skillet and fry mustard seeds until they pop. Add chilies, green beans, turmeric, and salt and cook gently about 5 minutes. Cover and cook until beans are tender, 6 to 8 minutes. Prepare mustard paste as directed on page 16. Add sugar, coconut, and mustard paste to skillet. Cook, stirring, until most of the liquid is absorbed. Serve with boiled rice or Indian bread.

SERVES 4

BUND GOBI FOOGATH
(*Cabbage with Coconut*)

5 to 6 tablespoons [about
3 ounces] vegetable oil
Pinch of mustard seeds
2 green chilies, seeded and
chopped
2 to 2½ pounds cabbage, finely
shredded
¼ teaspoon [⅕ E.] ground
turmeric

1¼ teaspoons [1 E.] salt
Pinch of sugar
¾ cup [⅗ E.] freshly grated
coconut
2½ teaspoons [2 E.] dry mustard
2 tablespoons [1⅗ E.] water

Heat vegetable oil in a heavy skillet and fry mustard seeds until they pop. Add chilies, cabbage, and turmeric; cook gently about 5 minutes. Cover and cook until cabbage is tender. Prepare mustard paste as directed on page 16. Add salt, sugar, coconut, and mustard paste to skillet. Cook, stirring, until most of the liquid is absorbed. Serve with boiled rice or Indian bread.

SERVES 4

PHUL GOBI FOOGATH
(*Cauliflower with coconut*)

¼ cup [2 ounces] vegetable oil
Pinch of mustard seeds
2 green chilies, seeded and
chopped
1 medium cauliflower, coarsely
chopped
¼ teaspoon [⅕ E.] turmeric
¼ teaspoon [⅕ E.] freshly grated
gingerroot
Pinch of sugar

½ teaspoon [⅓ E.] salt
½ cup [⅖ E.] freshly grated
coconut
2½ teaspoons [2 E.] dry mustard
2 tablespoons [1⅗ E.] water
2 to 4 tablespoons [1½ to 3 E.]
thinly sliced almonds
(optional)

Heat vegetable oil in a heavy skillet and fry mustard seeds until they pop. Add chilies, cauliflower, turmeric, and gingerroot; cook gently about 5 minutes. Cover and cook until cauliflower is tender. Prepare mustard paste as directed on page 16. Add sugar, salt, coconut, and almonds to skillet. Cook, stirring, until most of the liquid is absorbed. Serve with boiled rice or Indian bread.

SERVES 4

SAIM RASA
(*Green Bean Curry*)

2 tablespoons [1 ounce] vegetable oil
1 medium yellow onion, finely chopped
2 green chilies, seeded and chopped (optional)
¾ teaspoon [¼ inch] freshly minced gingerroot
1 pound green beans, trimmed
2½ teaspoons [2 E.] spiced onion

½ teaspoon [⅓ E.] salt
¾ teaspoon [⅗ E.] ground cumin
¼ teaspoon [⅕ E.] ground turmeric
3 tomatoes, cut into eighths
2½ teaspoons [2 E.] dry mustard
2 tablespoons [1⅗ E.] water
2 to 4 tablespoons [1½ to 3 E.] chopped coriander leaves

Heat oil in a large skillet with a cover and fry onion, chilies, and gingerroot for 2 minutes. Add beans, spiced onion, salt, cumin, and turmeric and cook over moderate heat about 5 to 8 minutes. Add tomatoes and cover. Cook gently until beans are tender, about 8 minutes. Uncover and boil off any excess liquid. Prepare mustard paste and add to pan. Simmer uncovered for 5 minutes. Be careful not to overcook the beans. They should stay slightly crisp. Garnish with coriander leaves.

SERVES 4

ALOO DOM
(*Potato Curry*)

1½ pounds small new potatoes,
   boiled in their jackets and
   peeled
¾ cup [⅗ E.] *ghee*
Pinch of salt
Pinch of turmeric
2 small bay leaves
Pinch of cumin seeds
2 red chilies (optional)
1½ teaspoons [½ inch] freshly
   minced gingerroot
1 large clove garlic, finely minced
2 medium yellow onions, thinly
   sliced

2½ tablespoons [2 E.] spiced onion
1¼ teaspoons [1 E.] ground cumin
1¼ teaspoons [1 E.] ground
   coriander
1¼ teaspoons [1 E.] salt
½ teaspoon [⅓ E.] ground
   turmeric
½ teaspoon [⅓ E.] cayenne
   pepper
½ teaspoon [⅓ E.] *garam masala*
¾ cup [⅗ E.] chicken stock
½ cup [3 ounces] plain yogurt
2½ teaspoons [2 E.] lemon juice

1. Heat ½ cup *ghee* in a skillet and fry potatoes with a pinch of salt and a pinch of turmeric until golden brown. Remove and set aside.

2. In another pan with a tight-fitting lid, heat ¼ cup *ghee*. Add bay leaves, cumin seeds, chilies, gingerroot, garlic, and onions and fry for 2 minutes. Add spiced onion, ground cumin, coriander, salt, turmeric, cayenne pepper, *garam masala*, and a tablespoon of water and cook for 2 to 3 minutes. Add fried potatoes and continue cooking another 2 minutes. Add chicken stock, cover, and cook gently for 10 minutes. Remove from heat, stir in yogurt, and return to heat. Simmer, covered, for 20 minutes. Sprinkle with lemon juice. Remove from heat. Garnish with chopped coriander leaves. Serve with Indian bread.

SERVES 6

PALAK BHUJJIA
(*Fried Spinach*)

1 cup cooked fresh spinach
 [10 ounces uncooked]
3 tablespoons [1½ ounces]
 vegetable oil
Pinch of black cumin seeds
Pinch of turmeric
Pinch of sugar
1¼ cups [1 E.] frozen mixed
 vegetables

½ teaspoon [⅓ E.] ground cumin
½ teaspoon [⅓ E.] ground
 coriander
½ teaspoon [⅓ E.] salt
Crushed, dried red pepper, to
 taste
¼ cup [⅕ E.] crushed fried *vadi*
 (page 20)
¼ cup [⅕ E.] chopped peanuts

Wash and finely chop spinach. Boil ¼ cup water. Add chopped spinach, cover, and cook about 6 minutes. Drain well. Heat vegetable oil in a skillet and add cumin seeds, turmeric, sugar, frozen vegetables, ground cumin, coriander, salt, and red pepper. Cook for 3 to 4 minutes, or until the moisture evaporates. Add spinach and continue cooking and stirring, over medium-low heat, about 5 more minutes. Stir in *vadi* and peanuts, and cook slowly for about 2 minutes. Remove from heat. Serve with boiled rice.

SERVES 2 to 4

BENGALI PALAK SAG
(*Bengali-Style Spinach*)

5 tablespoons [4 E.] vegetable oil
3 large yellow onions, thinly
 sliced
2 cloves garlic, finely minced
1¼ pounds (6 to 8) carrots, cut
 into 1-inch pieces
½ pound (medium) eggplant,
 sliced in 1-inch strips
1¼ teaspoons [1 E.] salt

¼ teaspoon [⅕ E.] ground
 turmeric
1¼ teaspoons [1 E.] ground cumin
¾ pound spinach, washed and
 drained
½ teaspoon [⅓ E.] crushed red
 chili
¼ cup [⅕ E.] crushed, fried *vadi*
 (optional)

Heat vegetable oil in a large skillet with a tight-fitting lid. Add onions and garlic and fry for 2 minutes. Add carrots, eggplant, salt, turmeric, and cumin and cook gently, covered, about 20 minutes, or until vegetables are tender. Uncover and, adding a handful of spinach at a time, stir over medium heat for 30 seconds; repeat until all the spinach is added. Cook another 5 to 8 minutes, stirring often. Sprinkle in chili and *vadi* and mix well. Remove from heat and keep covered until ready to serve.

SERVES 4 to 6

SHALGAM RASA
(*Turnip Curry*)

5 tablespoons [4 E.] vegetable oil
Pinch of fennel seeds
2 pounds turnip, sliced into 1-inch strips
2 teaspoons [1⅗ E.] salt
½ teaspoon [⅓ E.] ground turmeric

1¼ teaspoons [1 E.] ground cumin
1 cup [8 ounces] evaporated milk or whole milk
⅓ teaspoon [¼ E.] crushed red chili
2½ tablespoons [2 E.] chopped coriander leaves

Heat vegetable oil in a large skillet with a tight-fitting lid. Add fennel seeds and turnip strips. Fry, stirring, about 2 to 4 minutes over medium heat. Add salt, turmeric, and cumin and mix well. Cover and cook gently over low heat until turnip is soft, 8 to 10 minutes. Uncover and drain off excess oil. Stirring, add evaporated milk and cook over medium heat about 3 minutes. Remove from heat and sprinkle with chili and coriander leaves. Serve with boiled rice or Indian bread.

SERVES 4 to 6

PHUL GOBI DALNA
(*Cauliflower Curry*)

¼ cup [⅕ E.] vegetable oil
1 medium cauliflower, cut in flowerets
Pinch of salt
Pinch of turmeric
1 large baking potato, peeled and cut into dice
¼ cup [2 ounces] *ghee*
1 bay leaf
Pinch of cumin seeds
2 cardamoms, crushed
1½ teaspoons [½ inch] freshly minced gingerroot
1 medium yellow onion, finely chopped

2½ teaspoons [2 E.] spiced onion
1¼ teaspoons [1 E.] ground cumin
1¼ teaspoons [1 E.] ground coriander
1 cup [6 ounces] fresh green peas
2 large tomatoes, peeled, seeded, and chopped
1 teaspoon [⅘ E.] salt
Pinch of sugar
1 cup [8 ounces] thin coconut milk or warm water
2½ tablespoons [2 E.] chopped coriander leaves

1. Heat vegetable oil in a large skillet and fry cauliflower with a pinch of salt and a pinch of turmeric over medium heat until cauliflowerets are light brown. Remove from pan and set aside. Fry potatoes until golden; drain on paper toweling.

2. Heat *ghee* in another large skillet. Add bay leaf, cumin seeds, cardamoms, gingerroot, and chopped onion. Fry for 3 minutes, stirring. Add spiced onion, ground cumin, coriander, peas, tomatoes, salt, sugar, and fried potato. Cook slowly about 3 to 4 minutes. Add coconut milk and bring to a boil. Add fried cauliflowerets; cover and cook about 5 to 8 minutes, or until vegetables are tender. Sprinkle with coriander leaves and simmer, uncovered, for a few minutes.

NOTE: For variation, use 1 pound raw, cleaned shrimp fried in 2 tablespoons vegetable oil. Add shrimp when vegetables are tender. Or use 2 rainbow trouts, about 5 ounces each, cleaned and halved. Sprinkle fish with salt and turmeric, and gently rub spices on each side of the fish. Roll fish in all-purpose flour and fry in oil or *ghee* until lightly browned. Add fried trout 5 minutes before the cooking is over. One-half cup [⅖ E.] of plain yogurt may be added to the gravy when the vegetables are tender.

SERVES 4 to 6

BUND GOBI BHUJJIA
(*Shrimp and Cabbage*)

1 pound shrimp, shelled and
deveined
Pinch of salt
Pinch of turmeric
¼ cup [⅕ E.] vegetable oil
2 medium baking potatoes,
peeled and cut in ½-inch
cubes
2½ tablespoons [2 E.] *ghee*
Pinch of cumin seeds
2 small bay leaves
2 cardamoms, crushed
1 medium yellow onion, finely
chopped
1½ teaspoons [½ inch] finely
minced gingerroot
2 cloves garlic, finely minced
2½ teaspoons [2 E.] spiced onion
1 cup [6 ounces] fresh green peas
2½ teaspoons [2 E.] ground cumin

2½ teaspoons [2 E.] ground
coriander
½ teaspoon [⅓ E.] cayenne
pepper
½ teaspoon [⅓ E.] turmeric
½ teaspoon [⅓ E.] *garam masala*
¼ teaspoon [⅕ E.] paprika
¼ teaspoon [⅕ E.] sugar
1 medium cabbage, finely
shredded
1¼ teaspoons [1 E.] salt
2½ tablespoons [2 E.] raisins
2 tomatoes, peeled, seeded, and
chopped
¼ teaspoon [⅕ E.] cinnamon
½ cup [⅖ E.] crushed fried *vadi*
(optional)
2½ tablespoons [2 E.] chopped
coriander leaves

1. Mix shrimp with salt and turmeric. Heat vegetable oil in a large skillet and fry shrimp about 2 minutes, or until they are firm. Remove with a slotted spoon and set aside. Fry potatoes in the remaining vegetable oil until they are golden and almost cooked. Remove and set aside to drain.

2. To the same pan add *ghee*, cumin seeds, bay leaves, crushed cardamoms, and chopped onion and fry for 2 minutes, stirring. Add gingerroot, garlic, spiced onion, and peas and cook, stirring, about 2 minutes more. Add fried potato, ground cumin and coriander, cayenne pepper, turmeric, *garam masala*, paprika, sugar, and shredded cabbage. Cook, stirring, for 8 to 10 minutes. Add salt, raisins, and tomatoes and continue to cook until cabbage is reduced in bulk to about half. Cover and cook gently, taking care not to let the bottom burn, until vegetables are tender, about 10 minutes. Uncover and sprinkle with cinnamon, crushed *vadi*, and chopped coriander leaves.

Mix thoroughly and simmer for 10 to 15 minutes. Serve with Indian bread.

SERVES 6 to 8

UNDAY BRINJAL
(*Egg with Eggplant*)

5 to 6 tablespoons [2½ ounces] vegetable oil
Pinch of fennel seeds
1 bay leaf
2 medium yellow onions, thinly sliced
2 green chilies, seeded and chopped
1 tablespoon [1 inch] freshly grated gingerroot
1¼ teaspoons [1 E.] ground cumin
1¼ teaspoons [1 E.] ground coriander
¼ teaspoon [⅕ E.] cayenne pepper
¼ teaspoon [⅕ E.] turmeric
2 large eggplants, about 3 to 4 pounds, finely chopped
1 teaspoon [⅘ E.] salt
2 large eggs
½ teaspoon [⅓ E.] paprika
½ teaspoon [⅓ E.] *garam masala*
3 tablespoons [2 E.] chopped coriander leaves
3 tablespoons [2 E.] *ghee*

1. Heat vegetable oil in a large skillet with a tight-fitting lid. Fry fennel seeds, bay leaf, and onions about 2 minutes. Add chilies, gingerroot, cumin, coriander, cayenne pepper, turmeric, eggplant, and salt. Cook, stirring, for 5 to 8 minutes. Cover and simmer until the eggplant is very soft, about 20 minutes.

2. Mash the eggplant mixture to a cream-like consistency with a potato masher or put the eggplant mixture through a food mill. Add one egg at a time and stir in very quickly. Sprinkle mixture with paprika and *garam masala* and stir in chopped coriander leaves and *ghee*. Serve with Indian bread.

SERVES 4 to 6

MASSALEDARH BRINJAL
(*Eggplant with Tomatoes*)

1 large eggplant, about 2½ to 3 pounds
¼ cup [⅕ E.] vegetable oil
2 medium yellow onions, thinly sliced
Pinch of cumin seeds
1 bay leaf
¾ teaspoon [¼ inch] grated gingerroot
2 cloves garlic, finely minced
¾ teaspoon [⅗ E.] ground cumin
¾ teaspoon [⅗ E.] ground coriander
¼ teaspoon [⅕ E.] cayenne pepper
¼ teaspoon [⅕ E.] *garam masala*
¼ teaspoon [⅕ E.] turmeric
1 teaspoon [⅘ E.] salt
Pinch of sugar
7-ounce can Italian peeled tomatoes, drained and chopped
2 to 4 tablespoons [1½ to 3 E.] chopped coriander leaves

1. Preheat oven to 350°. Rub some vegetable oil on the skin of the eggplant. With a small knife, make 2 cuts about ½ inch deep in the skin. Bake eggplant for 40 to 50 minutes, or until it is very tender. Remove eggplant from the oven, cut in half, and remove pulp from the skin. Discard the skin; mash or finely chop the remaining pulp.

2. Heat vegetable oil and fry onions, cumin seeds, bay leaf, gingerroot, and garlic for 2 minutes. Add eggplant pulp, ground cumin, coriander, cayenne pepper, *garam masala*, turmeric, salt, sugar, and tomatoes. Cook about 15 minutes. Stir in chopped coriander leaves and simmer 10 minutes more.

SERVES 4 to 6

BAINGAN BHARTA
(Mashed Eggplant Curry)

1 large eggplant, 2½ to 3
    pounds
1¼ teaspoons [1 E.] ground
    roasted cumin
Big pinch of ground turmeric
Big pinch of paprika
Big pinch of sugar
½ teaspoon [⅓ E.] salt
5 to 6 tablespoons [3 ounces]
    ghee
2 large yellow onions, finely
    chopped

2 cloves garlic, finely minced
2 green chilies, seeded and
    chopped
1 tablespoon [1 inch] finely
    minced gingerroot
½ teaspoon [⅓ E.] garam masala
2½ tablespoons [2 E.] sour cream
2½ tablespoons [2 E.] chopped
    coriander leaves

1. Prepare eggplant pulp as directed in the recipe for Massaledarh Brinjal.

2. Combine eggplant pulp, cumin, turmeric, paprika, sugar, and salt and mix well. Heat ghee in a skillet and fry onions, garlic, chilies, and gingerroot for 2 minutes. Add eggplant mixture and cook until most of the liquid in the pan evaporates and mixture forms a mass. Remove from heat and sprinkle with garam masala; mix in sour cream and chopped coriander leaves. Serve hot with Indian bread.

SERVES 4 to 6

DILKHOSH BAINGAN KALIA
(*Bengali-Style Eggplant*)

2 medium eggplants, about
2½ pounds
½ teaspoon [⅓ E.] salt
½ teaspoon [⅓ E.] turmeric
Pinch of sugar
½ cup [⅖ E.] all-purpose flour
½ cup [⅖ E.] vegetable oil
Pinch of ground asafetida
(*hing*) (optional)
1½ tablespoons [1¼ E.] spiced
onion
¾ teaspoon [⅗ E.] grated
gingerroot

¾ teaspoon [⅗ E.] ground cumin
¾ teaspoon [⅗ E.] ground
coriander
¾ teaspoon [⅗ E.] cayenne
pepper
Big pinch of sugar
Big pinch of paprika
2 to 3 tablespoons [2 E.] water
1 cup [8 ounces] sour cream
3 to 4 tablespoons [3 E.]
crushed fried *vadi*
(optional)

1. Cut eggplant into ½-inch slices, sprinkle each slice with a little salt, turmeric, and sugar. Rub eggplant and set aside for 30 minutes. (The salt will remove any bitter flavor and draw out excess moisture.) Dredge each eggplant slice with flour. Fry in ¼ cup hot vegetable oil over medium heat until tender and brown on both sides. Remove with a slotted spoon and set aside to drain.

2. Heat ¼ cup vegetable oil in a large skillet. Cook asafetida, spiced onion, gingerroot, cumin, coriander, cayenne pepper, a big pinch of sugar, and paprika with water for one minute. Add sour cream and mix thoroughly. Add fried eggplant slices in a single layer and sprinkle crushed *vadi* on top. Simmer, covered, for 20 minutes or bake in a preheated 350° oven for 10 minutes. Garnish with chopped coriander leaves. Serve with Indian bread.

SERVES 6 to 8

GOURD BHUJJIA
(*Squash or Pumpkin with Onion*)

¼ cup [⅕ E.] vegetable oil
5 medium yellow onions, thinly sliced
1 green pepper, seeded and cut into strips
2 green chilies, seeded and sliced
1½ pounds yellow squash, peeled and cut into 1½-inch-long strips

Big pinch of ground turmeric
Big pinch of paprika
Big pinch of sugar
¾ teaspoon [⅘ E.] salt
3 to 4 tablespoons chopped coriander leaves

Heat vegetable oil in a large skillet. Fry onions with green pepper for one minute. Add chilies, squash, turmeric, paprika, sugar, and salt. Cook, stirring, for 5 minutes. Cover and simmer until vegetables are tender, 8 to 10 minutes. Remove from heat. Sprinkle with chopped coriander leaves. Serve with boiled rice.

SERVES 6

GOURD DALNA
(*Squash Curry*)

¼ cup [⅕ E.] vegetable oil
1½ pounds yellow squash, peeled and cut into 1-inch cubes
⅛ teaspoon [⅒ E.] salt
¼ teaspoon [⅕ E.] turmeric
1 large baking potato, peeled and cut into 1-inch cubes
2 tablespoons [1 ounce] *ghee*
Pinch of cumin seeds
1 bay leaf
¾ teaspoon [⅗ E.] grated gingerroot

¾ teaspoon [⅗ E.] crushed dried red pepper
¾ teaspoon [⅗ E.] ground coriander
1 green pepper, seeded and thinly sliced
1¼ teaspoons [1 E.] ground cumin
1½ teaspoons [1 ounce] creamed coconut
1 cup [8 ounces] warm water

1. Heat vegetable oil in a large skillet and fry squash with a pinch of salt and a pinch of turmeric until golden and almost cooked. Remove from pan and set aside to drain. Add potatoes with a pinch of

salt and a pinch of turmeric to vegetable oil remaining in pan and fry until almost cooked. Remove and set aside to drain.

2. Heat *ghee* in another pan; add cumin seeds, bay leaf, ginger-root, red pepper, coriander, remaining turmeric, green pepper, and ground cumin and cook about one minute, adding a tablespoon of water. Add coconut cream, water, and fried squash and potatoes. Mix well and taste for salt. Cook gently until vegetables are tender, 10 to 12 minutes. Garnish with *boras* (see page 20) and chopped coriander leaves. Simmer for 10 minutes. Serve with boiled rice or Indian bread.

SERVES 4 to 6

MASALA BHENDI
(*Okra Curry*)

1 pound fresh okra, trimmed
¼ cup [⅕ E.] vegetable oil
2 to 3 tablespoons [1½ ounces] mustard oil or vegetable oil
1 medium yellow onion, finely chopped
1 large clove garlic, finely minced
2 to 3 green chilies, seeded and halved (optional)
¾ teaspoon [⅗ E.] ground cumin

¼ teaspoon [⅕ E.] cayenne pepper
¼ teaspoon [⅕ E.] turmeric
½ teaspoon [⅓ E.] salt
Pinch of sugar
2 tablespoons water
2½ teaspoons [2 E.] dry mustard
2½ tablespoons [2 E.] ground *umchur* or lemon juice
2½ tablespoons [2 E.] sour cream

Slit okra on one side. Heat ¼ cup oil in a skillet and fry okra until light brown, about 10 minutes. Remove from oil and set aside to drain. In another pan, heat mustard oil and fry onion, garlic, and chilies for 2 minutes. Add fried okras, cumin, cayenne pepper, turmeric, salt, sugar, and water and cook about one minute. Cover and simmer until okra is tender. Uncover and add mustard paste, *umchur*, and sour cream. Mix well. Remove from heat.

NOTE: The whole dish can be steamed in a double boiler. After frying okra, combine with all the other ingredients and steam, covered, in a double boiler until okra is tender.

SERVES 4

SABZI KOFTA KALIA
(*Vegetable Balls Curry*)

Kofta:

1 pound fresh green peas, cooked and mashed

2 large potatoes, boiled and mashed

2½ tablespoons [2 E.] *besan* (chick-pea flour) or rice flour

2½ tablespoons [2 E.] chopped coriander leaves

1¼ teaspoons [1 E.] ground roasted cumin

1¼ teaspoons [1 E.] ground roasted coriander

¼ teaspoon [⅕ E.] turmeric

¼ teaspoon [⅕ E.] crushed dried red pepper

¼ teaspoon [⅕ E.] *garam masala*

Pinch of cumin seeds

Pinch of sugar

¾ teaspoon [⅘ E.] salt

2 eggs, lightly beaten

½ cup [⅖ E.] bread crumbs

¼ cup [⅕ E.] vegetable oil

Sauce:

¼ cup [⅕ E.] *ghee*

1 small yellow onion, finely chopped (optional)

Pinch of cumin seeds

2 cardamoms, crushed

1 cinnamon stick

1 bay leaf

1½ teaspoons [½ inch] grated gingerroot

2½ tablespoons [2 E.] spiced onion (optional)

1 large tomato, peeled, seeded, and chopped

1¼ teaspoons [1 E.] ground coriander

1¼ teaspoons [1 E.] ground cumin

¼ teaspoon [⅕ E.] turmeric

½ teaspoon [⅓ E.] cayenne pepper

½ teaspoon [⅓ E.] *garam masala*

1½ cups [12 ounces] coconut milk

½ teaspoon [⅓ E.] salt

3 to 4 tablespoons [3 E.] chopped coriander leaves

⅛ teaspoon [¹⁄₁₀ E.] paprika

1. Combine mashed peas, mashed potatoes, *besan*, coriander leaves, ground roasted cumin and coriander, turmeric, red pepper, *garam masala*, cumin seeds, sugar, and salt in a bowl and mix well. Form little balls about one inch in diameter. Dip them in lightly beaten eggs, then roll them in crumbs. Fry *koftas* in hot vegetable oil until brown. Remove from pan and set aside to drain.

2. Heat *ghee* in a large skillet. Fry chopped onion, cumin seeds,

cardamoms, cinnamon stick, bay leaf, gingerroot, and spiced onion for 2 to 3 minutes over moderate heat. Add tomato, coriander, ground cumin, turmeric, cayenne pepper, and *garam masala*; stir to blend well. Remove from heat and add coconut milk and salt. Return to high heat and boil for 5 minutes.

3. Preheat oven to 350°. Place *koftas* in a shallow baking dish and pour on the sauce. Sprinkle with chopped coriander leaves and paprika. Bake for 15 to 20 minutes, covered, or until the gravy is thick. Do not stir after adding *koftas*; just shake the pan a little to keep them from sticking. Serve with Indian bread.

SERVES 6 to 8

SABZI MOLEE
(*South Indian Vegetable Curry*)

¼ cup [⅕ E.] vegetable oil
Pinch of mustard seeds
1½ teaspoons [½ inch] grated gingerroot
1 large yellow onion, thinly sliced
2 green chilies, seeded
2½ teaspoons [2 E.] ground coriander
2½ teaspoons [2 E.] ground cumin
¼ teaspoon [⅕ E.] ground turmeric
1 small potato, cut into 1-inch cubes
2 carrots, scraped and cut into ¼-inch slices

1 eggplant, 1½-pounds, cut into 1-inch cubes
¼ pound green beans, trimmed and cut into 2-inch lengths
2 green peppers, seeded and roughly chopped
2 teaspoons [1¾ E.] salt
Big pinch of sugar
1½ cups [12 ounces] thick coconut milk
20 to 30 small *vadi*, fried (optional)
3 to 4 tablespoons [3 E.] chopped coriander leaves
¼ teaspoon [⅕ E.] paprika

Heat vegetable oil in a heavy pan over medium heat. Fry mustard seeds until they pop. Add gingerroot, onion, and chilies and fry about 2 minutes. Stirring constantly, add coriander, cumin, and turmeric and cook gently a few more seconds. Add potato, carrots, eggplant, and beans and cook, stirring, for about 5 minutes. Add green peppers, salt, sugar, and coconut milk; cover and cook gently until vegetables are tender, about 12 minutes. Add fried *vadi* and chopped coriander leaves and mix well. Sprinkle with paprika and simmer for 5 to 10 minutes. For more gravy, add more coconut milk. Garnish with toasted coconut. Serve with boiled rice.

SERVES 4 to 6

BEETROOT DALNA
(*Beet Curry*)

3 tablespoons [1½ ounces] vegetable oil or *ghee*
Pinch of cumin seeds
1 bay leaf
2½ tablespoons [2 E.] spiced onion
¼ teaspoon [⅕ E.] cayenne pepper
¼ teaspoon [⅕ E.] *garam masala*

1 medium potato, peeled and cut into dice
½ cup [⅖ E.] frozen green peas
1 15-ounce can diced beets and their liquid
½ teaspoon [⅓ E.] salt
20 small crushed fried *vadi* (optional)

Heat vegetable oil and fry cumin seeds, bay leaf, spiced onion, cayenne pepper, and *garam masala* for about one minute. Add potato, peas, and drained beets. Cook gently about 2 minutes. Add beet liquid and salt and cook until potato is tender, 8 to 10 minutes. Sprinkle with crushed *vadi* and simmer for 5 minutes. Serve with boiled rice.

SERVES 4 to 6

ALOO MATAR
(*Potato and Pea Curry*)

5 tablespoons [4 E.] *ghee*
  Pinch of *punch-phoron* seeds
1 bay leaf
1¼ teaspoons [1 E.] freshly grated
  gingerroot
1 medium yellow onion, finely
  chopped
2 medium potatoes, peeled and
  cut into ½-inch cubes
2 large tomatoes, peeled, seeded,
  and chopped
1 teaspoon [⅘ E.] salt
¾ teaspoon [⅗ E.] ground cumin

1¼ teaspoons [1 E.] ground
  coriander
¼ teaspoon [⅕ E.] cayenne
  pepper
¼ teaspoon [⅕ E.] turmeric
¼ teaspoon [⅕ E.] *garam masala*
2 cups [1⅗ E.] fresh green peas
1½ cups [12 ounces] coconut milk
  or warm water
3 to 4 tablespoons [3 E.]
  chopped coriander leaves
⅛ teaspoon [⅟₁₀ E.] paprika

Heat *ghee* in a large saucepan. Fry *punch-phoron* seeds, bay leaf, gingerroot, and onion for one minute. Add potatoes and continue cooking another 5 minutes. Stir in tomatoes, salt, ground cumin, coriander, cayenne pepper, turmeric, *garam masala,* and peas and cook about 4 to 5 minutes. Add coconut milk and boil rapidly for 3 minutes. Cover and cook gently until vegetables are tender, 10 to 15 minutes. Remove from heat. Sprinkle with chopped coriander leaves and paprika.

SERVES 4

TITORI BHUJJIA
(*Bean Sprouts Curry*)

¼ cup [⅕ E.] vegetable oil
½ pound raw shrimp, cleaned and
    chopped roughly
Pinch of ground turmeric
Pinch of salt
1 potato, partially cooked,
    peeled, and cut into small
    cubes
2 tablespoons [1 ounce] *ghee*
1 medium yellow onion, finely
    chopped
2 small bay leaves
2½ tablespoons [2 E.] fresh
    coconut, peeled and finely
    chopped

1¼ teaspoons [1 E.] ground cumin
1¼ teaspoons [1 E.] ground
    coriander
⅓ teaspoon [¼ E.] cayenne
    pepper
⅓ teaspoon [¼ E.] ground
    turmeric
⅓ teaspoon [¼ E.] *garam masala*
½ teaspoon [⅓ E.] salt
Pinch of sugar
½ cup [⅖ E.] water
1 pound bean sprouts
10 to 15 *boras* (page 20)

1. Heat vegetable oil in a skillet and fry shrimp with a pinch of salt and a pinch of turmeric about one minute, or until firm. Remove from pan and set aside to drain. Fry potato in remaining vegetable oil until golden brown. Remove and set aside to drain.

2. In another skillet, heat *ghee*; add onion and bay leaves and fry for one minute. Add coconut, cumin, coriander, cayenne pepper, turmeric, *garam masala*, salt, sugar, and one tablespoon of water and cook, stirring, about 2 minutes. Add fried potato and water. Cook gently until potato is tender. Stirring, add bean sprouts, and cook for 5 to 6 minutes. Mix in *boras* and shrimp, and simmer another 3 to 5 minutes. Sprinkle with chopped coriander leaves. Serve with Indian bread.

SERVES 4 to 6

LABRA
(*Mixed Vegetable Curry*)

5 to 6 tablespoons [3 ounces] vegetable oil
Pinch of black cumin seeds
2 green chilies, seeded and halved
1¼ teaspoons [1 E.] grated gingerroot
¼ pound green beans, cut into 2-inch lengths
½ medium cauliflower, cut into flowerets
½ pound yellow squash, peeled and cut into 1-inch cubes

2 small carrots, scraped and cut into ¼-inch-thick rounds
10 to 12 small radishes, halved
1 small eggplant, cut into ½-inch cubes
1 potato, peeled and cut into ½-inch cubes
1¼ teaspoons [1 E.] salt
Pinch of sugar
½ teaspoon [⅓ E.] ground turmeric

Heat vegetable oil in a large skillet with a tight-fitting lid. Fry cumin seeds, chilies, and gingerroot for one minute. Add green beans, cauliflower, squash, carrots, radishes, eggplant, and potato, and cook, stirring, for 5 to 8 minutes. Add salt, sugar, and turmeric; cover and cook gently until vegetables are tender, about 20 minutes. Uncover and cook a few more minutes. One tablespoon of all-purpose flour mixed with 2 tablespoons water may be added to the mixture if there is too much liquid. Sprinkle with coriander leaves or grated coconut.

SERVES 6

KUDDOO JHINGA
(*Zucchini or Cucumber with Shrimp*)

1 zucchini (3 to 3½ pounds) or large cucumbers

¼ cup [⅕ E.] vegetable oil

1½ pounds fresh shrimp, cleaned and deveined

Pinch of salt

Pinch of turmeric

3 to 4 tablespoons [3 E.] spiced onion

2 green chilies, seeded and halved

2 teaspoons [1⅗ E.] ground cumin

2 teaspoons [1⅗] ground coriander

⅓ teaspoon [¼ E.] turmeric

¼ teaspoon [⅕ E.] ground cinnamon

¼ teaspoon [⅕ E.] ground cardamom

1¼ teaspoons [1 E.] salt

¼ teaspoon [⅕ E.] paprika

10 to 15 *boras* (page 20)

1½ tablespoons [1¼ E.] chopped coriander leaves

2½ teaspoons [2 E.] all-purpose flour

Peel zucchini and cut into ½-inch cubes. (If using cucumbers, remove seeds before cutting.) In a large skillet, heat vegetable oil and fry shrimp with a pinch of salt and a pinch of turmeric for one minute. Add spiced onion, chilies, cumin, coriander, turmeric, and zucchini. Cook, stirring, 8 to 10 minutes. Cover and cook gently until vegetables are tender, about 10 minutes. Add cinnamon, cardamom, salt, paprika, and *boras* and mix well. Sprinkle with coriander leaves and flour. Stir well and simmer, uncovered, another 10 minutes. Serve with boiled rice or Indian bread.

SERVES 4 to 6

DHOKAR DALNA or CHANNA MATAR
(*Lentil Cake Curry or Cottage Cheese Curry*)

Dhokar Dalna, made from lentils, and *Channa Matar* are very popular among vegetarians. These are substitutes for meat or fish products. They are rich in protein and other vitamins and are easy to prepare. Make *dhokar* or *channa* and then prepare the curry.

Dhokar:

½ pound *gram dal* or yellow split peas, soaked overnight
¼ cup [⅕ E.] water
¼ cup [2 ounces] vegetable oil
Pinch of white cumin seeds
Pinch of ground asafetida (*hing*) (optional)
2½ tablespoons [2 E.] spiced onion
2½ tablespoons [2 E.] all-purpose flour
1¼ teaspoons [1 E.] ground cumin

1¼ teaspoons [1 E.] ground coriander
1¼ teaspoons [1 E.] finely minced gingerroot
¼ teaspoon [⅕ E.] cayenne pepper
¼ teaspoon [⅕ E.] turmeric
¼ teaspoon [⅕ E.] sugar
⅓ teaspoon [¼ E.] salt
¼ cup [⅕ E.] *ghee*

Channa:

½ gallon [64 ounces] milk
¼ cup [⅕ E.] white vinegar or about ¾ teaspoon [⅗ E.] citric acid

½ cup [4 ounces] water
¼ cup [⅕ E.] *ghee*

Gravy:

½ cup [4 ounces] *ghee*
1 large potato, peeled and cut into ½-inch cubes
Pinch of salt
Pinch of turmeric
Pinch of cumin seeds
2½ tablespoons [2 E.] spiced onion
½ teaspoon [⅓ E.] ground turmeric
½ teaspoon [⅓ E.] cayenne pepper

½ teaspoon [⅓ E.] ground cumin
Pinch of sugar
½ teaspoon [⅓ E.] salt
¼ teaspoon [⅕ E.] *garam masala*
Dash of paprika
1 cup [6 ounces] plain yogurt
1 cup [6 ounces] fresh green peas
2 to 2½ cups [16 to 20 ounces] chicken stock
3 to 4 tablespoons [3 E.] chopped coriander leaves

1. Combine *gram dal* and water in the container of a blender and blend at high speed for 30 seconds. Turn off blender, scrape down the sides of the jar with a rubber spatula, and blend again until the mixture is creamy. Heat vegetable oil in a large skillet and fry cumin seeds and asafetida for a few seconds. Add spiced onion, lentil paste, flour, ground cumin, coriander, gingerroot, cayenne pepper, turmeric, sugar, and salt and cook gently, stirring continuously, until most of the liquid in the pan evaporates and the mixture is thick enough to draw away from the sides and bottom of the pan in a solid mass. Spread *dal* mixture ¼ inch thick on a greased baking sheet. Set aside to cool. Cut into 1-inch cubes and fry in *ghee* until golden brown on both sides. Remove from pan and set aside to drain.

2. Prepare *channa* according to directions on page 19. Put the bag containing *channa* on a flat wooden board and press it with a weight to extract any remaining liquid. Chill. Cut into small ½-inch cubes. Fry *channa* cubes in *ghee* until browned. Remove and set aside to drain.

3. Heat ¼ cup of *ghee* in a skillet and fry potato cubes with a pinch of salt and a pinch of turmeric. (*Ghee* remaining from browning *dal* or *channa* cubes may be used.) Fry cubes until golden and almost cooked. Remove and set aside to drain.

4. Heat ¼ cup [⅕ E.] *ghee* in a large skillet. Add cumin seeds and spiced onion and fry gently about one minute. Add fried potatoes, turmeric, cayenne pepper, ground cumin, salt, and sugar. Cook, stirring regularly, about one or two minutes. Add *garam masala* and paprika and stir to blend well. Remove from heat and mix in yogurt. Return to heat, add peas, and cook another minute or so. Add chicken stock and cook over medium heat until vegetables are tender, about 10 minutes. Reduce heat to low and add either *dhokar* or *channa* cubes. Sprinkle with chopped coriander leaves and simmer for 10 minutes, or until the sauce has thickened. More liquid can be added if desired. Serve with Indian bread.

SERVES 6

CHANNA KOFTAS
(*Cheese Ball Curry*)

Channa Koftas:

7½ cups [60 ounces] milk
¼ cup [⅕ E.] white vinegar
Pinch of ground turmeric
Pinch of ground cloves
Pinch of ground cinnamon
Pinch of ground cardamom
Pinch of freshly ground black pepper
2½ tablespoons [2 E.] biscuit mix

2½ tablespoons [2 E.] sour cream
¼ teaspoon [⅕ E.] salt
¼ teaspoon [⅕ E.] ground cumin
Pinch of monosodium glutamate
20 pistachio nuts (about ¼ cup)
¼ cup [⅕ E.] raisins
Vegetable oil for deep fat frying

Curry:

¼ cup [⅕ E.] *ghee*
Pinch of white cumin seeds
1 bay leaf
2 cardamoms, crushed
2 small (1 inch) pieces cinnamon stick
2½ tablespoons [2 E.] spiced onion (optional)
¾ teaspoon [⅗ E.] finely minced gingerroot
⅓ teaspoon [¼ E.] ground turmeric
¼ teaspoon [⅕ E.] cayenne pepper

¼ teaspoon [⅕ E.] salt
¾ teaspoon [⅗ E.] ground cumin
½ cup [4 ounces] ground almonds
2½ tablespoons [2 E.] raisins
1 to 1½ cups [8 to 12 ounces] whey (*channa* liquid) or water
2½ tablespoons [2 E.] plain yogurt or sour cream
Pinch of sugar
Pinch of paprika
3 to 4 tablespoons [3 E.] chopped coriander leaves

1. Prepare *channa* according to directions on page 19, reserving whey for curry. Squeeze as much liquid as possible from the *channa*. In a bowl combine the *channa* with turmeric, cloves, cinnamon, cardamom, black pepper, biscuit mix, sour cream, salt, ground cumin, and monosodium glutamate and mix well. Shape the mixture into balls one inch in diameter. Stuff each ball with one pistachio nut and 2 raisins. Heat 2 inches vegetable oil in a heavy saucepan or deep fat fryer and fry *channa* balls over medium-low heat for 10 to 15 minutes, or until golden brown. Remove balls with a slotted spoon and set aside to drain.

2. To prepare curry, heat *ghee* in a large skillet. Add cumin seeds, bay leaf, cardamoms, cinnamon sticks, spiced onion, and gingerroot and fry for one minute. Add turmeric, cayenne pepper, salt, cumin, and ground almonds and cook for another minute. Mix in raisins and whey and boil for 2 to 3 minutes. Stir in yogurt, sugar, and paprika, reduce heat to low, and add a single layer of *channa* balls. Spoon sauce over *channa* balls and sprinkle with chopped coriander leaves. Simmer for 10 to 15 minutes. Shake pan occasionally to keep curry from sticking, but do not stir. Serve with *pullao*, *biryani*, or Indian bread.

SERVES 4 to 5

CHANNA KABAB KALIA
(*Cheese and Lentil Curry*)

Channa Kababs:

1¼ cups [1 E.] *tur dal* (*arhar dal*)
   or *chana dal*
3 cups [24 ounces] water
¾ teaspoon [⅗ E.] salt
¼ teaspoon [⅕ E.] turmeric
¼ teaspoon [⅕ E.] *sambhar* spice
   (see page 17)
¼ teaspoon [⅕ E.] *garam masala*
¼ teaspoon [⅕ E.] sugar
Pinch of saffron threads soaked
   in 1 tablespoon warm water
Pinch of monosodium
   glutamate (optional)

½ teaspoon [⅓ E.] ground cumin
½ teaspoon [⅓ E.] ground
   coriander
2½ tablespoons [2 E.] *ghee*
3 quarts [120 ounces] milk
⅓ cup [3 ounces] white vinegar
2½ teaspoons [2 E.] *suji* (farina)
2½ teaspoons [2 E.] plain yogurt or
   sour cream
½ teaspoon [⅓ E.] salt
Vegetable oil for deep fat
   frying

Curry:

3 tablespoons [1½ ounces] *ghee*
Pinch of cumin seeds
2 small bay leaves
2 small [1 inch] cinnamon sticks
1 large yellow onion, finely
   chopped (optional)
¾ teaspoon [⅗ E.] finely minced
   gingerroot
¾ teaspoon [⅗ E.] ground cumin
½ teaspoon [⅓ E.] cayenne
   pepper
½ teaspoon [⅓ E.] *garam masala*
Pinch of saffron threads soaked
   in 1 tablespoon warm water

2½ tablespoons [2 E.] tomato
   paste
2½ tablespoons [2 E.] ground
   almonds
2½ tablespoons [2 E.] raisins
½ teaspoon [⅓ E.] salt
1 to 1½ cups [8 to 12 ounces]
   coconut milk
2½ tablespoons [2 E.] slivered
   almonds
3 to 4 tablespoons [3 E.]
   chopped coriander leaves

---

1. Wash *dal*; boil in water with salt and turmeric for 20 to 30 minutes, or until tender. Drain *dal* and grind in a food mill to make a smooth paste. Combine ground *dal* with *sambhar* spice, *garam masala*, sugar, saffron and its soaking water, monosodium glutamate, ground cumin, and coriander in a bowl and mix well. Heat *ghee* in a large skillet; add *dal* mixture and cook until all moisture evaporates. Re-

move from heat, set aside to cool, and shape *dal* mixture into even-sized balls about 1½ inches in diameter.

2. Prepare *channa* according to directions on page 19. Place warm *channa* in a bowl and rub with your palms until creamy. Combine *channa* with *suji*, yogurt, and salt and mix well. Form *channa* into even-sized balls twice the size of the *dal* balls. Keeping your fingers moist with milk, make a depression in each *channa* ball, place a *dal* ball inside, and reform the *channa* ball into the shape of an egg, so that the *dal* ball is completely contained within. Heat vegetable oil to a depth of 2 to 3 inches in a deep fat fryer, add *channa* balls, and fry over very low heat until golden brown. Remove with a slotted spoon and set aside to drain.

3. To prepare curry, heat *ghee* in a large skillet. Add cumin seeds, bay leaves, cinnamon sticks, onion, gingerroot, ground cumin, cayenne pepper, *garam masala*, and saffron with its soaking water and fry for 2 minutes. Add tomato paste, ground almonds, raisins, and salt and cook for another 2 minutes. Add cocount milk and boil for 2 to 3 minutes. Reduce heat to low, add *channa kababs*, and simmer, covered, for 15 minutes. Sprinkle with slivered almonds and chopped coriander leaves.

SERVES 10 to 12

GHOOGNI
(*Yellow Peas with Lamb*)

1 pound whole yellow peas, soaked overnight in 5½ cups [44 ounces] water
2¾ teaspoons [2⅕ E.] salt
½ teaspoon [⅓ E.] turmeric
4 to 6 tablespoons [2 to 3 ounces] *ghee* or vegetable oil
2 medium yellow onions, thinly sliced
2 small bay leaves
4 cloves of garlic, finely minced
1½ teaspoons [½ inch] finely minced gingerroot
2 medium potatoes, peeled and cut into ¼-inch cubes
¼ cup [⅕ E.] spiced onion
1 pound lean lamb, cut into ½-inch cubes
¼ cup [⅕ E.] tomato paste
2½ teaspoons [2 E.] ground cumin

2½ teaspoons [2 E.] ground coriander
½ teaspoon [⅓ E.] cayenne pepper
¼ teaspoon [⅕ E.] ground cardamom
5 tablespoons [4 E.] raisins
¼ cup [⅕ E.] coconut, peeled and finely chopped
Big pinch of sugar
2 green chilies, seeded and halved (optional)
¼ teaspoon [⅕ E.] ground cinnamon
1¼ teaspoons [1 E.] ground roasted cumin
1¼ teaspoons [1 E.] ground roasted coriander
Juice of 1 lemon

1. Bring peas with their soaking water, 2 teaspoons salt, and the turmeric to a boil and simmer for 30 to 45 minutes, or until they are cooked but still a little firm. Try not to crush the peas during cooking. Remove from heat and keep uncovered. Do not drain.

2. Heat *ghee* in a large skillet. Brown onions, remove with a slotted spoon, and set aside. Add bay leaves, garlic, gingerroot, and potatoes and cook, stirring, about 5 minutes. Add spiced onion and lamb cubes and cook gently, stirring often, for 4 to 5 minutes. Add ¾ teaspoon salt, the tomato paste, cumin, and coriander and cook, covered, until meat is tender, about 15 minutes. Add cayenne pepper, cardamom, raisins, coconut, sugar, chilies, cinnamon, and boiled peas with the liquid in which they were cooked. Cook gently over low heat about 20 minutes. Add roasted cumin and coriander and fried onions and continue to simmer another 5 to 10 minutes. Sprinkle with lemon juice before serving. Garnish with chopped coriander leaves. Serve

with Indian bread. The flavor improves if *ghoogni* is made a day or two in advance.

SERVES 10 to 12

CHOLE
(*Chick-pea Curry*)

1 pound chick-peas, soaked over-
    night with 5 to 6 cups (40 to
    48 ounces) water
1½ teaspoons [1¼ E.] salt
¾ cup [⅗ E.] vegetable oil
2 large yellow onions, finely
    chopped
2 red chilies
3½ teaspoons [1¼ inches] finely
    chopped gingerroot

¾ teaspoon [⅗ E.] cayenne
    pepper
¾ teaspoon [⅗ E.] *garam masala*
2½ teaspoons [2 E.] ground cumin
2½ tablespoons [2 E.] ground
    umchur
2½ tablespoons [2 E.] lemon juice
3 to 4 tablespoons [3 E.]
    chopped coriander leaves

1. Simmer chick-peas, covered, in their soaking water and salt until they are almost cooked, about one hour. Uncover and continue cooking 30 minutes, or until the liquid evaporates.

2. Heat vegetable oil in a large skillet and fry onions, red chilies, and gingerroot for 2 minutes. Add cooked chick-peas, cayenne pepper, *garam masala*, cumin, and *umchur*. Cook another 15 minutes, adding more vegetable oil if necessary. Sprinkle with lemon juice and chopped coriander leaves and simmer for 20 more minutes. Garnish with chopped onion. Serve warm with Indian bread.

NOTE: Adjust hot spices to suit your taste.

SERVES 8 to 10

KABULI MATAR
(*Yellow Peas*)

1 pound dried whole yellow peas, soaked overnight in 5 to 6 cups [40 to 48 ounces] cold water
1¼ teaspoons [1 E.] salt
½ teaspoon [⅓ E.] ground turmeric
1 cup [⅘ E.] vegetable oil

1¼ tablespoons [1 E.] finely chopped gingerroot
2 to 4 green chilies, finely chopped
Pinch of cumin seeds
¼ cup [⅕ E.] lemon juice
1½ tablespoons [1¼ E.] *sambhar* spice

1. Bring peas with their soaking water to a boil and add salt and turmeric. Cover and simmer about ½ hour, or until peas are almost cooked, but still a little firm. Drain and refrigerate until cold.

2. Heat ¼ cup of the vegetable oil in a large skillet and add gingerroot, chilies, and cumin seeds. Fry a few seconds; add drained and chilled peas and cook for 2 to 4 minutes more, stirring gently with a fork, being careful not to break the peas. Reduce heat to low and sprinkle one tablespoon of lemon juice and one tablespoon of vegetable oil at a time over the peas, shaking the pan (but do not stir). Repeat adding juice and oil until all lemon juice and remaining vegetable oil are used. Sprinkle with *sambhar* spice; taste and add more salt if necessary. Simmer until the moisture evaporates and peas are crisp on the outside and tender inside, 20 to 30 minutes. Garnish with coriander leaves. Serve warm.

SERVES 8 to 10

RAJMA DALNA
(Vegetarian Red Kidney Beans)

1 pound dried kidney beans
½ teaspoon [⅓ E.] ground
   turmeric
2½ teaspoons [2 E.] salt
¼ cup [2 ounces] *ghee*
Pinch of cumin seeds
2 small bay leaves
1¼ teaspoons [1 E.] grated gingerroot
1¼ teaspoons [1 E.] ground cumin
1¼ teaspoons [1 E.] ground
   coriander

½ teaspoon [⅓ E.] cayenne
   pepper
½ teaspoon [⅓ E.] *garam masala*
¼ teaspoon [⅕ E.] ground
   cardamom
2 large tomatoes, peeled and
   chopped
½ cup [4 ounces] sour cream
3 to 4 tablespoons [3 E.]
   chopped coriander leaves
Pinch of sugar
Pinch of paprika

1. Wash kidney beans and cover with enough water so that water level is 1½ inches above the level of the beans. Cover and bring to a boil. Boil for 5 minutes, turn off heat, and let stand one hour. Add turmeric and salt. Cover and cook gently until beans are tender, about 1½ hours. If necessary, add a little warm water during cooking. Drain beans, reserving liquid.

2. Heat *ghee* in a large skillet and add cumin seeds, bay leaves, gingerroot, ground cumin, coriander, cayenne pepper, *garam masala*, cardamom, and tomatoes. Cook, stirring, 3 to 4 minutes. Add drained kidney beans and sour cream and mix well. Add ½ cup reserved liquid. Sprinkle with coriander leaves, sugar, and paprika and simmer for 15 minutes.

SERVES 8

Eggs

Like milk, eggs offer a rich source of good nutrition. Always cook eggs over medium heat; at high temperatures they become tough. They should be at room temperature before cooking or baking. Cover eggs with cold water in a pan, set over high heat, and bring just to a boil. Remove the pan from heat and let stand 20 minutes for hard-boiled eggs and 6 to 8 minutes for soft-boiled eggs. Then put the eggs under cold running water to cool quickly and shell. There are hundreds of ways to serve eggs. They can be particularly rich and delicious if they are properly cooked in the Indian manner. Here are a few ways you can serve them to your family and friends.

KAGINA
(*Indian Omelet*)

2 eggs, separated
1¼ teaspoons [1 E.] finely chopped onion
1 green chili, seeded and finely chopped
Pinch of finely chopped gingerroot
Pinch of chopped coriander leaves
Pinch of turmeric
1¼ teaspoons [1 E.] evaporated milk or cream
Dash of salt
2½ tablespoons [2 E.] *ghee*

1. Beat egg whites until stiff. Lightly beat egg yolks and gently fold into beaten egg whites. Add onion, chili, gingerroot, coriander leaves, turmeric, evaporated milk, and salt and mix lightly.

2. Heat a small skillet or omelet pan and add one tablespoon *ghee*.

Scrape egg mixture into pan and turn the heat to low. Cook gently for a few seconds; then gently swirl the pan in order to distribute the eggs evenly over the entire pan. As the omelet starts to cook, the edges begin to rise up the side of the pan. With a fork, pull cooked egg away from the edge of the pan and allow uncooked egg to run over the edge and beneath the cooked portion of the omelet. Repeat this a few times until the omelet is entirely cooked. Roll omelet like a pancake. Brush remaining *ghee* on both the top and bottom of the omelet and turn once. Serve immediately with sliced tomatoes.

MAKES 1 omelet

KAGINA DALNA
(*Omelet Curry*)

4 *Kagina* (page 115) or
   8 hard-cooked eggs
¼ cup [⅕ E.] vegetable oil
1 19-ounce can sliced Irish
   potatoes, drained, reserving
   the liquid
3 to 4 tablespoons [2 ounces]
   ghee
Pinch of cumin seeds
4 cardamoms, crushed
2 bay leaves
1½ teaspoons [½ inch] finely
   minced gingerroot
2 cloves garlic, minced
1 medium yellow onion, thinly
   sliced
1½ tablespoons [1¼ E.] spiced
   onion
2 tomatoes, peeled and chopped

1¼ teaspoons [1 E.] ground cumin
1¼ teaspoons [1 E.] ground
   coriander
¼ teaspoon [⅕ E.] cayenne
   pepper
¼ teaspoon [⅕ E.] *garam masala*
¼ teaspoon [⅕ E.] ground
   turmeric
Pinch of sugar
Pinch of ground cinnamon
Pinch of ground cloves
Pinch of paprika
1 cup [8 ounces] potato liquid,
   water, or chicken stock
½ teaspoon [⅓ E.] salt
½ cup [⅖ E.] plain yogurt
3 to 4 tablespoons [3 E.]
   chopped coriander leaves

1. If hard-cooked eggs are to be used, prick the eggs all over with a toothpick or fork and rub them gently with a pinch of turmeric and a pinch of salt. Heat vegetable oil in a pan and fry eggs until golden on all sides. Remove from oil and set aside to drain. Fry potatoes in vegetable oil remaining in pan in which eggs were browned. Remove

and set aside to drain. If *kagina* are used, fry potatoes in ¼ cup vegetable oil until golden brown. Remove and set aside to drain.

2. In another pan, heat *ghee*, add cumin seeds, cardamoms, bay leaves, gingerroot, garlic, and onion and fry about 2 minutes, stirring. Add spiced onion, tomatoes, ground cumin, coriander, cayenne pepper, *garam masala*, turmeric, sugar, cinnamon, cloves, and paprika and cook gently for a few seconds, before adding potato liquid. Add fried potatoes and salt and cook gently for 5 to 8 minutes. Remove from heat and stir in yogurt. If Indian omelets are being used, cut each omelet into 3 pieces. Return to heat and add omelet pieces or hard-cooked eggs and simmer about 10 minutes. Sprinkle with coriander leaves. Lemon juice may be added to your taste. Serve with boiled rice or Indian bread.

SERVES 4

NARGISI KABAB
(*Egg-stuffed Meatballs*)

1 pound ground lean lamb, ground beef, or uncooked ground turkey	½ teaspoon [⅓ E.] ground cumin
1 egg	½ teaspoon [⅓ E.] ground coriander
2½ teaspoons [2 E.] *besan* (chickpea flour) or all-purpose flour	½ teaspoon [⅓ E.] *garam masala*
Pinch of turmeric	2½ tablespoons [2 E.] spiced onion
Pinch of monosodium glutamate	2½ tablespoons [2 E.] chopped coriander leaves
Pinch of freshly ground black pepper	¾ teaspoon [⅗ E.] salt
Pinch of cayenne pepper	8 small hard-cooked eggs
Pinch of paprika	1 egg, lightly beaten
	½ cup [⅖ E.] bread crumbs
	1½ to 2 cups [1⅕ to 1⅗ E.] vegetable oil
	1 tablespoon lemon juice

Combine meat, egg, *besan*, turmeric, monosodium glutamate, black pepper, cayenne pepper, paprika, *garam masala*, spiced onion, coriander leaves, and salt in a bowl and mix well. Divide the meat mixture into 8 equal parts. Using moistened fingers, wrap each portion of meat around a hard-cooked egg, covering the egg completely. Dip each covered egg in the lightly beaten egg and roll it in bread crumbs. In a heavy saucepan or deep fat fryer, heat 2 to 3 inches oil. Fry meat-wrapped eggs until browned on all sides. Drain and sprinkle with lemon juice. Serve hot or cold, either whole or cut in half lengthwise. Garnish with lime slices and chopped coriander leaves.

SERVES 4 to 8

NARGISI KABAB RASA
(*Egg–Meatball Curry*)

8 *Nargisi Kababs* (see page 117)
3 tablespoons [1½ ounces] *ghee* or vegetable oil
1 large yellow onion, chopped
2 cloves garlic, finely minced
1¼ teaspoons [1 E.] freshly grated gingerroot
4 cardamoms, crushed
1 small bay leaf
1 or 2 green chilies, seeded and halved (optional)
½ cup [2 ounces] ground almonds
1¼ teaspoons [1 E.] ground cumin

1¼ teaspoons [1 E.] ground coriander
1 large green pepper, seeded and slivered
2 large tomatoes, peeled and roughly chopped
¼ teaspoon [⅕ E.] salt
¼ teaspoon [⅕ E.] cayenne pepper
1 7½-ounce can tomato sauce
3 to 4 tablespoons [3 E.] chopped coriander leaves

Prepare *Nargisi Kababs* according to directions on page 117. Heat *ghee* in a large skillet until it begins to smoke. Add onion, garlic, gingerroot, cardamoms, bay leaf, and chilies and fry for 2 to 3 minutes. Add almonds, cumin, coriander, green pepper, tomatoes, salt, and cayenne pepper. Cook, stirring, about one minute more. Add tomato sauce and mix well. Add *Nargisi Kababs* in single layer. Simmer for 15 minutes. Garnish with chopped coriander leaves.

SERVES 8

PARSI OMELET
(*Corn and Cheese Omelet*)

8 large eggs
5 tablespoons [4 E.] evaporated milk
⅓ teaspoon [¼ E.] salt
¼ teaspoon [⅕ E.] freshly ground black pepper
1¼ teaspoons [1 E.] finely chopped gingerroot
2 green chilies, seeded and finely chopped

5 to 6 tablespoons [3 ounces] *ghee*
2 large yellow onions, thinly sliced
1¼ cups [1 E.] frozen corn
½ cup [⅗ E.] grated cheddar cheese
½ teaspoon [⅓ E.] paprika

Beat eggs with evaporated milk, salt, pepper, gingerroot, and chilies. Heat *ghee* in a large skillet until it begins to smoke. Cook onions until soft but not brown. Add corn and cook another 2 to 3 minutes. Gently add egg mixture on top of the onion mixture; do not stir. Cook 2 to 3 minutes over very low heat until eggs start to set. Slip pan under a preheated broiler for a few seconds until eggs are barely cooked through. Sprinkle cheese on top and return to the broiler until cheese starts to melt. Remove from heat. Sprinkle paprika on top. Cut into portions and serve immediately with chutney.

SERVES 4

Fish

Seafoods are tasty and rich in vitamins and minerals. They offer an excellent source of easily digestible protein and are remarkably low 'n calories. In India people eat lots of fish fresh from ponds or lakes. Shrimp are also plentiful and are used in a variety of dishes. How to cook fish depends largely on the fat content of the particular fish. Care should be taken while cooking fish, because it cooks very quickly and can easily be ruined by overcooking.

MACHI DAHI
(Fish in Yogurt Sauce)

1 pound fish fillets (perch, flounder, sole, or haddock)
½ cup [⅖ E.] all-purpose flour (seasoned with a pinch each of garlic powder, salt, and turmeric)
½ cup [⅖ E.] vegetable oil
Pinch of cumin seeds
1 medium yellow onion, finely chopped
1 clove garlic, finely minced
½ teaspoon [⅓ E.] freshly grated gingerroot
1 bay leaf
1½ tablespoons [1¼ E.] spiced onion

¼ teaspoon [⅕ E.] turmeric
¼ teaspoon [⅕ E.] cayenne pepper
¼ teaspoon [⅕ E.] ground cinnamon
Pinch of monosodium glutamate
Pinch of paprika
Pinch of ground cardamom
½ cup [3 ounces] plain yogurt
¾ teaspoon [⅗ E.] salt
2½ teaspoons [2 E.] dry mustard
1 tablespoon water
3 to 4 tablespoons [3 E.] chopped coriander leaves

1. Cut fish fillets into 8 pieces. Place flour in a plastic bag; add garlic powder, salt, and turmeric and shake well. Add a few pieces of fish at a time to the bag and shake until fish is well coated. Heat ¼ cup vegetable oil in a skillet and fry fish fillets about 2 minutes or until lightly browned on each side. Remove fish and set aside to drain.

2. In another skillet heat remaining ¼ cup vegetable oil; add cumin seeds, onion, garlic, gingerroot, and bay leaf. Fry, stirring, about 2 minutes. Add spiced onion, turmeric, cayenne pepper, cinnamon, monosodium glutamate, paprika, and cardamom and cook another minute or so. Remove from heat and stir in yogurt and salt. Return to heat and carefully add fried fish in a single layer. Cover fish with the yogurt sauce. Simmer for 10 minutes, covered. Prepare mustard paste according to directions on page 16. Add mustard paste and chopped coriander leaves and continue simmering, uncovered, about 5 more minutes. Serve with boiled rice.

SERVES 4

MACHI KOFTA KALIA
(*Fish Ball Curry*)

Fish Kofta:

2½ pounds fish fillets (sole, flounder, haddock, or blue fish)	½ teaspoon [⅓ E.] cumin seeds
	½ teaspoon [⅓ E.] turmeric
	½ teaspoon [⅓ E.] cayenne pepper
2 tablespoons [1⅗ E.] rice flour	
2 tablespoons [1⅗ E.] all-purpose flour	½ teaspoon [⅓ E.] *sambhar* spice
1¼ teaspoons [1 E.] finely minced gingerroot	1½ teaspoons [1¼ E.] salt
1¼ teaspoons [1 E.] ground roasted cumin	2½ tablespoons [2 E.] plain yogurt or sour cream
	1 egg, lightly beaten
2½ tablespoons [2 E.] spiced onion	½ cup [⅓ E.] bread crumbs
2½ tablespoons [2 E.] chopped coriander leaves	1½ to 2 cups [1⅕ to 1⅗ E.] vegetable oil

Cut fish into 4-inch pieces and poach in boiling water to cover for about 5 minutes, or until fish flakes easily with a fork. Remove fish with a slotted spoon and carefully take out bones. Combine fish with rice flour, all-purpose flour, gingerroot, cumin, spiced onion, chopped coriander leaves, cumin seeds, turmeric, cayenne pepper, *sambhar* spice, salt, and yogurt in a bowl and mix well. Form fish balls about one inch in diameter. Dip fish balls in lightly beaten egg and roll in bread crumbs. Add vegetable oil to a deep fat fryer to a depth of 2 inches and heat to 375°. Add fish balls and fry until lightly golden in color. Remove and set aside to drain.

Shrimp Kofta:

2½ pounds fresh shrimp, cleaned, deveined, and finely chopped
1 medium yellow onion, finely minced
2 cloves garlic, finely minced
1½ teaspoons [½ inch] freshly grated gingerroot
1 or 2 green chilies, seeded and finely chopped
Big pinch of monosodium glutamate

Big pinch of ground turmeric
Big pinch of cumin seeds
½ teaspoon [⅓ E.] dry mustard
3 to 4 tablespoons [3 E.] bread crumbs
3 to 4 tablespoons [3 E.] chopped coriander leaves
1 egg
1¼ teaspoons [1 E.] salt
1½ cups [1⅕ E.] vegetable oil

Combine chopped shrimp, onion, garlic, gingerroot, chilies, monosodium glutamate, turmeric, cumin seeds, dry mustard, bread crumbs, chopped coriander leaves, egg, and salt in a bowl and mix well. Form small balls about the size of a walnut. Preheat vegetable oil to 375°. Add shrimp balls. As they brown, transfer them to paper toweling to drain.

Lobster Kofta:

2 cups cooked lobster or 3 5-ounce cans lobster meat
½ yellow onion, finely minced
1 clove garlic, finely minced
¾ teaspoon [⅗ E.] grated gingerroot
1 green chili, seeded and chopped
Pinch of monosodium glutamate

Pinch of cumin seeds
Pinch of turmeric
2½ tablespoons [2 E.] bread crumbs
2½ tablespoons [2 E.] chopped coriander leaves
1 small egg
½ teaspoon [⅓ E.] salt
1½ cups vegetable oil

Combine cooked lobster, onion, garlic, gingerroot, chili, monosodium glutamate, cumin seeds, turmeric, bread crumbs, chopped coriander leaves, egg, and salt in a bowl and mix well. Form balls one inch in diameter. Heat vegetable oil, add lobster balls, and fry until golden. Remove and set aside to drain.

NOTE: To prepare lobster stock: In a saucepan combine lobster claws and shells from 1 lobster, 1 cup water, 1 small onion (chopped), 2 small celery leaves, 1 small carrot (diced), 2 cloves, and 1 bay leaf. Cover, boil for 2 minutes, reduce heat, and simmer for 20 minutes. Strain, reserving liquid.

Gravy:

¼ cup [2 ounces] *ghee*
1 medium yellow onion, finely
    chopped
1 bay leaf
2½ tablespoons [2 E.] spiced onion
1¼ teaspoons [1 E.] ground cumin
1¼ teaspoons [1 E.] ground
    coriander
¼ teaspoon [⅕ E.] ground
    turmeric

¼ teaspoon [⅕ E.] cayenne
    pepper
¼ teaspoon [⅕ E.] *garam masala*
3 tomatoes, peeled and chopped
¼ teaspoon [⅕ E.] salt
1½ cups [12 ounces] coconut milk
    (lobster stock may be used
    for lobster *kofta* curry)
3 to 4 tablespoons [3 E.]
    chopped coriander leaves
½ teaspoon [⅓ E.] paprika

Heat *ghee* in a saucepan; add onion and bay leaf and cook about 2 minutes. Add spiced onion, cumin, coriander, turmeric, cayenne pepper, *garam masala*, tomatoes, and salt. Cook, stirring, another minute or so. Add coconut milk and bring to a boil. Add fish, shrimp, or lobster *koftas*, reduce heat to low, and simmer for 8 to 10 minutes, or until the sauce is slightly thickened. Sprinkle with coriander leaves and paprika. Serve with *pullao*, boiled rice, or Indian bread.

SERVES 8 to 10

JHINGA MALAI
(*Shrimp Curry*)

¼ cup [2 ounces] vegetable oil
2 pounds raw shrimp, cleaned
   and deveined
¼ teaspoon [⅕ E.] salt
¼ teaspoon [⅕ E.] ground
   turmeric
¼ teaspoon [⅕ E.] finely minced
   gingerroot
Big pinch of monosodium
   glutamate
1 bay leaf
4 to 6 cardamoms, crushed
2 to 3 small (1-inch) cinnamon
   sticks

2 green chilies, seeded and
   halved
1 medium yellow onion, finely
   minced
2 cloves garlic, finely minced
Pinch of saffron threads soaked
   in 1 tablespoon warm water
4 to 5 tablespoons [3 to 4 E.]
   ground almonds
½ teaspoon [⅓ E.] salt
Pinch of sugar
2½ tablespoons [2 E.] raisins
1 to 1¼ cups [8 to 10 ounces]
   coconut milk

Heat large skillet; then add vegetable oil. Fry shrimp with salt, turmeric, gingerroot, and monosodium glutamate for about 2 minutes. Remove from pan and set aside. Add bay leaf, cardamoms, cinnamon, chilies, onion, and garlic to vegetable oil remaining in pan and fry for another 2 minutes. Add saffron with its soaking water, ground almonds, salt, sugar, raisins, and coconut milk, and cook gently for 2 to 3 minutes. Add fried shrimp, cover, and cook gently for 5 to 8 minutes. Garnish with slivered almonds. Serve with *pullao*.

SERVES 8

BHAPA JHINGA
(*Steamed Shrimp*)

2½ teaspoons [2 E.] dry mustard
1 tablespoon water
1 pound raw shrimp, shelled and
   deveined
4 tablespoons [2 ounces]
   creamed coconut, grated
2 green chilies, seeded and
   halved

2 tablespoons [1 ounce] mustard
   oil or vegetable oil
Big pinch of ground turmeric
¼ teaspoon [⅕ E.] salt
½ cup [⅖ E.] coconut milk
Big pinch of paprika

1. Prepare mustard paste according to directions on page 16.
2. Combine shrimp, coconut, chilies, mustard oil, turmeric, salt, coconut milk, paprika, and mustard paste in the top of a double boiler and mix well. Cover and set aside for 30 minutes. Boil water rapidly in the bottom of the double boiler and set pan containing shrimp over the boiling water. Cover and cook gently for 16 to 20 minutes. Turn shrimp once and continue cooking another 10 to 15 minutes, or until shrimp are cooked and the sauce has thickened. Serve with boiled rice.

SERVES 4

MACHI QORMA
(*Rich Fish Curry*)

1½ pounds fish, cleaned and boned (carp, white fish, lake trout, or salmon)
½ teaspoon [⅓ E.] salt
½ teaspoon [⅓ E.] ground turmeric
¼ cup [⅕ E.] plus 2½ [2 E.] tablespoons vegetable oil
2 medium yellow onions, thinly sliced
2 cloves garlic
½ inch fresh gingerroot
2 red chilies
1¼ teaspoons [1 E.] cumin seeds
1¼ teaspoons [1 E.] poppy seeds

¼ teaspoon [⅕ E.] *garam masala*
1½ tablespoons [1¼ E.] lemon juice
1½ tablespoons [1¼ E.] tomato paste
1 bay leaf
½ cup [⅖ E.] fish or chicken stock
½ cup [⅖ E.] plain yogurt
2½ tablespoons [2 E.] slivered almonds
2½ tablespoons [2 E.] raisins
3 tablespoons [2½ E.] chopped coriander leaves

1. Cut fish into 8 equal pieces. Sprinkle with ¼ teaspoon salt and ¼ teaspoon turmeric, rub well, and set aside for 20 minutes. Heat ¼ cup vegetable oil in a skillet. When oil starts to smoke, add fish, a few pieces at a time, and fry for 2 minutes on each side, or until golden. Remove from pan and set aside to drain.
2. Combine half of the sliced onions, the garlic, gingerroot, chilies, cumin seeds, poppy seeds, remaining turmeric and salt, *garam masala*, lemon juice, and tomato paste in the container of a blender and blend until smooth and creamy, adding a little water if necessary.
3. Heat 2½ tablespoons vegetable oil in a large skillet. Add remain-

ing onion slices and fry until lightly browned. Remove with a slotted spoon and set aside. Add creamed spice mixture to oil remaining in skillet and fry for 2 minutes. Add bay leaf, fish stock, yogurt, almonds, raisins, and coriander leaves and cook for one minute. Add cooked fish pieces and simmer for 15 minutes. Sprinkle with fried onions.

SERVES 4

MASSALEDARH HADDOCK
(*Spiced Haddock*)

¼ cup [⅕ E.] spiced onion
¼ teaspoon [⅕ E.] turmeric
¼ teaspoon [⅕ E.] cayenne pepper
¼ teaspoon [⅕ E.] *garam masala*
½ teaspoon [⅓ E.] salt
1½ tablespoons [1¼ E.] lemon juice
1½ pounds haddock, cut into 8 pieces

1 egg, lightly beaten
½ cup [⅖ E.] bread crumbs
¼ cup [2 ounces] vegetable oil
2 tablespoons [1 ounce] *ghee*
4 cardamoms, crushed
1 green chili, seeded
1 bay leaf
1 medium yellow onion, thinly sliced
½ cup [5 ounces] sour cream

1. Combine spiced onion, turmeric, cayenne pepper, *garam masala*, salt, and lemon juice in a bowl. Add pieces of fish and mix well. Cover and set aside for one hour.

2. Heat vegetable oil in a skillet. Remove fish from the spice mixture, dip in egg and roll in bread crumbs. Add fish to oil and brown on both sides. Remove fish and set aside to drain. Heat *ghee* in another pan. Add cardamoms, chili, bay leaf, and onion and fry about 2 minutes. Add spice mixture in which fish pieces marinated and cook gently one minute. Add sour cream and mix well. Return fish to the sauce, cover, and cook gently for about 10 minutes. Turn once and cook another 5 minutes. Serve with boiled rice.

SERVES 4 to 6

RAI MACHI
(*Smelts with Mustard*)

Fresh smelts are delicate and therefore cook very quickly. They are bony, however, and must be carefully filleted. If smelts are frozen, thaw completely at room temperature for one or 2 hours before cooking.

1 pound smelts, heads and tails removed if desired
½ teaspoon [⅖ E.] salt
Dash of turmeric
½ cup [⅖ E.] all-purpose flour
½ cup [⅖ E.] vegetable oil
Pinch of black cumin seeds
2 to 3 green chilies, seeded
1 large yellow onion, finely chopped

¼ teaspoon [⅕ E.] ground turmeric
¼ teaspoon [⅕ E.] cayenne pepper
¼ teaspoon [⅕ E.] paprika
¼ cup [⅕ E.] water
1½ tablespoons [1¼ E.] dry mustard
1 tablespoon [⅘ E.] water
2 to 3 tablespoons [2 E.] scallions, finely chopped

1. Rub a dash of salt and turmeric into the fish. Set aside for 20 minutes. Roll each fish lightly in flour. Heat ¼ cup vegetable oil in a large skillet. Add fish and fry about one minute, turning once. Remove from oil and set aside to drain.

2. Heat ¼ cup vegetable oil in another pan. Add black cumin seeds, chilies, and chopped onion, and fry about 2 minutes. Add turmeric, cayenne pepper, and paprika, and cook a few more seconds. Add water, ⅓ teaspoon salt, and fried fishes, and cook gently for one minute. Prepare mustard paste according to directions on page 16. Reduce heat to simmer and add mustard paste and scallions. Simmer for 5 minutes. Serve with boiled rice.

SERVES 4

MACHI TANDOORI
(*Barbecued Fish*)

1 large yellow onion, chopped
1 inch fresh gingerroot
4 cloves garlic
1 or 2 green chilies
1 large tomato, peeled
½ green pepper, chopped
1¼ teaspoons [1 E.] ground
    coriander
1¼ teaspoons [1 E.] cumin seeds
½ teaspoon [⅓ E.] turmeric
1¼ teaspoons [1 E.] *garam masala*

5 tablespoons [4 E.] lemon juice
¼ cup [2 ounces] vegetable oil
1 whole fish about 3 to 3½
    pounds (salmon, bass, red
    snapper, white fish, lake
    trout, or pike) or 5 or 6
    eight-ounce fillets of sole
¾ teaspoon [⅗ E.] salt
3 to 4 tablespoons [3 E.]
    chopped coriander leaves

1. Place onion, gingerroot, garlic, chilies, tomato, green pepper, coriander, cumin seeds, turmeric, *garam masala*, and lemon juice in the container of a blender and blend until creamy. Heat vegetable oil in a heavy saucepan and cook blended ingredients over very low heat (do not boil), stirring occasionally, for 5 minutes. Set aside to cool.

2. Make one or two cuts on either side of the whole fish. Place whole fish or fish fillets in a close-fitting dish. Cover with the cooked spice mixture and add salt and coriander leaves. Gently rub the spice mixture into the cavity of the whole fish or over the fillets. Cover dish with aluminum foil and place in refrigerator to marinate for at least 24 hours, turning the fish several times.

3. Preheat oven to 350°. Arrange fish in buttered shallow baking pan. Bake fish about 40 to 50 minutes, or until fish flakes easily. During baking, brush remaining spice mixture over the fish every 15 minutes. Carefully turn fish once during baking. The fillets should be baked 10 to 15 minutes, or until golden brown. Slip fish or fillets under the hot broiler just for a few minutes until it is golden. Serve on a large warmed platter and garnish with more coriander leaves, lemon slices, and onion rings.

SERVES 10

MACHI KABAB
(*Fish Kababs*)

½ cup [⅖ E.] plain yogurt
2½ tablespoons [2 E.] lemon juice
2½ tablespoons [2 E.] chopped coriander leaves
¼ teaspoon [⅕ E.] turmeric
¼ teaspoon [⅕ E.] cayenne pepper
¼ teaspoon [⅕ E.] *garam masala*
¼ teaspoon [⅕ E.] salt

¾ teaspoon [⅗ E.] ground cumin
¾ teaspoon [⅗ E.] ground coriander
2 cloves garlic, finely minced
2½ tablespoons [2 E.] spiced onion
¼ cup [2 ounces] vegetable oil
1 pound fish (carp, white fish, or half-cooked lobster chunks)
¼ cup [⅕ E.] corn flake crumbs

1. Combine yogurt, lemon juice, chopped coriander leaves, turmeric, cayenne pepper, *garam masala*, salt, cumin, ground coriander, garlic, spiced onion, and vegetable oil in a bowl and mix with a fork. Cut fish into 6 to 8 portions. Marinate fish pieces in spice mixture for 4 to 6 hours, covered.

2. Preheat oven to 375°. Place buttered foil on a baking sheet. Remove fish from marinade and place fish on the foil in single layer and sprinkle it with corn flake crumbs. Bake about 10 to 15 minutes, or until golden brown. Brush remaining spice marinade over the fish at intervals. Turn once and bake another 5 minutes, or until fish flakes when tested with a fork. Serve on a heated platter, garnished with chopped coriander leaves and lemon slices.

SERVES 3 to 4

MACHI KALIA
(*Fish Curry*)

1½ pounds fish fillets (carp, salmon, lake trout, or pike), cut into 8 pieces
½ teaspoon [⅖ E.] salt
Dash of turmeric
6 tablespoons [3 ounces] vegetable oil
1 large potato, peeled and cut into 1-inch cubes
1 medium cauliflower, cut into flowerets
Pinch of cumin seeds
1 bay leaf
2½ tablespoons [2 E.] spiced onion
2 green chilies, seeded
⅓ teaspoon [¼ E.] ground turmeric

⅓ teaspoon [¼ E.] cayenne pepper
1¼ teaspoons [1 E.] ground cumin
1¼ teaspoons [1 E.] ground coriander
1 medium tomato, peeled and chopped
1 tablespoon water
1½ cups [12 ounces] fish stock, chicken stock, or water
½ cup [⅖ E.] plain yogurt
¼ teaspoon [⅕ E.] *garam masala*
¼ teaspoon [⅕ E.] paprika
Pinch of sugar
3 to 4 tablespoons [3 E.] chopped coriander leaves

1. Sprinkle ⅛ teaspoon [⅒ E.] salt and turmeric on the pieces of fish. Rub spices gently into fish and set aside for 10 minutes. Heat 4 tablespoons vegetable oil in a large skillet. Fry fish pieces until they are browned. Remove from pan and set aside to drain. Fry potato and cauliflower in remaining vegetable oil until light brown, adding more oil if necessary. Remove from pan and set aside to drain.

2. Heat 2 tablespoons vegetable oil in another pan and add cumin seeds, bay leaf, and spiced onion and cook, stirring, about one minute. Add chilies, turmeric, cayenne pepper, cumin, coriander, tomato, water and cook for a minute or so. Add fried vegetables and mix well. Add fish stock and remaining salt and cook gently, covered, about 10 minutes or until vegetables are tender but not mushy. Stir in yogurt, a little at a time. Add *garam masala*, paprika, and sugar, and simmer for 5 minutes. Add fish pieces to pan and spoon sauce over them. Sprinkle with chopped coriander leaves and continue simmering another 10 minutes. For lighter gravy, use more liquid. Serve with boiled rice.

SERVES 4 to 6

JHINGA or MACHI VINDALOO
(*Shrimp or Fish Sour Curry*)

2 medium yellow onions,
chopped
4 to 6 cloves garlic
2 red or green chilies, chopped
1 inch fresh gingerroot
¼ cup [2 ounces] white vinegar
1¼ teaspoons [1 E.] *garam masala*
1¼ teaspoons [1 E.] cumin seeds
½ teaspoon [⅓ E.] turmeric
1 to 2 teaspoons [2 E.] sugar

2 pounds raw shrimp, shelled and
deveined, or 2 pounds fish,
cut into 16 pieces
½ teaspoon [⅖ E.] salt
6 tablespoons [3 ounces]
vegetable oil
1 medium yellow onion, finely
chopped
½ cup [⅖ E.] water
4 to 6 tablespoons [3 to 5 E.]
lemon juice

Place onions, garlic, chilies, gingerroot, vinegar, *garam masala*, cumin seeds, turmeric, and sugar in the container of a blender and blend until creamy. Sprinkle ⅛ teaspoon salt and turmeric on the fish, and rub gently. Heat ¼ cup of vegetable oil in a large skillet and fry fish or shrimp for about 2 minutes. Remove from oil and set aside to drain. Heat 2 tablespoons of vegetable oil in another pan, add onion, and fry for 2 minutes. Add blended spice mixture and remaining salt and cook for another 3 to 4 minutes. Add water and fried fish or shrimp, and cook gently 5 to 8 minutes. Mix in lemon juice and remove from heat. Serve with boiled rice.

SERVES 8

MACHI
(*Bombay Style Fish*)

2 pounds fish fillets (haddock, sole, perch), cut into 16 pieces
Pinch of monosodium glutamate
⅓ teaspoon [¼ E.] salt
Pinch of turmeric
½ cup [⅖ E.] rice flour or all-purpose flour
½ cup [⅖ E.] vegetable oil
1 large yellow onion, chopped
2 cloves garlic, finely minced
1¼ teaspoons [1 E.] finely minced gingerroot
1¼ teaspoons [1 E.] ground cumin
4 cardamoms, crushed

1 small bay leaf
1 or 2 green chilies, seeded
⅓ cup [¼ E.] blanched almonds
1 green pepper, seeded and slivered
2 large tomatoes, peeled and roughly chopped
½ teaspoon [⅓ E.] cayenne pepper
7½-ounce can tomato sauce
½ cup [⅖ E.] crushed fried *vadi* (optional)
3 to 4 tablespoons [3 E.] chopped coriander leaves

1. Sprinkle fish fillets with monosodium glutamate, ⅛ teaspoon salt, and turmeric, and rub gently. Set aside for one hour at room temperature. Roll each fillet in flour to coat all sides. Heat ¼ cup vegetable oil in a skillet. Add a few flour-coated fillets at a time and fry about 2 minutes, or until lightly golden brown on all sides. Remove from oil and set aside to drain.

2. In a large skillet, heat remaining ¼ cup of vegetable oil until it smokes. Add onion, garlic, and gingerroot, and fry for 2 minutes. Add cumin, cardamoms, bay leaf, green chilies, almonds, and green pepper, and cook over medium heat about one minute. Add tomatoes and cayenne pepper and stir to blend well. Add tomato sauce and remaining salt, and bring to a boil. Add fried fish pieces in single layer. Cover and simmer 15 minutes, basting occasionally. Sprinkle with crushed *vadi* and chopped coriander leaves. Continue simmering another 2 to 4 minutes, uncovered. Serve with hot boiled rice.

SERVES 6 to 8

MACHI-WRAP
(*Fish Rolls*)

2½ pounds fillet of sole (lemon or grey) or flounder
½ teaspoon [⅖ E.] salt
Dash of monosodium glutamate
5 tablespoons [4 E.] finely chopped scallions
½ cup [⅓ E.] ground almonds
1 7-ounce carton creamed coconut

1¼ cups [1 E.] warm water
2½ tablespoons [2 E.] dry mustard
2 tablespoons [1 ounce] water
2 green chilies, seeded
½ teaspoon [⅓ E.] cayenne pepper
2½ tablespoons [2 E.] butter
2½ tablespoons [2 E.] slivered almonds

---

1. Split fish fillets in half lengthwise. Sprinkle fillets with ⅛ teaspoon salt and monosodium glutamate and rub gently. Put one teaspoon of scallion and ½ teaspoon of ground almonds in the center of each fillet. Roll fillets and fasten with a toothpick.

2. Preheat oven to 425°. Butter a baking dish just large enough to hold the fish rolls in a single layer. Place fish rolls in the dish. Combine creamed coconut and water in a saucepan and boil until creamed coconut becomes liquid. Prepare mustard paste as directed on page 16. Remove creamed coconut from heat; add mustard paste, chilies, cayenne pepper, remaining salt, butter, and slivered almonds and pour over fish rolls. Bake uncovered for 20 minutes, or until fish flakes. Serve with *pullao* or Indian bread.

SERVES 8 to 10

KAKRA KOFTA KALIA
(*Crab Ball Curry*)

Crab Kofta:

1½ pounds cooked crab meat
2½ tablespoons [2 E.] spiced onion
2½ tablespoons [2 E.] ground
   almonds
2½ tablespoons [2 E.] chopped
   coriander leaves

1¼ teaspoons [1 E.] finely minced
   gingerroot
2 tablespoons [2 ounces] sour
   cream
1 egg
⅓ teaspoon [¼ E.] salt
¼ cup [⅕ E.] vegetable oil

Curry:

2 to 3 tablespoons [1 to 1½
   ounces] vegetable oil or *ghee*
1 medium yellow onion, thinly
   sliced
2 small bay leaves
   Pinch of cumin seeds
2 green chilies, seeded
2½ tablespoons [2 E.] spiced onion
2½ tablespoons [2 E.] tomato paste
2½ tablespoons [2 E.] ground
   almonds

1¼ teaspoons [1 E.] ground cumin
1¼ teaspoons [1 E.] ground
   coriander
   Pinch of saffron threads soaked
   in 1 tablespoon warm water
1 cup [8 ounces] coconut milk
   Dash of salt
3 to 4 tablespoons [3 E.]
   chopped coriander leaves

---

1. Combine crab meat, spiced onion, ground almonds, chopped coriander leaves, gingerroot, sour cream, egg, and salt in a bowl and mix well. Shape the mixture into one-inch balls. Heat vegetable oil in a large skillet. Add crab balls to hot oil and fry, turning, until browned. Remove from oil and set aside to drain.

2. Heat vegetable oil and fry onions until light brown. Remove from pan and set aside to drain. Add cumin seeds, chilies, spiced onion, tomato paste, almonds, ground cumin, coriander, and saffron with its soaking water and cook for one minute. Add coconut milk and salt and boil for 2 minutes. Add *koftas*, fried onion, and coriander leaves. Simmer for 10 minutes.

SERVES 8 to 10

Poultry and Meat

Meat is an important food for everyday life. Meat curries made with chicken, duck, lamb, goat, or mutton are very popular in India. The success of the dish depends very frequently on using the right sauce. Chicken is a relatively inexpensive, high-quality protein food. It is enjoyed by rich and poor from all over the world. The soft and delicate chicken meat can be prepared in so many ways that are not only attractive but delicious. Here are a few ways that I like best.

MURGHI KHASA
(*Chicken Curry*)

3-pound frying chicken, cut into serving pieces
2½ tablespoons [2 E.] lemon juice
2½ teaspoons [2 E.] salt
¾ teaspoon [⅗ E.] ground turmeric
5 tablespoons [4 E.] *ghee*
Pinch of cumin seeds
1 bay leaf
3 cloves garlic, finely minced
1½ teaspoons [½ inch] finely minced gingerroot
1 large yellow onion, chopped
2½ tablespoons [2 E.] spiced onion
2½ tablespoons [2 E.] tomato paste

2½ tablespoons [2 E.] sour cream
2 large tomatoes, peeled and chopped
2½ teaspoons [2 E.] ground cumin
2½ teaspoons [2 E.] ground coriander
½ teaspoon [⅓ E.] cayenne pepper
½ teaspoon [⅓ E.] *garam masala*
½ teaspoon [⅓ E.] paprika
¼ teaspoon [⅕ E.] ground cinnamon
¼ teaspoon [⅕ E.] ground cardamom
½ cup [3 ounces] plain yogurt

1. Remove skin and fat from chicken pieces. Sprinkle chicken with lemon juice, 1¼ teaspoons of salt, and ¼ teaspoon turmeric, and rub each piece well.
2. Heat *ghee* in a large skillet. Brown chicken pieces lightly on both sides. Remove and set aside. Add cumin seeds, bay leaf, garlic, ginger-root, and onion, and fry for 2 minutes. Add spiced onion, tomato paste, and sour cream, and cook, stirring, for 3 to 4 minutes. Add tomatoes, ground cumin, coriander, cayenne pepper, *garam masala*, paprika, cinnamon, cardamom, fried chicken pieces, 1¼ teaspoons of salt, and ½ teaspoon of turmeric, and mix well. Cover and cook gently about 40 minutes, or until meat is tender. Add yogurt and continue to simmer, uncovered, another 10 to 15 minutes. Serve with boiled rice.

SERVES 6

MURGH MALAI
(*Chicken with Coconut Milk*)

5 tablespoons [4 E.] *ghee* or vegetable oil
2 large potatoes, peeled and cut into 1½-inch cubes
2 teaspoons [1⅗ E.] salt
¾ teaspoon [⅗ E.] ground turmeric
3-pound frying chicken, cut into serving pieces
1 medium yellow onion, chopped
2 small bay leaves

6 cardamoms, crushed
2 medium [1½ inch] cinnamon sticks
2 cloves
¼ cup [⅕ E.] spiced onion
¾ teaspoon [⅗ E.] cayenne pepper
¾ teaspoon [⅗ E.] *garam masala*
2 cups [16 ounces] coconut milk
2½ tablespoons [2 E.] raisins

Preheat oven to 350°. Heat *ghee* in a large Dutch oven and fry potato cubes with a dash of salt and a dash of turmeric until golden. Remove and set aside to drain. Add chicken pieces to *ghee* remaining in pot and brown on both sides. Remove and set aside to drain. Add onion, bay leaves, cardamoms, cinnamon, and cloves, and fry about 2 minutes. Stirring, add spiced onion, cayenne pepper, and *garam masala*, and cook another minute. Add coconut milk and bring mixture to a boil. Add chicken, potatoes, and raisins, cover, and bake in preheated oven for 50 to 60 minutes, or until meat is tender. Serve hot with boiled rice or Indian bread.

SERVES 6

MURGHI DOOPIAZA
(*Chicken with Onions*)

5 tablespoons [4 E.] *ghee*
2 pounds yellow onions, cut into thick slices
3 whole chicken breasts, cut in half lengthwise to make 6 halves
½ teaspoon [⅓ E.] turmeric
½ teaspoon [⅓ E.] cayenne pepper
¼ teaspoon [⅕ E.] ground cinnamon
¼ teaspoon [⅕ E.] ground cardamom
1¼ teaspoons [1 E.] paprika
1½ teaspoons [½ inch] finely minced gingerroot
1¼ teaspoons [1 E.] salt
2 to 4 cloves garlic, finely minced
2 large tomatoes, peeled and chopped
1 large yellow onion, finely minced

1. Heat *ghee* in a large skillet and fry the sliced onions until light brown. Remove with a slotted spoon and set aside. Add the chicken breasts and fry over moderate heat, about 5 minutes a side, or until chicken pieces are well browned. As chicken breasts brown, transfer them to a large shallow baking dish.

2. Preheat oven to 350°. Add turmeric, cayenne pepper, cinnamon, cardamom, paprika, gingerroot, salt, garlic, tomatoes, and onion to *ghee* remaining in pan in which chicken was browned, adding a little more *ghee* if necessary. Cook over moderate heat, scraping up any browned bits from the bottom, for two minutes. Pour sauce over chicken in the baking dish. Cover sauce and chicken with fried onions. Cover baking dish with aluminum foil and bake in preheated oven for 30 minutes, or until chicken is tender and sauce has thickened. Serve with *pullao*.

Serves 6

BATAKH DOOPIAZA
(*Duck with Onions*)

5 tablespoons [4 E.] *ghee*
2 pounds yellow onions, cut into
　　thick slices
4 to 5 pounds duck, cut into
　　serving pieces
½ teaspoon [⅓ E.] turmeric
½ teaspoon [⅓ E.] cayenne
　　pepper
¼ teaspoon [⅕ E.] ground
　　cinnamon

¼ teaspoon [⅕ E.] ground
　　cardamom
1¼ teaspoons [1 E.] paprika
1½ teaspoons [½ inch] minced
　　gingerroot
2 teaspoons [1⅗ E.] salt
4 cloves garlic, minced
3 large tomatoes, peeled and
　　chopped
2½ tablespoons [2 E.] spiced onion
1 cup [⅘ E.] warm water

1. Heat *ghee* in a large skillet and fry the sliced onions until light brown. Remove with a slotted spoon and set aside. Add duck pieces and fry over moderate heat about 5 minutes, or until they are well browned. As duck pieces brown, transfer them to a large shallow baking dish.

2. Preheat oven to 350°. Add turmeric, cayenne pepper, cinnamon, cardamom, paprika, gingerroot, salt, garlic, tomatoes, and spiced onion to *ghee* remaining in pan in which duck was browned, adding a little more *ghee* if necessary. Cook over moderate heat for 2 minutes, scraping up any browned bits from the bottom. Add water and bring to a boil. Pour sauce over duck pieces in the baking dish. Cover sauce and duck with half of the fried onions. Cover baking dish with aluminum foil and bake in preheated oven for 1 to 1½ hours, or until meat is tender.

3. Remove from oven and add remaining fried onions. Stir lightly and bake uncovered another 15 to 20 minutes.

SERVES 6

MURGH MASALA
(*Spiced Chicken*)

Masala Paste:

1 large yellow onion, chopped
1 large clove garlic
1 inch fresh gingerroot
2½ tablespoons [2 E.] coriander
   leaves
1¼ teaspoons [1 E.] cumin seeds
1¼ teaspoons [1 E.] coriander
   seeds*
4 cardamoms, peeled

2 cloves
2 peppercorns
Pinch of nutmeg
Pinch of mace
½ teaspoon [⅓ E.] ground
   turmeric
½ teaspoon [⅓ E.] ground
   cinnamon
2 green chilies, seeded

3-pound broiler chicken
½ teaspoon [⅓ E.] salt
½ cup [⅖ E.] *ghee*
1 medium yellow onion, chopped
2 tomatoes, peeled and chopped
¼ teaspoon [⅕ E.] saffron threads
   soaked in 1 tablespoon warm
   water

1 cup [8 ounces] plain yogurt
¼ cup [⅕ E.] sliced almonds
½ cup [⅖ E.] freshly grated
   coconut
3 hard-cooked eggs, chopped
3 to 4 tablespoons [3 E.]
   chopped coriander leaves
6 tomatoes, cut into wedges

1. Prepare *masala* paste: Place onion, garlic, gingerroot, coriander leaves, cumin seeds, coriander seeds, cardamoms, cloves, peppercorns, nutmeg, mace, turmeric, cinnamon, and chilies in the container of a blender and blend until creamy.

2. Pat chicken completely dry, inside and out, with paper toweling. Make 2 cuts about 2 inches long and ¼ inch deep on either side of each breast. Place chicken in a baking dish and rub the *masala* paste with salt into body cavity and the cuts and then over the skin of the chicken. Marinate at room temperature for at least 2 to 4 hours.

3. Heat *ghee* in a large skillet. Brown onion over medium heat. Add tomatoes and chicken with spices and cook for 5 to 8 minutes, stirring constantly. Cover and cook gently about 40 minutes. Combine saffron with its water and yogurt and stir in a little hot gravy from the cooked chicken; then slowly stir the yogurt mixture into the pan. Remove chicken and place on a platter. Stir in almonds, coconut,

and chopped eggs into the gravy remaining in the pan. Pour over chicken. Garnish with coriander leaves and tomato wedges.

SERVES 5 to 6

MURGH DEHIN
(*Chicken with Buttermilk*)

2 cups [16 ounces] buttermilk
2½ tablespoons [2 E.] spiced onion
2½ tablespoons [2 E.] catsup
2½ tablespoons [2 E.] chopped coriander leaves
1¼ to 1½ teaspoons [1 to 1¼ E.] salt
2½ to 3 pounds chicken pieces
2 tablespoons [1 ounce] vegetable oil
¼ teaspoon [⅕ E.] *garam masala*
2 tablespoons [1 ounce] *ghee*
1 medium yellow onion, thinly sliced
2 cloves garlic, finely minced

1¼ teaspoons [1 E.] finely minced gingerroot
1¼ teaspoons [1 E.] ground cumin
2½ teaspoons [2 E.] ground coriander
1 large tomato, seeded and chopped
¾ teaspoon [⅗ E.] turmeric
¾ teaspoon [⅗ E.] cayenne pepper
2 to 2½ tablespoons [2 E.] all-purpose flour

1. Combine buttermilk, spiced onion, catsup, coriander leaves, and salt in a bowl. Add chicken pieces and gently rub the paste into the chicken. Marinate overnight (or at least 5 to 6 hours) in the refrigerator.

2. Heat vegetable oil and *ghee* in a large skillet. Add onion, garlic, and gingerroot, and fry for 2 minutes. Mix in cumin, coriander, tomato, turmeric, cayenne papper and *garam masala*, and cook another 2 minutes. Remove chicken pieces from marinade and place in skillet. Cook, stirring, 4 to 5 minutes, or until *ghee* comes to the surface. Add flour to the buttermilk and spices in which the chicken marinated. Mix well, making certain there are no lumps. Pour marinade over chicken, cover, and cook slowly for about one hour, or until chicken is tender. Serve with boiled rice.

SERVES 4 to 6

KORMA BADAM MALAI
(*Creamed Chicken*)

3 pounds chicken, cut into serving
   pieces
2 cups [16 ounces] milk
¼ teaspoon [⅕ E.] salt
3 tablespoons [1½ ounces] *ghee*
1 cup [⅘ E.] sliced almonds
¼ teaspoon [⅕ E.] ground
   cardamom

3 medium yellow onions, thinly
   sliced
1 cup [⅘ E.] raisins
4 eggs, hard-cooked and chopped
3 cups [24 ounces] heavy cream
Pinch of saffron threads soaked
   in 1 tablespoon warm water
½ cup [⅖ E.] chicken stock

1. Put chicken in a large pot and cover with water. Heat to boiling, turn heat to medium, cover, and cook gently for 30 minutes, or until meat can easily be pulled away from bones. Drain, reserving about ½ cup [⅖ E.] liquid. Remove skin and bones from chicken and break flesh into bite-size pieces. Cook shredded chicken with milk and salt over medium-high heat until most of the milk evaporates, about 20 minutes. Remove from heat and set aside.

2. Heat *ghee* in a skillet, and fry almonds, cardamom, and onions until pale brown. Stir in raisins and chopped eggs and remove from heat. Combine heavy cream and saffron with its soaking water in a bowl.

3. Preheat oven to 325°. Grease one large baking dish. Spread one-half of the milk-cooked chicken in the dish, cover chicken with one-half of the fried onion mixture, and cover onions with one-half of the cream-and-saffron mixture. Repeat these layers using remaining chicken, onions, and cream. Pour chicken stock over the top. Cover baking dish with aluminum foil and bake in preheated oven for about 20 minutes. Serve with *pullao* or Indian bread. Garnish with chopped coriander leaves.

SERVES 4 to 6

PARSI MURGH
(*Special Chicken Curry*)

½ teaspoon [⅓ E.] turmeric
½ teaspoon [⅓ E.] cayenne
  pepper
½ teaspoon [⅓ E.] paprika
1¼ teaspoons [1 E.] salt
  Pinch of garlic powder
  Pinch of ginger
  Pinch of sugar
2½ tablespoons [2 E.] vegetable oil
2½ tablespoons [2 E.] lemon juice
3 pounds chicken breasts, cut
  into serving pieces
2 to 3 tablespoons [1 to 1½
  ounces] *ghee*

2 large yellow onions, thinly
  sliced
1 bay leaf
  Pinch of cumin seeds
1¼ teaspoons [1 E.] finely chopped
  gingerroot
1¼ teaspoons [1 E.] chopped
  coriander leaves
10 tiny white onions, boiled for
  8 minutes in salted water,
  and drained
1¼ tablespoons [1 E.] all-purpose
  flour
¼ teaspoon [⅕ E.] ground
  cardamom

1. Preheat oven to 350°. Combine turmeric, cayenne pepper, paprika, salt, garlic powder, ginger, sugar, vegetable oil, and lemon juice in a bowl and mix well. Place chicken breasts in a baking dish, pour spice mixture over them, and cover dish with aluminum foil. Bake the chicken in a preheated oven for 40 minutes.

2. Heat *ghee* in a large skillet. Add sliced onions and fry until brown. Remove onions from *ghee*. Add bay leaf, cumin seeds, gingerroot, coriander leaves, and boiled onions to *ghee* remaining in pan. Fry about 5 minutes, stirring most of the time. Remove chicken pieces from the gravy, place them in the frying pan, and sprinkle with flour. Fry to a rich brown color. Pour chicken gravy over the fried chicken, sprinkle with fried onions and cardamom, and mix well. Simmer covered for 20 minutes. Serve with *pullao* or *kitchuri*.

SERVES 6 to 8

MURGH TANDOORI
(*Barbecued Chicken Curry*)

Barbecued Chicken:

1½ cups [8 to 12 ounces] plain yogurt

2½ tablespoons [2 E.] tomato paste

2½ tablespoons [2 E.] lemon juice

1 medium yellow onion, finely minced

1½ tablespoons [1½ inches] finely minced gingerroot

6 to 8 cloves garlic, finely minced

2½ teaspoons [2 E.] ground coriander

1¼ teaspoons [1 E.] ground cumin

1¼ teaspoons [1 E.] *garam masala*

1¼ teaspoons [1 E.] salt

Big pinch of sugar

¼ cup [2 ounces] vegetable oil

3 pounds chicken, legs and thighs

1½ cups [1⅕ E.] corn flake crumbs

Curry:

2 tablespoons [1 ounce] *ghee*

1 large yellow onion, chopped

1 green pepper, seeded and slivered

6 cardamoms, crushed

2 cloves

2 1-inch cinnamon sticks

1 bay leaf

1 15-ounce can tomato sauce

3 to 4 tablespoons [3 E.] toasted coconut

---

1. Combine yogurt, tomato paste, lemon juice, onion, gingerroot, garlic, coriander, cumin, *garam masala*, salt, sugar, and vegetable oil in a large bowl and mix well. Add chicken pieces and rub chicken well with spice mixture. Cover bowl with plastic wrap and place in refrigerator to marinate at least overnight, preferably for 24 hours. Turn chicken several times and baste with the marinade.

2. Preheat oven to 350°. Line a baking sheet with aluminum foil. Remove chicken pieces from marinade and dip in corn flake crumbs to coat lightly. Place chicken on prepared pan, meat side up. Place the sheet in the middle level of the preheated oven and bake for one hour, or until chicken is tender and golden. Place a piece of foil over chicken if it begins to brown too much. At this stage, chicken may be served hot with *kitchuri* or *pullao*, or it may be prepared with a curry sauce, as follows.

3. Heat *ghee* in a large pot or Dutch oven. Brown onion and green pepper for one minute. Add cardamoms, cloves, cinnamon sticks, and bay leaf, and fry for a few more seconds. Add tomato sauce and

mix well. Put in cooked chicken pieces and simmer, covered, for 20 minutes. Garnish with toasted coconut. Serve with Indian bread.

NOTE: *Murgh Tandoori* is delicious barbecued on a grill. Just omit corn flake coating and cook chicken 40 to 50 minutes, or until chicken is tender, turning once or twice.

SERVES 6 to 8

MOGHLAI CHIRGA
(*Roasted Whole Chicken*)

1 large yellow onion, chopped
2½ teaspoons [2 E.] coriander
    seeds
1¼ teaspoons [1 E.] cumin seeds
1½ inches gingerroot
2½ tablespoons [2 E.] tomato paste
2½ tablespoons [2 E.] white
    vinegar
2½ tablespoons [2 E.] coriander
    leaves
2 red or green chilies
1¼ teaspoons [1 E.] *garam masala*

1¼ teaspoons [1 E.] *sambhar* spice
1¼ teaspoons [1 E.] paprika
¼ teaspoon [⅕ E.] saffron threads
¼ teaspoon [⅕ E.] nutmeg
¼ teaspoon [⅕ E.] ground
    cardamom
½ teaspoon [⅓ E.] salt
1 cup [8 ounces] plain yogurt
¼ cup [2 ounces] vegetable oil
1 3-pound broiler chicken
1¼ teaspoons [1 E.] lemon juice

1. Combine onion, coriander seeds, cumin seeds, gingerroot, tomato paste, vinegar, coriander leaves, chilies, *garam masala*, *sambhar* spice, paprika, saffron, nutmeg, and cardamom in the container of a blender and blend until the mixture is very creamy, adding a little water if necessary. Combine creamed spice mixture, salt, yogurt, and vegetable oil in a large bowl and stir to blend well. Cover and set aside for half an hour before using.

2. Make a few cuts in the chicken breast and rub lemon juice and a dash of salt into the body cavity of the chicken. Cover and set aside for half an hour. Place chicken in a dish with a close-fitting cover, and pour marinade over the chicken. Rub the spice mixture first into the cuts and cavities, then over the whole chicken. Marinate chicken, covered, for one to 2 days in the refrigerator. During that time, turn and rub marinade into the chicken several times.

3. Preheat oven to 350°. Bake chicken and marinade in a covered

roasting pan in a preheated oven for one hour. Remove chicken from oven, and place it on a greased rack. Pour liquid left in roaster into a saucepan and boil down rapidly until it is reduced to a spreading consistency. Slip chicken under preheated (550°) broiler, about 6 inches from source of heat, and broil until chicken is browned. During broiling, brush chicken with thickened sauce several times. To cook chicken on a rotisserie, roast chicken in a 350° oven about 1½ hours, basting with the sauce every 15 minutes. The cooking time depends upon the weight of the chicken and the length of time it has marinated. Adjust time according to your taste. Serve chicken on a large platter garnished with thinly sliced onions, silver leaf, nuts, and wedges of lime. Serve with *naan* or *pullao*.

SERVES 4 to 6

BAGDADI MURGH
(*Stuffed Chicken Curry*)

Stuffing:

2 tablespoons [1 ounce] *ghee*

½ cup [⅖ E.] freshly grated coconut

½ cup [⅖ E.] powdered milk

2½ tablespoons [2 E.] raisins

1½ tablespoons [1¼ E.] chopped pistachio nuts

2½ tablespoons [2 E.] chopped almonds

Big pinch of salt

Pinch of saffron, soaked in 1 tablespoon warm water

2½ tablespoons [2 E.] heavy cream

Chicken Curry:

1 roasting chicken, about 4 pounds

½ teaspoon [⅓ E.] salt

Dash of freshly ground black pepper

1¼ teaspoons [1 E.] lemon juice

5 tablespoons [4 E.] *ghee*

2 medium yellow onions, thinly sliced

1 bay leaf

6 cardamoms, crushed

⅓ teaspoon [¼ E.] cayenne pepper

¼ cup [⅕ E.] slivered almonds

1¼ teaspoons [1 E.] ground cumin

¼ teaspoon [⅕ E.] ground turmeric

¼ teaspoon [⅕ E.] *garam masala*

1 15-ounce can tomato sauce or 2 cups [1⅗ E.] coconut milk

1. To prepare stuffing, heat *ghee* over low heat. Add in coconut, powdered milk, raisins, pistochios, almonds, salt, saffron with its soaking water, and heavy cream and cook for 2 minutes. Remove from heat and set aside to cool.

2. Pat the chicken completely dry, inside and out, with paper toweling. Rub inside with a dash of salt, pepper, and lemon juice. Set aside for 20 minutes. Spoon stuffing into cavity of chicken. Skewer opening closed and lace tightly with string.

3. Preheat oven to 350°. Heat *ghee* in a large ovenproof pot or Dutch oven. Fry sliced onion until limp but not brown. Add bay leaf, cardamoms, cayenne pepper, remaining salt, almonds, cumin, turmeric, and *garam masala* and stir to blend well. Place stuffed chicken in the pot, turning the chicken to coat it evenly with the spice mixture. Cook over medium heat for 5 minutes.

4. Place pot in the oven and bake chicken, covered, for one hour, or until the meat is tender. When the chicken is cooked, remove from the pot and cook remaining liquid over medium heat until the *ghee* comes to the surface. Return the chicken to the pot, add tomato sauce, and simmer on top of the stove for 20 minutes. Serve on a large meat platter, garnished with coriander leaves and more almonds.

SERVES 10 to 12

KERALA MURGH
(*South Indian Chicken Curry*)

2 tablespoons [1 ounce] *ghee*	2 green chilies, seeded, chopped
½ cup [⅖ E.] cashew nuts	2 bay leaves
½ cup [⅖ E.] freshly grated coconut	½ teaspoon [⅓ E.] turmeric
	½ teaspoon [⅓ E.] cayenne
5 tablespoons [4 E.] vegetable oil	pepper
1 3-pound fryer, cut into serving pieces	½ teaspoon [⅓ E.] *garam masala*
	1 to 1½ cups [8 to 12 ounces]
1 large yellow onion, thinly sliced	coconut milk
1¼ teaspoons [1 E.] finely minced gingerroot	1 tablespoon [⅘ E.] lemon juice
	3 to 4 tablespoons [3 E.]
1¼ teaspoons [1 E.] salt	chopped coriander leaves

Heat *ghee* in a large skillet and fry cashews for 2 minutes. Add coconut to pan and stir for a few seconds. Remove mixture with a slotted spoon and set aside. Heat vegetable oil in the same skillet and add the chicken pieces. Cook over moderate heat, about 5 minutes, or until chicken pieces are well browned. Remove from pan and set aside. Add onion, gingerroot, salt, chilies, bay leaves, turmeric, cayenne pepper, and *garam masala* to the pan, and cook, stirring, for one minute. Return chicken pieces to pan and add coconut milk. Bring to a boil and cook, covered, about 40 minutes or until meat is tender. Serve curry in a deep heated bowl. Drizzle with lemon juice and garnish with fried cashews, coconut, and chopped coriander leaves.

SERVES 6 to 8

MURGH JHAL FREZI
(*Spicy Chicken*)

1½ cups [9 ounces] plain yogurt
½ cup [⅖ E.] spiced onion
1¼ teaspoons [1 E.] ground cumin
1¼ teaspoons [1 E.] *garam masala*
1¼ teaspoons [1 E.] salt
¾ teaspoon [⅗ E.] turmeric
¾ teaspoon [⅗ E.] finely minced gingerroot

3 pounds chicken, legs and thighs
¼ cup [⅕ E.] *ghee*
2 large yellow onions, thinly sliced
4 cloves garlic, finely minced
2½ teaspoons [2 E.] tomato paste
1¼ teaspoons [1 E.] crushed red chili

1. Combine ½ cup yogurt, the spiced onion, cumin, *garam masala*, salt, turmeric, and gingerroot in a bowl. Add the chicken pieces to this marinade, stirring until each piece is well coated. Let chicken marinate for 2 to 4 hours, covered.

2. Heat *ghee* in a large skillet and fry onions until they are light brown. Push fried onions to one side of skillet, add garlic and tomato paste and cook gently for one minute. Add chicken and cook, stirring continuously, another 5 minutes. Cover and simmer 40 minutes, or until meat is tender. Mix in 1 cup yogurt and sprinkle with crushed chili. Simmer another 20 minutes, turning chicken pieces occasionally. Serve hot with boiled rice.

SERVES 6 to 8

BATAKH VINDALOO
(Sour Duck Curry)

3½ to 4 pounds duck, cut into
   serving pieces
2 cardamoms, crushed
2 cloves
2 peppercorns
2 cinnamon sticks
2 bay leaves
3 to 4 cups [24 to 32 ounces]
   water
2 large yellow onions, chopped
1 1-inch piece gingerroot
2 to 4 cloves garlic
1¼ teaspoons [1 E.] cumin seeds

1¼ teaspoons [1 E.] coriander
   seeds
1¼ teaspoons [1 E.] poppy seeds
2 to 4 red chilies
¾ teaspoon [⅗ E.] turmeric
¾ teaspoon [⅗ E.] garam masala
¾ to 1 cup [6 to 8 ounces] white
   vinegar (according to your
   taste)
3 tablespoons [1½ ounces] ghee
1 large potato, parboiled, peeled,
   and cut into 1-inch cubes
1¼ teaspoons [1 E.] salt

1. Remove skin and most of the fat from the duck pieces. Combine crushed cardamoms, cloves, peppercorns, cinnamon sticks, bay leaves, water, and duck pieces in a large pot. Cook gently until meat is tender, about 1½ hours. Drain, reserving liquid.

2. Blend onion, gingerroot, garlic, cumin seeds, coriander seeds, poppy seeds, chilies, turmeric, and garam masala with ¼ cup of white vinegar in a blender until creamy. Heat ghee and fry duck pieces until light brown. Remove from pan and set aside to drain. Add blended spice mixture and potato to ghee remaining in pan and cook for 2 to 3 minutes. Return duck pieces to pan, add remaining vinegar and salt, and simmer for 20 to 30 minutes. Add sugar to taste if necessary. Garnish with chopped chilies. Serve with boiled rice.

SERVES 8 to 10

GOSHT CURRY
(*Lamb Curry*)

2½ pounds lean leg of lamb, boned
   and cut into 1-inch cubes
5 tablespoons [4 E.] spiced onion
5 tablespoons [4 E.] sour cream
2½ teaspoons [2 E.] ground cumin
2½ teaspoons [2 E.] ground
   coriander
¾ teaspoon [⅗ E.] turmeric
¾ teaspoon [⅗ E.] cayenne
   pepper

¾ teaspoon [⅗ E.] *garam masala*
1¼ teaspoons [1 E.] salt
¼ cup [⅕ E.] *ghee*
2 medium potatoes, peeled and
   cut into 1-inch cubes
2 cardamoms, crushed
2 cinnamon sticks
2 bay leaves
1 medium yellow onion, finely
   chopped

Trim off any bits of fat remaining on the lamb. Combine spiced onion, sour cream, cumin, coriander, turmeric, cayenne pepper, *garam masala*, salt, and lamb, and mix well. Heat *ghee* in a large skillet, add potatoes, and fry until light golden. Remove from pan and set aside to drain. Add cardamoms, cinnamon, bay leaves, and onion to *ghee* remaining in pan. Fry, stirring, about 2 minutes. Add lamb mixture and cook gently about 10 minutes. Mix in potatoes, cover, and cook until meat is tender, 40 to 45 minutes. Serve with rice.

SERVES 6 to 8

ROGAN JOSH
(*North Indian Lamb Curry*)

1 cup [8 ounces] plain yogurt
½ cup [⅖ E.] spiced onion
2½ tablespoons [2 E.] ground cumin
2½ tablespoons [2 E.] ground coriander
1¼ teaspoons [1 E.] cayenne pepper
1¼ teaspoons [1 E.] *garam masala*
Pinch of saffron threads soaked in 1 tablespoon warm water
2½ to 3 teaspoons [2 to 2½ E.] salt
Pinch of ground mace
Pinch of nutmeg
Pinch of monosodium glutamate
1 4-pound leg of lamb, cut into 1-inch cubes

½ cup [⅖ E.] *ghee*
2 medium yellow onions, thinly sliced
2 bay leaves
2 small (1 inch) cinnamon sticks
2 cloves
4 to 6 cloves garlic, finely minced
1¼ teaspoons [1 E.] finely chopped gingerroot
6 cardamoms, crushed
2 large tomatoes, peeled and chopped
½ cup [2 ounces] ground almonds
¼ teaspoon [⅕ E.] paprika
3 to 4 tablespoons [3 E.] chopped coriander leaves

1. In a large bowl, combine yogurt, spiced onion, cumin, coriander, cayenne pepper, *garam masala*, saffron, salt, mace, nutmeg, and monosodium glutamate. Add lean lamb and mix thoroughly. Cover and set aside to marinate in the refrigerator overnight, or at least 4 hours.

2. Heat *ghee* in a large ovenproof casserole or Dutch oven. Fry sliced onions until they are golden. Remove with a slotted spoon and set aside. Add bay leaves, cinnamon sticks, cloves, garlic, gingerroot, and cardamoms to the remaining *ghee*. Fry about one minute, then stir in tomatoes and lamb mixture. Cook, stirring most of the time, about 10 minutes. Mix in ground almonds and paprika.

3. Preheat oven to 300°. Cover pan and seal the lid with strips of aluminum foil. Bake in the middle level of the oven for 1½ hours, or until meat is tender. Remove from the oven, add fried onions, and sprinkle with coriander leaves. Simmer for 10 minutes. This North Indian curry is served with Indian bread.

SERVES 10 to 12

MASSALEDARH BHOGAR
(*Asafetida-flavored Lamb Curry*)

2½ pounds lean shoulder of lamb, cut into 1½-inch cubes
1 cup [8 ounces] plain yogurt
1¼ teaspoons [1 E.] salt
¾ teaspoon [⅗ E.] cayenne pepper
¾ teaspoon [⅗ E.] ground cumin
⅓ teaspoon [¼ E.] turmeric
⅓ teaspoon [¼ E.] paprika
⅓ teaspoon [¼ E.] *garam masala*
5 tablespoons [4 E.] *ghee*

¼ to ½ teaspoon [⅕ to ⅓ E.] ground asafetida (*hing*)
2 medium yellow onions, finely chopped
4 cloves garlic, finely minced
1¼ teaspoons [1 E.] freshly grated gingerroot
1¼ teaspoons [1 E.] tomato paste
Pinch of cumin seeds
1 bay leaf

1. Combine yogurt, salt, cayenne pepper, cumin, turmeric, paprika, and *garam masala* with lamb cubes in a bowl and mix well. Set aside for one hour.

2. Heat *ghee* in a large skillet with a tight-fitting lid, and add asafetida, onions, garlic, and gingerroot. Fry gently for 2 minutes. Add tomato paste, cumin seeds, bay leaf, and lamb cubes and their marinade. Cook, stirring, over medium heat, about 15 to 20 minutes. Cover and cook about 40 minutes, or until meat is tender. Uncover and simmer for another 10 minutes. Garnish with chopped coriander leaves. Serve with Indian bread.

SERVES 6

BADSAHI KOFTA
(Lamb Balls Stuffed with Nuts)

20 raisins
20 roasted pistachio nuts
20 roasted almonds
1½ pounds ground lean lamb
2 eggs, 1 lightly beaten
4 tablespoons [3 E.] besan
   (chick-pea flour) or rice flour
½ teaspoon [⅓ E.] salt
Pinch of saffron threads soaked
   in 1 tablespoon warm water
½ cup [⅖ E.] bread crumbs
½ cup [⅖ E.] ghee or vegetable
   oil
1 large yellow onion, finely
   chopped
¼ cup [⅕ E.] spiced onion
1 bay leaf

Pinch of cumin seeds
½ teaspoon [⅓ E.] turmeric
½ teaspoon [⅓ E.] cayenne
   pepper
½ teaspoon [⅓ E.] garam masala
Pinch of sugar
¼ teaspoon [⅕ E.] ground
   cardamom
¼ teaspoon [⅕ E.] paprika
½ cup [⅖ E.] chicken stock or
   warm water
1 cup [8 ounces] plain yogurt
2½ tablespoons [2 E.] sliced
   almonds
3 to 4 tablespoons [3 E.]
   chopped coriander leaves

---

1. Place raisins, pistachios, and almonds in a bowl and cover with boiling water. Set aside to soak for one hour. Combine ground lamb, egg, besan, salt, and saffron and mix well. Divide lamb mixture into 16 to 20 equal portions. Take one raisin, one pistachio, and one almond, and place them in the center of each meatball. Reform the meat into a ball with the nuts enclosed. Dip each meatball in egg and roll in bread crumbs. Heat ¼ cup ghee in a skillet. Brown meatballs; remove and set aside to drain.

2. Heat ¼ cup ghee in a large skillet. Add chopped onion and fry over medium heat about 2 minutes. Stir in spiced onion, bay leaf, cumin seeds, turmeric, cayenne pepper, garam masala, sugar, cardamom, and paprika. Cook, stirring, another 2 minutes. Add chicken stock and boil for one minute. Remove from heat and stir in yogurt. Return to heat, add meat koftas, and simmer, covered, for 10 to 15 minutes. Add sliced almonds and coriander leaves and continue simmering for another 5 minutes. Remove from heat; keep covered until ready to serve. Serve with Indian bread.

SERVES 4 to 5

GOSHT QORMA
(*Spiced Lamb Curry*)

5 tablespoons [4 E.] *ghee*
2 pounds lean lamb, cut into
    1-inch cubes
1 large yellow onion, sliced
8 cloves garlic, finely chopped
1¼ teaspoons [1 E.] finely minced
    gingerroot
2 green chilies, seeded and
    chopped
2 cardamoms, crushed

2 cloves
2 cinnamon sticks
2 bay leaves
½ teaspoon [⅓ E.] turmeric
1½ cups [8 to 12 ounces] plain
    yogurt
1¼ teaspoons [1 E.] salt
½ teaspoon [⅓ E.] crushed chili
3 to 4 tablespoons [3 E.]
    chopped coriander leaves

Preheat oven to 350°. Heat 3 tablespoons *ghee* in a flameproof casserole and fry lamb cubes for 2 minutes. Add onion, garlic, gingerroot, chilies, cardamoms, cloves, cinnamon sticks, and bay leaves, and fry gently for 5 to 8 minutes. Mix in turmeric, yogurt, and salt. Cover and bake in a preheated oven for 50 minutes, or until meat is tender. Remove from oven; add crushed chili, coriander leaves, and remaining *ghee*, and cook slowly on the top of the stove about 8 to 10 minutes, or until meat is nicely browned. Serve with boiled rice.

SERVES 6

BADSAHI BADAM QORMA
(*Lamb Curry with Almonds*)

2 pounds lean leg of lamb, boned
    and cut into 1-inch cubes
8 cloves garlic, crushed
½ cup [⅖ E.] water
6 tablespoons [3 ounces] *ghee*
4 medium yellow onions, thinly
    sliced
¾ cup [⅗ E.] slivered almonds
1¼ teaspoons [1 E.] finely chopped
    gingerroot

1¼ teaspoons [1 E.] ground cumin
1 bay leaf
¾ to 1 teaspoon [⅗ to ⅘ E.] salt
½ teaspoon [⅓ E.] turmeric
½ teaspoon [⅓ E.] cayenne
    pepper
½ teaspoon [⅓ E.] ground
    cardamom
1 cup [8 ounces] plain yogurt or
    sour cream

Trim off any bits of fat that may have been left on the lamb. Soak garlic in boiling water for 30 minutes. Drain, reserving liquid and discarding the garlic. Heat *ghee* in a large skillet and fry 2 onions until golden brown; remove them with a slotted spoon and set aside. Fry almonds in remaining *ghee* until light brown. Remove with a slotted spoon and set aside. Add gingerroot, remaining 2 onions, cumin, and bay leaf to the pan, adding more *ghee* if necessary, and fry about 2 minutes. Add lamb cubes, salt, turmeric, cayenne pepper, and cardamom, and cook gently, sprinkling with garlic water, for 5 to 7 minutes or until brown. Care must be taken not to burn the meat. Cover and simmer about one hour, or until meat is tender. Add fried onions and almonds, mix in yogurt, and simmer for 10 minutes.

SERVES 6

BHOONA FREZI
(*Lamb Oriental*)

2½ tablespoons [2 E.] rice flour
2½ tablespoons [2 E.] paprika
1¼ teaspoons [1 E.] salt
2 to 4 tablespoons [1½ to 3 E.]
    chopped coriander leaves
½ teaspoon [⅓ E.] ground cumin
½ teaspoon [⅓ E.] crushed chili
2½ pounds lean shoulder lamb,
    cut into 1-inch cubes

¼ cup [2 ounces] *ghee* or
    vegetable oil
1 large yellow onion, thinly sliced
½ pound raw mushrooms, sliced
7½-ounce can tomato sauce with
    mushrooms
1 green pepper, seeded and
    slivered

Preheat oven to 350°. Combine rice flour, paprika, salt, coriander leaves, cumin, and chili in a flat dish. Roll lamb cubes in flour mixture to coat all sides. (Reserve any leftover flour mixture.) Heat *ghee* in a flameproof pan. Add coated lamb cubes and brown for 2 minutes. Add onions and mushrooms. Stirring, add tomato sauce. Sprinkle leftover flour mixture on top. Bake, covered, in a preheated oven for 30 minutes. Add green pepper and bake, uncovered, for 10 minutes more. Serve over boiled rice.

SERVES 6 to 8

MOGHLAI HUSENI KABAB
(*Lamb Kabobs with Moghlai Sauce*)

Moghlai Sauce:

2 tablespoons [1 ounce] *ghee*

2½ tablespoons [2 E.] pistachio
nuts, crushed

¾ cup [3 ounces] ground
almonds

¼ teaspoon [⅕ E.] ground
cardamom

Pinch of saffron, soaked in one
tablespoon warm water

1½ cups [12 ounces] half-and-half

Lamb Kabob:

1 pound ground lean lamb

1 small yellow onion, finely
minced

¾ teaspoon [⅗ E.] finely minced
gingerroot

3 cloves garlic, finely minced

¼ cup [2 ounces] dried yellow
split peas, cooked, drained,
and pureed in a food mill

2 green chilies, seeded and
chopped

2½ tablespoons [2 E.] ground
almonds

1 teaspoon [⅘ E.] salt

¼ teaspoon [⅕ E.] turmeric

¼ teaspoon [⅕ E.] *garam masala*

1½ tablespoons [1¼ E.] lemon
juice

1½ tablespoons [1¼ E.] chopped
coriander leaves

2 tablespoons [1 ounce] *ghee*

1 egg, lightly beaten

½ cup [⅓ E.] bread crumbs

Vegetable oil for deep fat
frying

¼ teaspoon [⅕ E.] paprika

3 to 4 tablespoons [3 E.] slivered
almonds

1. Heat *ghee* in a saucepan and add crushed pistachio nuts, ground almonds, cardamom, and saffron with its soaking water. Cook for a few seconds over low heat. Add half-and-half, increase heat to medium, and cook, stirring, until sauce is slightly thickened. Remove from heat and set aside.

2. Combine ground lamb, onion, gingerroot, garlic, ground peas, chilies, almonds, salt, turmeric, *garam masala*, lemon juice, and coriander leaves in a bowl, and mix well. Heat *ghee* in a large skillet and fry meat mixture over medium heat for 5 minutes. Remove from heat and set aside until cool enough to handle. Divide the lamb mixture into 16 to 20 equal portions and shape them into balls. Dip lamb balls in egg and roll in bread crumbs. Deep fry in vegetable oil 5 to 6 at a time, turning with a slotted spoon, for about 3 to 4 minutes, or until golden brown. As lamb balls brown, mound them

attractively on a warm platter. Pour Moghlai Sauce over them just before serving. Sprinkle with paprika and sliced almonds.

NOTE: To crush pistachio nuts, roll nuts between two layers of waxed paper with a rolling pin.

SERVES 6

SEEKH KABABS
(*Marinated Lamb on Skewers*)

1½ pounds leg or shoulder lamb, boned and cut into 1½-inch cubes
¼ cup [⅕ E.] plain yogurt
¾ teaspoon [⅜ E.] salt
¼ cup [2 ounces] vegetable oil
6 slices lemon peel
4 bay leaves
2½ tablespoons [2 E.] spiced onion
1½ tablespoons [1¼ E.] lemon juice
1½ tablespoons [1¼ E.] chopped coriander leaves

½ teaspoon [⅓ E.] cayenne pepper
½ teaspoon [⅓ E.] turmeric
2 green peppers, each seeded and cut into 6 slices
12 mushroom caps
2 large yellow onions, each cut into 12 wedges
2 large tomatoes, each cut into 6 wedges
⅓ teaspoon [¼ E.] *garam masala*
2 to 3 tablespoons [2 E.] chopped coriander leaves

1. Combine lamb cubes, yogurt, salt, vegetable oil, lemon peel, bay leaves, spiced onion, lemon juice, chopped coriander leaves, cayenne pepper, and turmeric in a bowl and mix well. Cover, and put in the refrigerator, covered, to marinate for about 4 hours.

2. Remove lamb cubes from the marinade and thread tightly on greased skewers placing a slice of green pepper, one mushroom cap, and one onion wedge between each cube of meat. Place the skewers side by side on a rack and brush with marinade. Place skewers under broiler about 4 to 6 inches from heat, turning the skewers occasionally, for 10 to 15 minutes, or until lamb is done as desired. Thread tomato wedges on a separate skewer, brush with spice mixture, and broil for 3 to 5 minutes. Slide the kabobs off the skewers with a fork and mound them on a heated platter. Garnish with onion rings and wedges of lime. Sprinkle with *garam masala* and chopped coriander leaves.

SERVES 6

SHAMI KABABS
(*Ground Lamb Patties*)

1½ pounds ground lean lamb
½ cup [⅖ E.] boiled chick-peas, drained and ground
4 cloves garlic, finely minced
¼ teaspoon [⅕ E.] freshly ground black pepper
¼ teaspoon [⅕ E.] cayenne pepper
¼ teaspoon [⅕ E.] *garam masala*
Big pinch of turmeric
1¼ teaspoons [1 E.] salt

1 large egg
1 medium yellow onion, finely chopped
2 to 3 green chilies, seeded and finely chopped
1 tablespoon [1 inch] ginger-root, finely chopped
2 to 3 tablespoons [2 E.] chopped coriander leaves
1 large hard-cooked egg, chopped
¼ cup [2 ounces] vegetable oil

1. Combine ground lamb, ground chick-peas, garlic, black pepper, cayenne pepper, *garam masala*, turmeric, and salt and puree in a food mill. Beat in egg. Divide the mixture into 10 to 15 equal portions and form into balls.

2. Combine onion, chilies, gingerroot, coriander leaves, and egg in a bowl and mix well. Take one lamb ball and place ¼ to ½ teaspoon mixed chopped ingredients in the center of each ball. Reform the ball and flatten it into thick round shape. Heat vegetable oil in a large frying pan. Add lamb balls and cook, turning, until brown. Remove with a slotted spoon and drain. Serve hot with chopped raw onion and lemon slices.

SERVES 5 to 6

KOFTA QORMA
(Meatball Curry)

1 pound ground lean lamb, ground round steak, or uncooked ground turkey
1½ tablespoons [1¼ E.] spiced onion
1½ tablespoons [1¼ E.] rice flour
1½ tablespoons [1¼ E.] sour cream
½ cup [⅖ E.] powdered milk
½ teaspoon [⅓ E.] salt
1 large egg
½ teaspoon [⅓ E.] turmeric
½ teaspoon [⅓ E.] garam masala
½ cup [⅖ E.] ghee
Pinch of cumin seeds
1 bay leaf
2½ tablespoons [2 E.] chopped onion
2½ tablespoons [2 E.] spiced onion

1¼ teaspoons [1 E.] ground cumin
1¼ teaspoons [1 E.] ground coriander
¼ teaspoon [⅕ E.] crushed dried red pepper
¼ teaspoon [⅕ E.] ground cardamom
1 tomato, chopped
4 to 6 ounces chicken stock or warm water mixed with 2½ tablespoons [2 E.] creamed coconut
½ cup [⅖ E.] slivered almonds
2½ tablespoons [2 E.] raisins
¼ teaspoon [⅕ E.] salt
2½ tablespoons [2 E.] chopped coriander leaves
1 cup [8 ounces] plain yogurt

1. Combine ground lamb, spiced onion, rice flour, sour cream, powdered milk, salt, egg, ¼ teaspoon turmeric, and ¼ teaspoon garam masala in a bowl, and stir to blend well. Form small balls about the size of a walnut. Heat ¼ cup ghee in a skillet, add meatballs, and fry, turning, until brown. Remove and set aside.

2. Heat ¼ cup ghee in large skillet. Fry cumin seeds, bay leaf, and chopped onion, for one minute. Add spiced onion, cumin, coriander, ¼ teaspoon turmeric, red pepper, ¼ teaspoon garam masala, cardamom, and tomato, and cook gently, stirring, about 2 minutes. Add chicken stock, almonds, and raisins, and bring to a boil. Add salt and coriander leaves, and cook for one minute. Place yogurt in a bowl, remove a few tablespoons of gravy from the pan, and mix yogurt and gravy well. Stir yogurt mixed with hot gravy into remaining hot mixture in pan. Reduce heat, add fried koftas, cover, and cook for 10 minutes. Uncover and simmer another 5 minutes, or until the sauce has thickened. Serve with Indian bread.

SERVES 5 to 6

KHEEMA CURRY
(*Minced Meat Curry*)

3 tablespoons [1½ ounces] *ghee*
1 large yellow onion, finely
    chopped
Pinch of cumin seeds
1 bay leaf
4 cloves garlic, finely minced
1¼ teaspoons [1 E.] grated ginger-
    root
1 or 2 green chilies, seeded and
    halved
1½ pounds ground lean beef or
    ground uncooked turkey
¾ teaspoon [⅗ E.] ground
    cumin
¾ teaspoon [⅗ E.] ground
    coriander

¾ teaspoon [⅗ E.] paprika
¼ teaspoon [⅕ E.] turmeric
¼ teaspoon [⅕ E.] *garam masala*
1¼ cups [1 E.] chopped cauliflower
    or carrot
1 large potato, parboiled, peeled,
    and cut into ½-inch cubes
1 cup [about 6 ounces] frozen
    green peas
1¼ teaspoons [1 E.] salt
3 tomatoes, peeled and chopped
½ cup [4 ounces] sour cream
4 hard-cooked eggs, chopped
3 to 4 tablespoons [3 E.]
    chopped coriander leaves

Heat *ghee* in a large skillet. Add onion, cumin seeds, bay leaf, garlic, and gingerroot, and fry for 2 minutes. Add chilies, ground beef, cumin, coriander, paprika, turmeric, and *garam masala,* and stir to blend well. Add cauliflower or carrots, potatoes, green peas and salt, and cook, stirring, about 5 minutes. Add tomatoes, cover, and cook gently until vegetables are tender but firm, about 10 minutes. Uncover, mix in sour cream, and simmer for 5 minutes. Remove from heat and stir in chopped eggs and coriander leaves. Serve with Indian bread. This dish is even better when reheated.

SERVES 6 to 8

MOGHLAI FREZI
(*Beef Curry*)

1 cup [8 ounces] coconut milk
2 pounds lean stewing beef, cut into 1-inch cubes
5 tablespoons [4 E.] *ghee*
2 large yellow onions, thinly sliced
4 to 6 cloves garlic, finely minced
1¼ teaspoons [1 E.] finely minced gingerroot
1¼ teaspoons [1 E.] ground cumin
1¼ teaspoons [1 E.] ground coriander
¼ teaspoon [⅕ E.] turmeric
¼ teaspoon [⅕ E.] cayenne pepper
¼ teaspoon [⅕ E.] *garam masala*
2 cardamoms, crushed
2 bay leaves
2 small (1 inch) cinnamon sticks
2 chilies
1¼ teaspoons [1 E.] salt
1½ tablespoons [1¼ E.] tomato paste
1 cup [8 ounces] plain yogurt

1. Bring coconut milk to a boil, add beef cubes, and cook, covered, over medium heat about 40 minutes, or until meat is almost tender. Drain, discarding coconut milk.

2. Heat *ghee* in a large skillet and fry onions until light golden. Remove and set aside. Add garlic, gingerroot, cumin, coriander, turmeric, cayenne pepper, *garam masala*, cardamoms, bay leaves, cinnamon sticks, and chilies to *ghee* remaining in pan. Fry, stirring, about one minute. Add beef cubes, salt, and tomato paste, and fry gently until rich brown in color, 8 to 10 minutes. Stir in yogurt, add fried onions, and simmer for 20 minutes. Garnish with chopped coriander leaves. Serve with boiled rice or Indian bread.

SERVES 6

SOOR VINDALOO
(*Pork Curry*)

2 pounds loin of pork, trimmed of all fat and cut into 2-inch cubes
½ cup [⅓ E.] white vinegar or lemon juice
1¼ teaspoons [1 E.] salt
¾ teaspoon [⅗ E.] crushed chili
¾ teaspoon [⅗ E.] ground cumin
¼ cup [2 ounces] *ghee* or vegetable oil
1 large yellow onion, chopped

1½ teaspoons [½ inch] grated gingerroot
1½ teaspoons [1¼ E.] ground coriander
4 cloves garlic, finely minced
¼ teaspoon [⅕ E.] turmeric
¼ teaspoon [⅕ E.] paprika
¼ teaspoon [⅕ E.] cinnamon
¼ teaspoon [⅕ E.] sugar
2 large tomatoes, peeled and chopped

Combine pork cubes, vinegar, salt, chili, and cumin, and mix well. Cover and set aside for 2 hours. Drain meat and reserve marinade. Heat *ghee* and fry pork cubes, turning frequently, about 4 to 5 minutes. As meat browns, remove with a slotted spoon and set aside. Add onion, gingerroot, coriander, garlic, turmeric, paprika, cinnamon, and sugar to *ghee* remaining in pan and cook until onion is soft. Add tomatoes and fried meat, and fry a few more minutes. Cover and cook gently until meat is tender, about 1¼ hours. Add reserved marinade and simmer for another 10 to 15 minutes. Add more vinegar or lemon juice according to your taste. Serve with boiled rice.

SERVES 4 to 6

GURDA RASA
(*Kidney Curry*)

3 pounds beef or veal kidneys
1½ teaspoons [½ inch] finely
    minced gingerroot
¼ teaspoon [⅕ E.] ground
    cardamom
¼ teaspoon [⅕ E.] cinnamon
    Pinch of saffron threads soaked
    in 1 tablespoon warm water
3 to 4 tablespoons [1½ to 2
    ounces] *ghee*

2 medium yellow onions, thinly
    sliced
2½ tablespoons [2 E.] catsup
1½ teaspoons [1¼ E.] salt
¼ teaspoon [⅕ E.] cayenne
    pepper
1 cup [8 ounces] plain yogurt
6 hard-cooked eggs, chopped

Remove the white membrane and cut lobes away from the fat and tubes of each kidney. Cut kidneys into ½-inch slices. Combine kidneys, gingerroot, cardamom, cinnamon, and saffron mixture in a bowl, and mix well. Set aside for one or 2 hours. Heat *ghee* in a large skillet, add onions, and fry until brown. Add catsup, kidneys, and kidney marinade, and cook, stirring, about 2 to 3 minutes. Add salt, cayenne pepper, and yogurt; cover, and cook gently until kidneys are done, about one hour. Garnish with chopped eggs. Kidney curry may be served as a side dish.

SERVES 8 to 10

KALEJI RASA
(*Liver Curry*)

3 tablespoons [1½ ounces] *ghee*
Pinch of cumin seeds
1 bay leaf
2 cardamoms, crushed
2 cinnamon sticks
2 cloves garlic, finely minced
1 medium yellow onion, finely chopped
2½ tablespoons [2 E.] spiced onion
¾ teaspoon [⅗ E.] ground cumin
¾ teaspoon [⅗ E.] ground coriander

¾ teaspoon [⅗ E.] salt
¼ teaspoon [⅕ E.] turmeric
¼ teaspoon [⅕ E.] cayenne pepper
¼ teaspoon [⅕ E.] *garam masala*
1½ pounds calves liver, cut into 1-inch pieces
4 tomatoes, peeled and chopped
1 large potato, parboiled and cut into 1-inch cubes
4 to 8 tablespoons [2 to 4 ounces] chicken stock or warm water
2½ tablespoons [2 E.] plain yogurt

Heat *ghee* in a large skillet, fry cumin seeds, bay leaf, cardamoms, cinnamon, garlic, and onion for 2 minutes. Add spiced onion, cumin, coriander, salt, turmeric, cayenne pepper, and *garam masala*, and cook, stirring, for a few seconds. Add liver and fry 2 to 3 minutes more. Mix in tomatoes and potato, and continue cooking until *ghee* comes to the surface. Add chicken stock, cover, and cook gently until liver and potato are tender, about 20 minutes. Uncover, stir in yogurt, and simmer 5 minutes, uncovered. Garnish with chopped coriander leaves. Liver curry may be served with Indian bread or boiled rice as a side dish.

SERVES 4 to 6

Fried Foods

Fried foods are always tasty. But there are some special techniques for frying foods. Cook only a few pieces of food at a time so the temperature of the oil remains constant. Do not overheat oils and fats; this spoils them for cooking. Foods deep fat fried should never be greasy. Deep frying is not costly if the oil is treated and kept for further use. After you are through frying, heat the fat slowly and add 2-inch pieces of 2 to 3 unpeeled raw potatoes. Let the potatoes cook until they become brown; then remove them with a slotted spoon. The unpeeled potatoes will absorb leftover flavors, and you can store the oil for further use. Cool the oil and pour it through a sieve lined with cheese-cloth. Store it in a covered bottle in the refrigerator.

For deep fat frying, the fat should be heated to 375°, or when a one-inch cube of bread turns golden brown in one minute. Add the food only when the oil has become hot enough. Some fried foods need to be reheated; in that case, fry for a few minutes less the first time. When the food is cooked but not very brown or crisp, remove it from the oil, drain, and store. Just before serving, heat oil to the same temperature and then fry a few pieces at a time just for a minute or two until they look crisp.

Some foods are fried in small amounts of oil. Always drain fried foods well on absorbent paper toweling. Here are some fried foods from my kitchen. You will notice that there is an advantage to most of my recipes—they can be made in advance to set and should be fried just before serving time.

BAGADI JHINGA
(*Butterfly Shrimp*)

1 pound large shrimp, peeled and deveined, with tail left on

1 medium yellow onion, chopped

4 cloves garlic

1 tablespoon [1 inch] roughly chopped fresh gingerroot

2 green chilies

2½ tablespoons [2 E.] chopped coriander leaves

2 tablespoons [1 ounce] creamed coconut

¼ teaspoon [⅕ E.] ground turmeric

2½ tablespoons [2 E.] lemon juice

½ teaspoon [⅓ E.] *garam masala*

½ teaspoon [⅓ E.] paprika

½ teaspoon [⅓ E.] salt

½ cup [⅓ E.] bread crumbs

1 large egg, lightly beaten

Vegetable oil for deep fat frying

1. Split shrimp lengthwise up to the tail and open flat to resemble a butterfly. Place shrimp between layers of waxed paper and pound them lightly. Combine onion, garlic, gingerroot, chilies, coriander leaves, creamed coconut, turmeric, lemon juice, *garam masala*, paprika, and salt in the container of a blender and blend until creamy. Place shrimp on a large platter, and cover with blended spice mixture. Rub spice mixture gently into the shrimp, cover, and set aside to marinate for at least 2 hours in a cool place.

2. Remove shrimp from marinade. Roll body, not the tail, of each shrimp in crumbs, dip in egg, and then roll again in bread crumbs. Set aside for one hour, or until coating is dry.

3. Heat 2 to 3 inches vegetable oil in a deep fat fryer to 375°. Using a frying basket, lower 3 to 4 shrimp at a time into the hot oil. Fry about 2 minutes, or until golden brown. Remove and drain on paper toweling. Keep shrimp hot in a 300° oven until all are browned. Serve with desired chutney.

SERVES 4

MACHI CUTLET
(*Salmon Cutlet*)

½ pound salmon, canned or
   cooked
½ cup [4 ounces] condensed
   cream of mushroom soup
¾ to 1 cup [⅗ to ⅘ E.] cooked
   rice, mashed
¾ teaspoon [⅗ E.] finely minced
   gingerroot
¾ teaspoon [⅗ E.] ground
   roasted cumin
¾ teaspoon [⅗ E.] ground
   roasted coriander

2 green chilies, finely chopped
1½ tablespoons [1¼ E.] finely
   chopped onion
1½ tablespoons [1¼ E.] chopped
   coriander leaves
2 tablespoons [1 ounce] *ghee*
½ cup [⅓ E.] all-purpose flour
2 eggs, lightly beaten
½ cup [⅓ E.] bread crumbs
Vegetable oil

1. Combine salmon, mushroom soup, mashed rice, gingerroot, cumin, coriander, chilies, onion, and coriander leaves in a bowl. Blend thoroughly with fingers. Heat *ghee* in a skillet and fry salmon mixture for 2 to 4 minutes, or until sticky. Spread the salmon mixture in a layer about ½ inch thick in a greased pan. Refrigerate until chilled and cut into desired shape.

2. Have ready 3 shallow bowls containing flour, eggs, and bread crumbs. Roll cutlets in flour to coat, dip in egg, and roll in crumbs to cover completely. Transfer cutlets to a platter and refrigerate for one hour, or until coating is set.

3. Heat vegetable oil to depth of one inch in a skillet and fry cutlets until deep golden, turning once to brown evenly. Drain on paper toweling. Place cutlets in a 200° oven to keep warm until ready to serve. Garnish with tomato slices and coriander leaves.

SERVES 4 to 6

SABZI CUTLET
(*Vegetable Cutlet*)

10-ounce package frozen sliced or French-style green beans, cooked, drained, and chopped

10-ounce package frozen broccoli spears, cooked, drained, and chopped

10-ounce package frozen green peas, cooked, drained, and mashed

2 large potatoes, boiled, drained, and mashed

4 to 6 carrots, boiled, drained, and mashed

14-ounce can diced beets, drained

1½ tablespoons [1½ inches] finely chopped gingerroot

1¼ teaspoons [1 E.] ground roasted cumin

1¼ teaspoons [1 E.] ground roasted coriander

2 to 4 green chilies, seeded and chopped

¼ teaspoon [⅕ E.] turmeric

¼ teaspoon [⅕ E.] onion powder (optional)

¼ teaspoon [⅕ E.] ground cardamom

Salt to taste

1¼ teaspoons [1 E.] *sambhar* spice

5 tablespoons [4 E.] vegetable oil

Pinch of cumin seeds

½ cup [⅓ E.] all-purpose flour

2 eggs, lightly beaten

½ cup [⅓ E.] bread crumbs

Vegetable oil

1. Combine green beans, broccoli, peas, potatoes, carrots, beets, gingerroot, cumin, coriander, chilies, turmeric, onion powder, cardamom, salt, and *sambhar* spice in a bowl. Mix thoroughly with fingers (mixture will be sticky). Heat vegetable oil in a large skillet and fry cumin seeds for a few seconds. Add vegetable mixture and continue frying about 8 to 10 minutes. Set aside to cool.

2. Take a portion of vegetable mixture about the size of a small egg and form it into a cutlet (heart shaped). Repeat with remaining mixture. Roll cutlets in flour, dip in eggs and roll in bread crumbs until well coated. Transfer cutlets to a platter and refrigerate for one hour, or until coating is set. Heat vegetable oil to a depth of one inch in a skillet and fry cutlets until deep golden, turning once to brown evenly. Drain cutlets on paper toweling. Serve with tomato catsup and chopped onion.

SERVES 4 to 6

MURGHI CUTLET
(*Chicken Cutlet*)

1 large chicken breast
¾ teaspoon [⅗ E.] salt
3 eggs, 2 lightly beaten
2 slices bread, soaked in cold
   water and squeezed dry
1 green chili, seeded and
   chopped
1¼ teaspoons [1 E.] chopped
   gingerroot
   Pinch of turmeric
   Pinch of cumin seeds
   Pinch of garlic powder
   Pinch of onion powder
1½ tablespoons [1¼ E.] chopped
   coriander leaves

1½ tablespoons [1¼ E.] lemon
   juice
½ teaspoon [⅓ E.] ground
   roasted cumin
½ teaspoon [⅓ E.] ground
   roasted coriander
½ teaspoon [⅓ E.] *sambhar* spice
2 tablespoons [1 ounce] *ghee* or
   vegetable oil
½ cup [⅖ E.] all-purpose flour
½ cup [⅖ E.] bread crumbs
   Vegetable oil
1 lemon

1. Wrap chicken breast in aluminum foil and bake in preheated 350° oven for about one hour, or until the meat is tender. Bone breast and chop meat finely. Combine chopped chicken, salt, one egg, bread, chili, gingerroot, turmeric, cumin seeds, garlic powder, onion powder, coriander leaves, lemon juice, cumin, coriander and *sambhar* spice in a bowl and mix well. Heat *ghee* in a large skillet and fry the chicken mixture about 5 minutes over medium heat. Remove from heat and set aside to cool.

2. With lightly floured palms, shape 4 even-sized, ½-inch-thick cutlets. Refrigerate to chill.

3. Roll cutlets in flour, dip in eggs, and roll in bread crumbs until well coated. Transfer cutlets to a platter and refrigerate for one hour, or until coating is set. Heat vegetable oil to a depth of one inch in a skillet and fry cutlets until deep golden, turning once to brown evenly. Drain cutlets on paper toweling. Serve hot with tomato relish and onion rings. Sprinkle with lemon juice before serving.

SERVES 2

CHOP
(*Indian-Style Cutlets*)

Cutlets:

2 pounds potatoes, boiled and mashed

1¼ teaspoons [1 E.] salt

1¼ teaspoons [1 E.] ground roasted cumin

1¼ teaspoons [1 E.] ground roasted coriander

1¼ teaspoons [1 E.] *sambhar* spice

1¼ teaspoons [1 E.] grated ginger-root

Pinch of garlic powder

Pinch of sugar

Pinch of roasted cumin seeds

Pinch of ground cardamom

3 eggs, lightly beaten

½ teaspoon [⅓ E.] *garam masala*

½ teaspoon [⅓ E.] turmeric

½ teaspoon [⅓ E.] cayenne pepper

2½ tablespoons [2 E.] lemon juice

2½ tablespoons [2 E.] chopped coriander leaves

5 tablespoons [4 E.] *ghee* or vegetable oil

2 large yellow onions, finely chopped

15 meat, egg, or fish balls

¾ cup [⅗ E.] bread crumbs

Vegetable oil

1. In a large bowl, combine mashed potatoes, salt, cumin, coriander, *sambhar* spice, gingerroot, garlic powder, sugar, cumin seeds, cardamom, one egg, *garam masala*, turmeric, cayenne pepper, lemon juice, and coriander leaves, and mix well. Heat *ghee* in a large skillet and fry onions about 2 minutes, or until soft. Add potato mixture and cook, stirring, about 15 minutes, or until the potato mixture is light brown in color and somewhat sticky. Be careful to prevent potato mixture from sticking to the bottom of the pan and burning. When the potato mixture pulls away from the edges of the pan easily, remove from heat and divide into 15 equal portions. Form into balls while potato mixture is still hot.

2. Take one potato ball and, with your thumb, make a cup-shaped depression in the center. Fill this depression with one meat, egg, or fish ball (see fillings below). Reform the potato ball with the filling enclosed, flatten, and shape into round cakes about 2 inches in diameter. Take care not to crack or break the potato covering.

3. Roll prepared potato chops in bread crumbs, dip chops in egg, and roll again in bread crumbs. Refrigerate at least one hour, or until ready to cook. Heat vegetable oil to depth of one inch in a skillet, add

chops, and fry, turning, until evenly browned. Serve warm with chutney and chopped onion.

NOTE: Chops can be prepared ahead of time and frozen. About 30 to 40 minutes before serving, heat oven to 450°, place frozen chops on a baking sheet, and bake about 10 minutes. Reduce heat to 300° and continue baking in the middle level of the oven about 20 minutes more, or until chops are hot.

SERVES 7 to 8

Meat Filling:

2 tablespoons [1 ounce] *ghee*
1 large yellow onion, finely chopped
1¼ teaspoons [1 E.] grated gingerroot
1 green chili, seeded and chopped
½ cup [⅖ E.] frozen peas
½ pound ground beef, lamb, or uncooked turkey
Big pinch of turmeric
Big pinch of garlic powder
Big pinch of cayenne pepper

Big pinch of monosodium glutamate
¼ teaspoon [⅕ E.] salt
¼ teaspoon [⅕ E.] ground roasted cumin
¼ teaspoon [⅕ E.] ground roasted coriander
2½ tablespoons [2 E.] raisins
2½ tablespoons [2 E.] mashed potatoes
2½ tablespoons [2 E.] chopped coriander leaves
¼ cup [⅕ E.] chopped peanuts

Heat *ghee* in a large skillet. Add onion and gingerroot and fry about 2 minutes, or until onion is soft. Add chili and peas, cover, and cook gently until peas are tender. Mash peas without removing them from the skillet. Increase heat and add ground beef, turmeric, garlic powder, cayenne pepper, monosodium glutamate, salt, cumin, and coriander and fry for a few seconds. Mix in raisins, mashed potatoes, and coriander leaves and cook about 8 minutes, or until meat is cooked through. Remove from heat and stir in peanuts. Set aside until cool. Divide meat mixture into 15 even portions and form into balls.

Egg Filling:

3 tablespoons [1½ ounces] *ghee*
1 medium yellow onion, finely chopped
1½ teaspoons [½ inch] grated gingerroot
1 green chili, finely chopped
2½ tablespoons [2 E.] cooked and mashed green peas

6 hard-cooked eggs, chopped
1½ tablespoons [1¼ E.] lemon juice
1½ tablespoons [1¼ E.] chopped coriander leaves
⅓ teaspoon [¼ E.] salt
2½ tablespoons [2 E.] raisins
1 egg, lightly beaten

Heat *ghee* in a large skillet and fry onions until soft. Add ginger-root, chili, and peas, and cook, stirring, over medium heat about 2 minutes. Mix in chopped eggs, lemon juice, coriander leaves, salt, and raisins and cook for another 3 to 5 minutes. Quickly stir lightly beaten egg into cooked mixture. Remove from heat and set aside until cool. Divide egg mixture into 15 equal portions and form into balls.

Fish Filling:

1½ tablespoons [1¼ E.] butter
1 pound sole fillets (lemon or grey)
2½ tablespoons [2 E.] mashed potatoes
2½ tablespoons [2 E.] chopped coriander leaves
½ teaspoon [⅓ E.] salt
2 green chilies, seeded and chopped
Pinch of turmeric

Pinch of garlic powder
Pinch of cumin seeds
1¼ teaspoons [1 E.] ground roasted cumin
2 tablespoons [1 ounce] *ghee*
1 medium yellow onion, finely chopped
¾ teaspoon [⅗ E.] grated ginger-root
2½ tablespoons [2 E.] raisins

Melt butter in a skillet and sauté fish fillets for 10 minutes. Flake fish into a bowl, combine with mashed potatoes, coriander leaves, salt, chilies, turmeric, garlic powder, cumin seeds, and ground roasted cumin and mix well. Heat *ghee* in another skillet and fry onion and gingerroot about 2 minutes, or until onion is soft. Add fish mixture and cook, stirring, about 5 minutes. Mix in raisins and cook another minute or so. Remove from heat and set aside to cool. Divide fish mixture into 15 equal portions and form into balls.

MACHI TALAWI
(*Fish Cakes*)

1 pound fish fillets (sole, had-
　dock, perch, or blue fish)
2½ cups [2 E.] mashed potatoes
1 egg, lightly beaten
1¼ teaspoons [1 E.] chopped
　gingerroot
1¼ teaspoons [1 E.] ground
　roasted cumin
¼ teaspoon [⅕ E.] garlic powder

¼ teaspoon [⅕ E.] onion powder
¼ teaspoon [⅕ E.] turmeric
1¼ teaspoons [1 E.] *sambhar* spice
1¼ teaspoons [1 E.] lemon juice
¾ teaspoon [⅗ E.] salt
¼ teaspoon [⅕ E.] cayenne
　pepper
2½ tablespoons [2 E.] chopped
　coriander leaves

Batter:

1 egg yolk
½ cup [⅖ E.] water
½ cup [⅖ E.] *besan* (chick-pea
　flour)
¼ cup [⅕ E.] rice flour
½ teaspoon [⅓ E.] ground cumin

½ teaspoon [⅓ E.] cayenne
　pepper
½ teaspoon [⅓ E.] salt
Pinch of cumin seeds
1¼ teaspoons [1 E.] poppy seeds
Vegetable oil for deep fat
　frying

1. Preheat oven to 350°. Bake fillets in the middle level of the pre-heated oven for 15 minutes, or until the fish flakes easily. Bone fillets and finely mince. Combine fish with mashed potatoes, egg, ginger-root, cumin, garlic powder, onion powder, turmeric, *sambhar* spice, lemon juice, salt, cayenne pepper, and coriander leaves in a bowl and mix well. Divide fish mixture into 12 equal portions and form into ½-inch-thick round cakes.

2. Combine egg yolk and water and beat until frothy. Add *besan*, rice flour, cumin, cayenne pepper, salt, cumin seeds, and poppy seeds and beat with a wire whisk.

3. Heat 2 to 3 inches of vegetable oil in a deep fat fryer. Dip each fish cake into the batter, allow to drip for a moment, and place gently in hot oil. Fry until golden and crisp. Remove with a slotted spoon and set aside to drain on paper toweling. Serve hot with chopped chili, fresh coriander leaves, and lemon slices.

SERVES 4 to 6

PAKORAS
(*Fritters*)

1 large yellow onion, finely
   chopped
2 green chilies, finely chopped
½ cup [⅖ E.] chopped celery
   leaves (very young leaves
   from the center of the stalk)
   or *methi* leaves
2 to 3 tablespoons [2 E.]
   chopped coriander leaves

Pinch of turmeric
Pinch of cumin seeds
Pinch of sugar
2 tablespoons [1⅗ E.] *besan*
   (chick-pea flour)
2 tablespoons [1⅗ E.] rice flour
¼ teaspoon [⅕ E.] salt
Vegetable oil
Dash of cayenne pepper

Combine onion, chilies, celery, coriander leaves, turmeric, cumin seeds, sugar, *besan*, rice flour, salt, and cayenne pepper in a bowl and mix well. Dough will be sticky. Heat one or 2 inches of vegetable oil in a skillet. Take a teaspoonful of dough and, with another teaspoon, form a rough ball. Scrape dough ball from spoon into hot oil and fry gently on both sides until crisp. Press *pakoras* lightly with a spatula during frying. As *pakoras* brown, transfer them to paper toweling to drain. Serve with tea or coffee, or as a side dish with *dal*.

YIELD: 15 to 20 *pakoras*

ALOO PAKORAS
(*Potato Fritters*)

1 pound potatoes, boiled, peeled,
   and finely chopped
2 eggs, separated
2 tablespoons [1⅗ E.] *besan*
   (chick-pea flour) or all-
   purpose flour
1¼ teaspoons [1 E.] ground
   roasted cumin
1¼ teaspoons [1 E.] *sambhar* spice
¾ teaspoon [⅗ E.] salt
Dash of cayenne pepper

1½ tablespoons [1¼ E.] lemon
   juice
1½ tablespoons [1¼ E.] chopped
   coriander leaves
2½ tablespoons [2 E.] freshly
   grated coconut
¼ teaspoon [⅕ E.] turmeric
¼ teaspoon [⅕ E.] cumin seeds
1 medium yellow onion, finely
   chopped
2 green chilies, finely chopped
Vegetable oil for deep fat
   frying

1. Combine potatoes, egg yolks, *besan*, cumin, *sambhar* spice, salt, cayenne pepper, lemon juice, coriander leaves, coconut, turmeric, cumin seeds, onion, and chilies in a large bowl and mix well. In a small bowl, beat egg whites with an electric mixer or a wire whisk until stiff peaks form. Gently fold egg whites into potato mixture.

2. Heat 2 inches of vegetable oil in a deep fat fryer. Drop potato mixture by heaping tablespoons into the hot oil, a few at a time, and fry for 5 minutes, or until golden. Remove with a slotted spoon and drain well on paper toweling. Serve hot with chutney.

YIELD: 20 to 30 *pakoras*

DAHI BORAS
(*Lentil Cakes in Yogurt Sauce*)

1 cup [⅘ E.] split white *urad dal*
1⅓ cups [11 ounces] water
2 to 4 green chilies, seeded
¾ teaspoon [⅗ E.] salt
¼ cup [⅕ E.] chopped coriander
    leaves
½-inch-piece gingerroot
    Big pinch of ground asafetida
    (*hing*) or more to taste

Vegetable oil for deep fat
    frying
4 cups [32 ounces] plain yogurt
1¼ teaspoons [1 E.] ground
    roasted cumin
¼ teaspoon [⅕ E.] *garam masala*
¼ teaspoon [⅕ E.] paprika
5 tablespoons [4 E.] chopped
    coriander leaves
    Pinch of salt

1. Wash *dal* and soak in water for 24 hours in hot weather and 48 hours in cold weather. *Dal* should be fermented for light *boras*. Combine *dal* and soaking water (do not use extra water) with chilies, salt, coriander leaves, gingerroot, and asafetida in the jar of a blender and blend at high speed for a few seconds. Turn off the blender, scrape down the sides of the jar with a rubber spatula, and blend again until the mixture is reduced to a thick purée.

2. Heat 3 to 4 inches vegetable oil to 350° in a deep fat fryer. Drop lentil mixture into the hot oil, a tablespoonful at a time. Do not crowd *boras* because they will puff to almost twice their original size as they cook. Fry *boras* about 3 to 5 minutes, turning them with a slotted spoon, until they are golden brown on all sides. As they brown, transfer them to paper toweling to drain.

3. Soak *boras* in warm water for one minute (this degreases them

and makes them soft enough to hold the yogurt sauce). Take *boras* from water, squeeze slightly without changing their shape, and set aside.

4. Combine yogurt, cumin, *garam masala*, paprika, coriander leaves, and salt in a bowl. Beat with a fork. Add fried *boras*, turning them with a spoon until they are evenly coated with the yogurt sauce. (Or arrange soaked lentil balls on a deep platter and pour the yogurt sauce over them.) Sprinkle with *garam masala*. Refrigerate until ready to serve. Serve with tamarind or date chutney.

NOTE: *Boras* can be frozen before being soaked in water. Thaw *boras* in the refrigerator and continue with remainder of recipe.

SERVES 5 to 6

DOSA
(*Lentil and Rice Bread with Shrimp Filling*)

1 cup split white *urad dal*
2 cups [1 pound] uncooked rice
2 to 3 tablespoons [1 to 1½ ounces] *ghee* or vegetable oil
Pinch of fenugreek
Pinch of mustard seeds
2 large yellow onions, chopped

1 tablespoon [1 inch] finely minced gingerroot
2½ tablespoons [2 E.] chopped coriander leaves
1 or 2 green chilies, seeded and chopped
2 teaspoons [1⅗ E.] salt
2½ cups [20 ounces] buttermilk

1. Wash *dal* and rice and place each in separate bowls. Cover with cold water and let them soak at room temperature for 6 to 8 hours. Drain rice and combine with 6 tablespoons of water in the jar of a blender. Blend at high speed until rice is completely pulverized and the mixture becomes a thick batter. With a rubber spatula, scrape the rice into a deep bowl. Drain *dal* and combine with another 6 table- spoons of water in the jar of the blender and blend until *dal* is creamy and reduced to a batter. Combine the two pastes, cover, and set aside at room temperature for at least 10 to 12 hours to ferment.

2. Heat *ghee* in a large skillet and fry fenugreek and mustard seeds for a few seconds. Add onions and gingerroot and fry until onions are limp and light brown. Combine onion mixture, coriander leaves, chilies, and salt with rice-and-*dal* paste and add enough buttermilk to make a thin-pouring batter.

3. In a heavy skillet (preferably with a non-stick coating), heat one tablespoon of *ghee* over moderate heat until it begins to smoke. Pour in ½ cup [⅖ E.] of the batter and spread out in a very thin pancake with the back of a spoon or a rubber spatula. Spread batter as thin as possible for a crisper pancake. Cook for 2 to 3 minutes, or until bubbles begin to form on the surface. Turn pancake with a wide metal spatula and cook another minute or two, or until golden brown. If necessary, pour a little oil around the edges. Serve with chutney or spread with 3 to 4 tablespoons of shrimp filling folded or rolled in the center of the *dosa*. Serve with coconut chutney.

Shrimp Filling:

4 tablespoons [2 ounces] *ghee* or vegetable oil
1 large yellow onion, finely chopped
½-inch gingerroot, finely chopped
1 or 2 green chilies, finely chopped
Pinch of cumin seeds
1 bay leaf
½ cup [⅖ E.] peeled and finely chopped fresh coconut
½ pound fresh shrimp, cleaned, deveined, and chopped
1 large potato, boiled and mashed

½ teaspoon [⅓ E.] ground turmeric
1¼ teaspoons [1 E.] ground roasted cumin
1¼ teaspoons [1 E.] ground roasted coriander
½ teaspoon [⅓ E.] cayenne pepper
1 teaspoon [¼ E.] salt
½ pound bean sprouts
2½ tablespoons [2 E.] lemon juice
2 to 4 tablespoons [1½ to 3 E.] chopped coriander leaves

Heat *ghee* in a large skillet. Fry onion, gingerroot, and chilies about 2 minutes. Stirring, add cumin seeds, bay leaf, coconut, and shrimp and cook for one minute. Add potato, turmeric, ground roasted cumin and coriander, cayenne pepper, and salt. Cook, stirring, for 2 to 3 minutes over medium heat. Add bean sprouts and mix well. Cook for another 5 minutes. Mix in lemon juice and coriander leaves. Stirring most of the time, cook the whole mixture about 2 to 4 minutes more, or until brown.

SERVES 12 to 14

MASALA IDLI
(*Spicy Steamed Rice Cakes*)

1 cup [½ pound] uncooked rice
½ cup [⅔ E.] split white *urad dal*
1¼ teaspoons [1 E.] salt
½ teaspoon [⅓ E.] baking powder
Pinch of baking soda
Pinch of ground cumin
1 or 2 green chilies, seeded and
finely chopped

2 tablespoons [1 ounce] *ghee*
Pinch of mustard seeds
2½ tablespoons [2 E.] finely
minced onion
2½ tablespoons [2 E.] freshly
grated coconut

1. Wash and soak rice and *dal* overnight in separate bowls. Drain and grind each in the blender until thick and creamy, adding a little water if necessary. Combine the two pastes in a large pan; add salt, baking powder, baking soda, cumin, chilies, and only enough water to form a very thick cakelike batter. For light *idli*, the batter should be fermented. Cover and set aside in a warm place overnight.

2. Heat *ghee* and fry mustard seeds until they pop. Add onion and fry until soft. Add mustard seeds, onion, and coconut to rice-and-*dal* batter and beat well. Generously grease *idli* cups or muffin cups. Spoon batter into prepared cups, filling them about two-thirds full. Pour boiling water into a large wide pan. Place cups on a rack over the boiling water, and cover to steam. The cake is done when a toothpick inserted in the center comes out clean, about 5 to 10 minutes. Remove from steam and let stand 2 minutes before removing from cup. Serve with coconut chutney.

SERVES 10

Chutney and Rayta

Chutneys occupy a position of great importance in the food of almost any part of India, and they offer an astonishing diversity of flavors. They are made with fruits, spices, tamarind (sour fruit—a very important ingredient), vinegar, lemon juice, salt, and a large amount of sugar. Chutney is served with many different Indian dishes. But in some parts of India, it is always served just before the dessert. Mangos are considered one of the best fruits for chutney. The exotic mango is no longer as mysterious as it used to be. Most of the time, it is available in the supermarket.

In India, chutney is prepared daily. But here you can prepare chutney ahead of time and store it in a jar or container that has a very tight lid. Store in the coldest part of the refrigerator. It will stay fresh for several days. Some of the chutneys are very hot due to the spices, but there are many sweet chutneys, too.

Rayta helps digest rich, spicy foods. It is a combination of yogurt and chopped vegetables or fruits. Sometimes other ingredients such as *bundi* (lentil balls) are added.

AAM CHUTNEY
(*Mango Chutney*)

1 pound green, unripened
   mango, peeled and sliced
Dash of salt
Pinch of turmeric
1¼ cups [1 E.] sugar
1¼ teaspoons [1 E.] vegetable oil
Pinch of fennel seeds

1 or 2 whole red chilies
   (optional)
1¼ teaspoons [1 E.] finely chopped
   gingerroot
¼ pound fresh plums, seeded and
   chopped
2½ tablespoons [2 E.] white
   vinegar or lemon juice

1. Sprinkle salt and turmeric on sliced mango and set aside for 2 to 3 hours. Combine mango and sugar in a saucepan, and cook covered, over low heat, until mango is tender, about 15 minutes. Do not add any liquid. The mixture will form a thick, tangy sauce.

2. Heat vegetable oil in a small skillet, add fennel seeds, and fry for 2 seconds. Add chilies, gingerroot, and plums and cook, stirring, for one or 2 minutes. Combine spiced plums with mango mixture and continue cooking over very low heat about 30 minutes, or until plums are tender. Mix in vinegar, remove from heat, and set aside to cool.

YIELD: 3 cups

MOOLI CHUTNEY
(*Radish Chutney*)

20 to 25 small red radishes,
   cleaned and trimmed
2 green chilies, fresh or pickled
2 cloves garlic
½ inch gingerroot
4 to 5 tablespoons [3 to 4 E.]
   lemon juice

Pinch of black cumin seeds
½ teaspoon [⅓ E.] sugar
¼ teaspoon [⅕ E.] salt
1½ tablespoons [1¼ E.] mustard
   oil or vegetable oil

Combine radishes, chilies, garlic, gingerroot, lemon juice, black cumin seeds, sugar, and salt in the container of a blender and blend until creamy. Scrape chutney from blender container into a bowl, add mustard oil or vegetable oil, and mix well. Refrigerate until ready to serve.

YIELD: 1 cup

TAMATTAR CHUTNEY
(*Tomato Chutney*)

- 1¼ teaspoons [1 E.] vegetable oil
- Pinch of *punch-phoron* seeds
- 1 large clove garlic, finely minced (optional)
- 2 pounds ripe tomatoes, peeled, seeded, and chopped
- 1½ teaspoons [½ inch] finely minced gingerroot
- 1 whole red chili
- 10 to 15 pitted prunes
- ¼ cup [⅕ E.] water
- ½ cup [⅖ E.] sugar
- ½ teaspoon [⅓ E.] salt
- 2½ tablespoons [2 E.] raisins
- ¼ teaspoon [⅕ E.] paprika
- 1½ tablespoons [1¼ E.] white vinegar

Heat vegetable oil in a large skillet, add *punch-phoron* seeds and garlic, and fry for a few seconds. Add tomatoes, gingerroot, chili, and prunes, and cook, stirring, for 2 minutes. Add water, sugar, salt, and raisins; cover and cook gently for 10 to 15 minutes, or until tomatoes and prunes are tender. Uncover and cook until the sauce is thick. Mix in paprika and vinegar, remove from heat, and refrigerate until ready to serve.

YIELD: 3 cups

ALUBOKHRA CHUTNEY
(*Prune Chutney*)

- 2 cups [16 ounces] water
- ½ pound prunes
- 1¼ teaspoons [1 E.] vegetable oil
- Pinch of *punch-phoron* seeds or fennel seeds
- ¾ teaspoon [⅗ E.] freshly grated gingerroot
- ¼ pound dried pitted dates, chopped
- Dash of salt
- 2 to 3 tablespoons [2 E.] molasses
- 2½ tablespoons [2 E.] brown sugar
- ¼ cup [⅕ E.] raisins
- 2½ tablespoons [2 E.] slivered almonds or chopped pistachio nuts

1. Bring water to a boil, add prunes, and boil for 5 minutes. Remove from heat and set aside to cool. Remove pits and chop prunes. Reserve liquid in which prunes were cooked.
2. Heat vegetable oil in a saucepan, add *punch-phoron* seeds, ginger-

root, and dates, and cook, stirring, for one minute. Mix in salt, prunes, and reserved prune liquid. Cover and cook gently until the consistency is like thick jam. Add molasses, brown sugar, raisins, and almonds, and cook 2 minutes more. Remove from heat, set aside to cool, and refrigerate until ready to serve.

YIELD: 3 cups

SAYOO CHUTNEY
(*Apple Chutney*)

2 to 3 pounds cooking apples,
   peeled, cored, and sliced
2 cloves
2 cinnamon sticks
½ teaspoon [⅓ E.] salt
¼ cup [⅕ E.] raisins
   Red food coloring

2½ tablespoons [2 E.] water
1¼ teaspoons [1 E.] vegetable oil
1 or 2 red chilies (optional)
½ cup [⅖ E.] brown sugar
¼ teaspoon [⅕ E.] ground
   roasted cumin
2½ tablespoons [2 E.] lemon juice

Combine apples, cloves, cinnamon sticks, salt, raisins, and a few drops of food coloring in a saucepan. Add water, cover, and cook gently until apples are tender, about 15 minutes. Heat vegetable oil in a small skillet and fry chilies for a few seconds. Add chilies to apple mixture. Stir in brown sugar and cumin and cook for 5 minutes, or until the mixture is thick. Remove cloves and cinnamon sticks and mix in lemon juice. Refrigerate until ready to serve. Apple chutney goes particularly well with fried foods.

YIELD: 3½ cups

ANANAS CHUTNEY
(Pineapple Chutney)

1¼ teaspoons [1 E.] vegetable oil
Pinch of mustard seeds
1 red chili (optional)
1 15-ounce can crushed pineapple or 1 large fresh pineapple, peeled, cored, and
finely chopped
1½ ounces tamarind, soaked in
¼ cup [⅕ E.] water (2½
tablespoons [2 E.] lemon
juice may be used)

2½ tablespoons [2 E.] raisins
¼ teaspoon [⅕ E.] salt
Yellow food coloring
1¼ teaspoons [1 E.] all-purpose
flour
1¼ teaspoons [1 E.] ground
roasted cumin

Heat vegetable oil and fry mustard seeds until they pop. Add chili, pineapple and its canned juices (if you use fresh pineapple, add a little sugar to taste), tamarind pulp (see page 19), raisins, salt, and a few drops food coloring, and cook over medium heat about 10 minutes. Mix flour with one tablespoon water and stir into the pineapple mixture; cook for 2 minutes. Mix in cumin. Remove from heat, set aside to cool, and refrigerate until ready to serve.

YIELD: 2½ cups

NAVARATNA CHUTNEY
(Tomato Relish)

2½ pounds ripe tomatoes, peeled,
seeded, and chopped
2 large yellow onions, finely
chopped
3 cloves garlic, finely minced
1 tablespoon [1 inch] freshly
grated gingerroot
3 cups [¼ pound] sugar
¾ teaspoon [⅗ E.] salt

¼ teaspoon [⅕ E.] cayenne
pepper
¼ teaspoon [⅕ E.] freshly ground
black pepper
¼ teaspoon [⅕ E.] ground cloves
1¼ teaspoons [1 E.] ground cumin
1¼ teaspoons [1 E.] paprika
½ teaspoon [⅓ E.] cinnamon
5 tablespoons [4 E.] white
vinegar, or to taste

Combine tomatoes, onions, garlic, gingerroot, sugar, salt, cayenne pepper, black pepper, cloves, cumin, paprika, and cinnamon in a large saucepan. Bring to a rapid boil and cook slowly 1 to 1½ hours, or until relish thickens and big bubbles appear. (Drop a spoonful of relish onto a plate; if no water exudes, the relish is done.) Mix in vinegar and cook one minute longer. Remove the pan from heat and set aside to cool. If cooked properly, tomato relish can be kept in the refrigerator for several weeks.

YIELD: 3¾ cups

NAREAL CHUTNEY
(*Coconut Chutney*)

1 cup peeled and coarsely chopped fresh coconut
1 medium yellow onion, chopped
1¼ tablespoons [1¼ inch] freshly grated gingerroot
2 green chilies, seeded
2 small cloves garlic
½ teaspoon [⅓ E.] ground cumin

2½ tablespoons [2 E.] chopped coriander leaves
2 to 3 tablespoons [2 E.] lemon juice
½ teaspoon [⅓ E.] salt
1 tablespoon [1 ounce] vegetable oil
Pinch of mustard seeds

Combine coconut, onion, gingerroot, chilies, garlic, cumin, coriander leaves, lemon juice, and salt in the jar of a blender, and blend at high speed for one minute. Stop machine, scrape down the sides of the jar with a rubber spatula, and blend again until the coconut is reduced to a smooth paste. Heat oil in a skillet and fry mustard seeds until they pop. Add coconut mixture and cook for one minute, being sure not to let the coconut brown. Remove from heat and set aside to cool. Refrigerate until ready to serve.

YIELD: 1½ cups

IMLEE CHUTNEY
(*Tamarind Chutney*)

4 ounces tamarind
1½ to 2 cups [12 to 16 ounces]
    water
1¼ tablespoons [1¼ inches] finely
    minced gingerroot
2 to 3 tablespoons [2 E.]
    chopped coriander leaves

1¼ teaspoons [1 E.] ground roasted
    cumin
½ teaspoon [⅓ E.] cayenne
    pepper
2½ tablespoons [2 E.] lemon juice
½ cup [⅖ E.] brown sugar
¼ teaspoon [⅕ E.] salt

Prepare tamarind pulp with tamarind and water (see page 19). Combine tamarind pulp, gingerroot, coriander leaves, cumin, cayenne pepper, lemon juice, brown sugar, and salt in the jar of a blender and blend until creamy. Refrigerate until ready to serve.

YIELD: 1½ cups

PUDEENA CHUTNEY
(*Mint Chutney*)

1 or 2 ounces tamarind
½ cup [4 ounces] water
1¼ cups [1 E.] chopped fresh mint
    leaves
1¼ cups [1 E.] chopped coriander
    leaves

2 green chilies, seeded
1 large yellow onion, chopped
⅓ teaspoon [¼ E.] salt
1¼ to 2 teaspoons [1 to 1½ E.]
    sugar
¼ teaspoon [⅕ E.] ground cumin

Prepare tamarind pulp with tamarind and water (see page 19).

Combine tamarind pulp, mint leaves, coriander leaves, chilies, onion, salt, sugar, and cumin in the container of a blender and blend at high speed until mixture becomes a creamy paste. Pour the chutney into a jar, cover tightly, and keep in the refrigerator until ready to serve. Serve cold with fried foods. Mint chutney can be kept up to one week in the refrigerator.

YIELD: 1½ cups

MAJUR CHUTNEY
(*Date Chutney*)

½ pound pitted dates
½ cup [4 ounces] water
1 green chili
⅛ teaspoon [⅒ E.] salt

2½ tablespoons [2 E.] lemon juice
2½ tablespoons [2 E.] chopped
   coriander leaves

Combine dates, water, chili, salt, lemon juice, and coriander leaves in the container of a blender and blend until creamy. Chill and serve with *dahi bora* (page 174).

YIELD: 1½ cups

UMCHUR CHUTNEY
(*Mango and Walnut Chutney*)

1 cup [⅘ E.] sliced *umchur*
1 to 1¼ cups [8 to 10 ounces]
   water
1½ tablespoons [1¼ E.] vegetable
   oil
Pinch of fennel seeds
2 red chilies

1 pound pitted dates
½ cup [⅖ E.] raisins
¼ teaspoon [⅕ E.] salt
2½ tablespoons [2 E.] sugar
1¼ teaspoons [1 E.] ground
   roasted cumin
½ cup [⅖ E.] chopped walnuts

Soak washed *umchur* in water for 20 minutes. Drain and reserve liquid. Heat vegetable oil in a large skillet and fry fennel seeds and chilies for a few seconds. Add drained *umchur* and dates and cook, stirring, for one or 2 minutes. Add raisins, salt, and sugar. Stirring, add *umchur* liquid. Cover and cook gently until *umchur* is tender, about 10 minutes, adding more water if necessary. Stir in cumin and walnuts, remove from heat, and set aside to cool. Umchur chutney will be very thick, almost like a soft dough. It will stay fresh in a jar with a tight fitting lid in the refrigerator for several weeks.

YIELD: 3½ cups

KHEERA RAYTA
(*Cucumber with Spicy Yogurt*)

1½ cups [12 ounces] plain yogurt
½ teaspoon [⅓ E.] salt
¼ teaspoon [⅕ E.] cayenne
  pepper
⅓ teaspoon [¼ E.] ground
  roasted cumin

1 or 2 green chilies, seeded and
  chopped (optional)
2½ tablespoons [2 E.] chopped
  coriander leaves
1 large green cucumber, peeled,
  seeded, and finely grated
¼ teaspoon [⅕ E.] paprika

Combine yogurt, salt, cayenne pepper, cumin, chilies, and coriander leaves in a bowl. Stir to blend well. Drain cucumber juice from grated cucumber and add cucumber to yogurt mixture. Sprinkle with paprika. Serve chilled in a crystal bowl.

YIELD: 2 cups

BUNDI RAYTA
(*Rice Puff with Spicy Yogurt*)

4 cups [32 ounces] plain yogurt
¼ teaspoon [⅕ E.] salt
⅛ teaspoon [⅒ E.] cayenne
  pepper

1½ tablespoons [1¼ E.] lemon
  juice
2 to 2½ cups [1⅗ to 2 E.] *bundi*
¼ teaspoon [⅕ E.] *garam masala*

Prepare *bundi* as directed on page 204 through step 3. Combine yogurt, salt, cayenne pepper, and lemon juice and mix well. Add *bundi* and stir with a fork. Sprinkle *garam masala* on top. Serve chilled.

BRINJAL RAYTA
(*Eggplant with Spicy Yogurt*)

2 to 2½ pounds eggplant
1¼ cups [10 ounces] sour cream
1¼ teaspoons [1 E.] ground
    roasted cumin
1 or 2 green chilies, seeded and
    chopped

2½ tablespoons [2 E.] chopped
    coriander leaves
¾ teaspoon [⅗ E.] salt
Pinch of sugar
½ cup [⅖ E.] chopped walnuts
Dash of paprika

1. Rub a little oil on the skin of the eggplant. With a small knife, make 2 cuts about ½ inch deep in the skin. Bake in preheated oven (350°) for 40 to 45 minutes, or until the eggplant is very tender. Peel, drain the liquid, and mash the pulp until creamy.

2. Combine sour cream, cumin, chilies, coriander leaves, salt, sugar, walnuts, and paprika in a large bowl. Add creamed eggplant and stir with a fork. Cover and refrigerate until ready to serve.

YIELD: 2 cups

ALOO RAYTA
(*Potato with Spicy Yogurt*)

1 pound potatoes, boiled, peeled,
    and cut into ¼-inch cubes
2½ tablespoons [2 E.] vegetable oil
½ teaspoon [⅓ E.] black mustard
    seeds
1¼ teaspoons [1 E.] finely chopped
    gingerroot
2 green chilies, seeded and
    chopped

¾ teaspoon [⅗ E.] salt
Pinch of *garam masala*
1½ cups [9 to 10 ounces] plain
    yogurt or sour cream
1½ tablespoons [1¼ E.] lemon
    juice
2 to 4 tablespoons [1½ to 3 E.]
    chopped coriander leaves

Chill cubed potatoes. Heat vegetable oil in a large skillet and fry mustard seeds for a few seconds. Add gingerroot, chilies, and chilled potatoes and fry for one minute. Mix in salt and *garam masala* and stir until potato cubes are well coated with the seasonings. Remove from heat. In a bowl, beat together yogurt and lemon juice with a fork. Add potato mixture and coriander leaves and mix well. Serve chilled.

YIELD: 4 cups

PALAK RAYTA
(*Spinach with Spicy Yogurt*)

10-ounce package spinach,
  steamed, drained, and
  finely chopped
1 tablespoon [½ ounce]
  vegetable oil
Pinch of fenugreek seeds
½ teaspoon [⅓ E.] salt

¼ teaspoon [⅕ E.] cayenne
  pepper
½ teaspoon [⅓ E.] ground
  roasted cumin
2 cups [16 ounces] plain yogurt
2½ tablespoons [2 E.] lemon juice
Big pinch of paprika
Big pinch of *garam masala*

1. Squeeze out any excess liquid from cooked spinach. Heat vegetable oil in a large skillet and fry fenugreek seeds for a few seconds. Add spinach, salt, cayenne pepper, and cumin and stir well. Remove from heat and set aside to cool. Chill in refrigerator.

2. Combine yogurt, lemon juice, and paprika in a bowl and mix with a fork. Add chilled spinach and mix well. Chill again. Sprinkle with *garam masala* before serving.

YIELD: 3 cups

Sweetmeats

Indian sweets are not candies. They are delicious desserts, usually made from a milk-based preparation. However, there are some other sweets that are made from flour, sugar, and other ingredients. Sweets play an important, traditional role in Indian hospitality, and their preparation requires a lot of care and skill. But with practice anybody can learn this art, and they're so good, it's well worth the effort.

RASGULLAS
(Cheese Puffs in Syrup)

Rasgullas is a delicious Bengali sweetmeat. It is a white, spongy ball, the size of a golf ball, prepared from channa (Indian homemade cottage cheese), cooked in sugar syrup, and flavored with rose essence.

7½ cups [60 ounces] milk	3 sugar cubes
¼ cup [2 ounces] white vinegar	3¾ cups [3 E.] sugar
½ cup [4 ounces] water	8 cups [64 ounces] water
1¼ teaspoons [1 E.] suji (farina)	1¼ teaspoons [1 E.] rose water

1. Prepare channa according to directions on page 19. Place warm channa in a bowl and break it into small pieces with a rubber spatula. Mix in suji, and knead it with your palms until smooth and creamy. Divide channa into 12 equal-sized balls. Place ¼ of a sugar cube in the center of each ball, and reform the channa ball.

2. Combine 1¼ cups of sugar with 6 cups of water in a deep 3 to 4 quart pan. Boil for 10 minutes to make a thin sugar syrup. Put in

channa balls, cover, and boil over high heat for 5 minutes. Reduce heat to medium-high, and continue cooking for another 40 minutes. During cooking, the *rasgullas* will puff.

3. While *rasgullas* are cooking in the thin syrup, prepare heavy syrup: Combine 2½ cups of sugar with 2 cups of water in another deep pan. Boil for 5 minutes, reduce heat, and keep warm until ready to use. After *rasgullas* have cooked in the thin syrup, remove them with a slotted spoon and transfer them into the thick warm syrup. Remove syrup from heat and set aside to cool, uncovered. Soak *rasgullas* overnight, or at least 4 to 6 hours. Remove from syrup and sprinkle with rose water before serving. Do not keep *rasgullas* in the refrigerator, as it will harden them.

Alternate method for cooking channa *balls*:

Prepare *channa* balls as directed in master recipe. Boil 5 to 6 cups of water in a 3½-quart pressure cooker. Add *channa* balls to boiling water, close cover securely, place pressure regulator on vent pipe, and cook over high heat until regulator begins to vibrate. Reduce heat to medium-high and continue cooking 12 minutes. Remove pressure cooker from heat and allow pressure to drop of its own accord. Remove cover of pressure cooker and, with a slotted spoon, transfer balls to warm sugar syrup.

NOTE: Both syrups can be strained and used for other kinds of sweets, such as *gilipis*, *pantua*, or any kind of *gauja*. The syrups are also delicious with pancakes.

SERVES 3 to 6

RASOMALAI
(*Rasgullas with Cream Sauce*)

5 cups [40 ounces] half-and-half
   or 10 cups [80 ounces] milk
   plus 2 to 4 tablespoons
   [1½ to 3 E.] sweet butter
½ cup [⅖ E.] sugar, or to taste
8 tablespoons [6⅖ E.] ground
   almonds

¼ teaspoon [⅕ E.] ground
   cardamom
1¼ teaspoons [1 E.] rose water
2½ tablespoons [2 E.] chopped
   unsalted roasted pistachio
   nuts

1. Prepare the *rasgullas* as directed on page 189. Bring half-and-half to a boil in a large saucepan. Stirring continuously with wooden spoon to prevent sticking, boil rapidly for 20 minutes. Reduce heat to medium-low and cook until half-and-half is reduced to two cups, about 25 minutes. (For homogenized milk, cooking will take a longer time.) Reduced half-and-half will be the consistency of heavy cream. Add sugar and mix well. Gradually stir in almonds a little at a time. Sprinkle cream sauce with cardamom and rose water.

2. Remove *rasgullas* from thin syrup and arrange in a deep serving bowl. Pour the *malai* over the *rasgullas*. Sprinkle with chopped pistachio nuts and garnish with silver leaf. Chill before serving.

SERVES 3 to 6

KAMLA-BHOG
(*Orange Cheese Puffs in Syrup*)

7½ cups [60 ounces] milk
¼ cup [2 ounces] white vinegar
½ cup [4 ounces] water
1¾ teaspoons [1⅓ E.] orange extract
Orange food coloring

2 teaspoons [1⅗ E.] instant orange drink powder or ground almonds
5 tablespoons [4 E.] confectioners' sugar
4 cups [3⅕ E.] sugar
7 cups [56 ounces] water

1. Prepare *channa* as directed on page 19. Combine hot *channa*, 1¼ teaspoons orange extract, and a few drops of orange food coloring in a bowl. Knead with the heel of the hand until it becomes creamy. Divide into 13 equal-sized balls. Take 3 flavored *channa* balls and add orange-drink powder and ½ teaspoon orange extract. Mix together until it becomes a creamy paste. Sprinkle with 2 to 3 teaspoons confectioners' sugar. Divide into 10 equal-sized balls and dust with remaining confectioners' sugar. Refrigerate to chill.

2. Form a cup-shaped depression in the center of one of the large *channa* balls and place a small *channa* ball in the center. Carefully reform the large ball with the smaller ball enclosed. Take care not to break or crack the *channa*.

3. Dissolve sugar in water. Add a few drops of orange food coloring. Bring to a boil for 10 minutes. Drop prepared *channa* balls in hot boiling syrup, cover, and cook over high heat for 5 minutes. Reduce

heat to medium high and continue cooking for about 60 to 80 minutes, or until the syrup thickens and feels sticky to the touch. Remove from heat. Allow balls to soak for a few hours before serving. Remove balls from syrup and serve cold with a little syrup.

YIELD: 10 *kamla-bhog*

CHAM-CHAM
(*Cheese Fingers in Syrup*)

1½ quarts [60 ounces] milk
¼ cup [2 ounces] white vinegar
½ cup [4 ounces] water
4 cups [3⅕ E.] sugar
7 cups [56 ounces] water
Orange food coloring

1. Prepare *channa* as directed on page 19. Take warm *channa* and knead until creamy. Add food coloring and mix well. Divide *channa* into 12 equal-sized portions. Shape each portion like a tongue about 1½ inches long and ⅙ inch thick.

2. Dissolve sugar in water. Add a few drops of food coloring. Bring to a boil for 10 minutes. Drop tongues in boiling syrup, cover, and cook over high heat for 5 minutes. Reduce heat to medium high and continue cooking for about 60 to 80 minutes, or until syrup thickens and forms a thread when dripped from a spoon. Remove from heat. Allow tongues to soak for at least a few hours before serving. *Cham-cham* may be served with syrup or drained *cham-cham* may be rolled in ground almonds. *Cham-cham* always tastes better if it has soaked in syrup for several days.

YIELD: 12 *cham-cham*

MALAI-CHOP
(*Cham-Cham with Cream Sauce*)

12 *cham-cham*
1 can [16 ounces] evaporated milk
2 to 3 tablespoons [1 to 1½ ounces] sweet butter
¼ cup [⅕ E.] sugar
Rose or vanilla extract
¼ teaspoon [⅕ E.] ground cardamom
2½ tablespoons [2 E.] chopped pistachio nuts
2½ tablespoons [2 E.] slivered almonds

1. Prepare *cham-cham* as directed on page 192 and soak in syrup overnight or longer.

2. Boil milk with butter over medium heat about 5 to 8 minutes, stirring all the time with a wooden spoon. Reduce heat to medium-low and cook slowly until milk thickens to heavy cream consistency. Add sugar and rose or vanilla extract and continue cooking and stirring a few minutes more. As milk begins to thicken, stir continuously and vigorously so that it does not stick to the bottom of the pan. The consistency of the *malai* will be like thick batter. Cooking will take about 40 to 50 minutes. Remove from heat and mix in cardamom.

3. Preheat oven to 350°. Drain *cham-cham*. Place *cham-cham* on a baking sheet and spread *malai* on one side of each *cham-cham*. Sprinkle pistachios and almonds on top of *malai*. Increase oven heat to a broil, and slide *malai-chop* under the broiler for 2 minutes, or until the *malai* puffs and lightly browns. Serve immediately.

SERVES 4 to 6

KHIR KADAMBO
(*Stuffed Cheese Balls*)

Kadambo:

1½ quarts [60 ounces] milk

¼ cup [2 ounces] white vinegar

6½ cups [52 ounces] water

4 cups [3⅕ E.] sugar

Khir:

1 quart [40 ounces] half-and-half

2½ tablespoons [2 E.] sweet butter

¾ cup [⅗ E.] sugar, or to taste

10 tablespoons [2½ ounces] ground almonds

4 drops of rose essence or 1½ tablespoons [1¼ E.] rose water

¼ teaspoon [⅕ E.] ground cardamom

1. Prepare *channa* as directed on page 19, using ½ cup water. Place warm *channa* in a bowl and break it into small pieces with a rubber spatula. Knead *channa* with your palms until creamy. Divide *channa* into 15 to 20 equal portions and roll to form balls.

2. Dissolve sugar in 6 cups water, bring to a boil, and boil for 10 minutes. Add *channa* balls, cover, and cook over high heat for 5 minutes. Reduce heat to medium-high and continue cooking for about 60 minutes, or until syrup thickens and feels sticky to the touch.

Remove from heat and allow *kadambo* to soak for 2 days in sugar syrup.

3. Heat half-and-half in a heavy pan, stirring with a wooden spoon. Boil rapidly for 15 minutes, then cook slowly until half-and-half is reduced to half its original volume. Add butter and continue stirring and cooking until the mixture is like thick batter. Gradually add sugar and mix well. Cooking will take about 2 hours. Stir in almonds a little at a time and mix well after each addition. Scrape bottom and sides of the pan and stir in the cooked batter. Add rose essence or rose water and cardamom. When the mixture looks like very soft dough, remove from heat. Let stand 5 to 6 hours, or overnight, to dry out the excess moisture from the milk preparation. The consistency will be a little softer than pie-crust dough.

4. Warm *khir* over *very low heat*. Place in a bowl and knead until it is very smooth, adding a little sugar syrup if necessary. Divide *khir* mixture into equal portions, slightly larger than the *channa* balls. If the *khir* is too dry, wet your palms with syrup. Form each *khir* ball into a round bowl. Place one drained *channa* ball inside and close the opening very carefully with moistened fingers. If there are any cracks, join them carefully with a little sugar syrup. Roll *khir* balls between your palms to make a round ball. Roll each ball in ground almonds. Place in a jar and cover tightly. *Khir kadambo* will stay fresh for 7 to 10 days in the refrigerator. It can also be frozen; just thaw at room temperature before serving.

SERVES 8 to 10

Alternate method for cooking kadambo:

Combine 4 cups [3⅓ E.] sugar and 4 cups [3⅓ E.] water in a 3-quart pressure cooker, bring to a boil over high heat, and boil for 5 minutes. Add *channa* balls, close cover securely, place pressure regulator on vent pipe, and cook over high heat until regulator begins to vibrate. Reduce heat to medium-high and continue cooking 15 minutes. Remove pressure cooker from heat and allow pressure to drop of its own accord. Remove cover and separate balls with a fork. Boil rapidly, uncovered, 1 or 2 minutes, or until syrup is thick and balls are light golden. Remove from heat and let *kadambo* soak for 2 days in sugar syrup.

Alternate method for preparing khir:

1 quart [40 ounces] milk	½ cup [⅖ E.] sugar, or to taste
4 to 6 tablespoons [2 to 3 ounces] sweet butter	2½ tablespoons [2 E.] rose water or a few drops of rose essence
1 16-ounce can evaporated milk	¼ teaspoon [⅕ E.] ground cardamom
1¼ cups [1 E.] powdered milk	½ cup [⅘ E.] ground almonds

Heat milk in a heavy pan, stirring with a wooden spoon. Boil rapidly for 15 minutes, and then cook slowly, stirring most of the time, until ⅔ of the milk evaporates. Add one ounce butter and evaporated milk, continue to cook, stirring, and add powdered milk, about one heaping tablespoon at a time. Mix well after each addition. Scrape bottom and sides of the pan and mix well. Add rest of the butter and continue cooking over low heat until the mixture is a soft thin dough. Add sugar and mix well. Stir in rose water and cardamom. Gradually add ground almonds and mix thoroughly. Remove from heat and set aside to cool. Let stand 4 to 5 hours, or overnight.

SANDESH
(*Cheese Fudge*)

3 quarts [120 ounces] milk	½ cup [⅖ E.] confectioners' sugar
⅓ cup [3 ounces] white vinegar	
1 cup [8 ounces] warm water	¼ teaspoon [⅕ E.] ground cardamom
¾ cup [⅗ E.] sugar, or to taste	
Green food coloring (optional)	Pistachio flavoring (optional)
1½ tablespoons [1¼ E.] sweet butter	½ cup [⅖ E.] chopped unsalted pistachio nuts

1. Prepare *channa* as directed on page 19.

2. Place warm *channa* in a bowl and knead with the heel of your hand until creamy. Mix in granulated sugar and a few drops of food coloring. Cook *channa* over medium heat, stirring continuously with a wooden spoon, until it leaves sides and bottom of the pan and makes a single lump. Gradually add confectioners' sugar and mix well. Mixture should be sticky, not crumbly. Mix in cardamom and pistachio flavoring. Total cooking time should be 20 to 25 minutes. Do not

allow *channa* to become too dry, or it will crumb. If it does become too dry, add a few teaspoons of cold milk at a time until a single lump forms again. Stir in chopped pistachio nuts and ground cardamom and remove from heat. Divide into 20 to 25 equal portions and press each portion into a small greased mold. If the mold gets too sticky, wash and grease it again. If a mold is not available, spread *channa* mixture about ½ inch thick in a greased square pan. Garnish with extra chopped pistachio nuts on top. Press lightly with the back of a spoon to set nuts on top. Cool and cut into diamond shapes.

YIELD: 20 to 25 *sandesh*

Sandesh Variations:

1. Use almond flavoring rather than pistachio. Omit green food coloring and substitute 2 ounces of ground almonds and ¼ cup [⅕ E.] of slivered almonds for chopped pistachio nuts.

2. Use maple sugar and maple flavoring instead of granulated sugar. Omit nuts. Use maple leaf mold for the shape or cut into diamond shape. Garnish with silver leaf.

3. After *channa* has cooked, remove from heat. Take ⅓ of cooked *channa* and color with a pinch of saffron, soaked in one tablespoon warm milk. Divide yellow *channa* into 10 small balls and divide the remaining white *channa* into 10 larger balls. Carefully place yellow ball inside white ball and reform the white ball so the yellow one is entirely contained within. Immediately cut ball in half with a sharp knife and sprinkle with nuts.

BHADA SANDESH
(*Baked Sandesh*)

3 quarts [120 ounces] milk
⅓ cup [3 ounces] white vinegar
1 cup [8 ounces] warm water
¾ cup [⅗ E.] sugar, or to taste
¾ cup [⅗ E.] powdered milk
1½ tablespoons [1¼ E.] sour cream or plain yogurt

Food coloring (any color, if desired)
¼ cup [⅕ E.] chopped nuts, walnuts, almonds, or pistachios

1. Prepare *channa* as directed on page 19.
2. Preheat oven to 300°. Place warm *channa* in a bowl and knead with the heel of the hand until creamy. Add sugar and mix well. Gradually add powdered milk and mix well. Mix in sour cream. Color half the *channa*, if desired, with a few drops of food coloring. Grease an 8-inch square pan with butter. Spread white *channa* evenly on the bottom. Sprinkle with nuts and press lightly with the back of a spoon. Spread colored *channa* evenly on top and sprinkle with more nuts. Cover with foil and bake in the middle level of the preheated oven for about 40 to 50 minutes, or until a toothpick inserted in the center comes out clean. Remove from the oven, allow to cool, chill, and cut into squares.

YIELD: 16 to 20 *sandesh*

CHANNA BURFI
(*Sweet Cheese Diamonds*)

3 quarts [120 ounces] milk
⅓ cup [3 ounces] white vinegar
1 cup [8 ounces] warm water
1½ cups [1¼ E.] sugar
¼ pound sweet butter
3½ cups [2⅖ E.] powdered milk
1 cup [8 ounces] milk

½ cup [⅔ E.] chopped unsalted nuts, walnuts, pistachios, or almonds
¼ teaspoon [⅕ E.] ground cardamom
Few drops of rose essence or 1½ tablespoons [1¼ E.] rose water

1. Prepare *channa* as directed on page 19.
2. Rub warm *channa* with the heel of the hand until creamy. Mix in sugar and cook over medium-low heat, stirring all the time with a wooden spoon, for about 15 to 20 minutes. Add butter and mix well. Remove from heat, add powdered milk and liquid milk, and mix thoroughly. Return to heat and cook for another 15 to 20 minutes over medium-low heat, or until the mixture leaves the sides of the pan and makes a single lump. Take care not to allow *channa* to brown. Mix in nuts, cardamom, and rose essence and remove from heat. Spread *channa* about ½ inch thick on a buttered dish. Press silver leaf on top or use walnut halves for garnish. Chill and cut into small squares or diamond shapes with a sharp knife. *Channa burfi* always tastes better after a few days in the refrigerator.

YIELD: 20 to 30 *channa burfi*

CHANNA GILIPI
(*Cheese Spirals in Syrup*)

3 quarts [120 ounces] milk
⅓ cup [3 ounces] white vinegar
1 cup [8 ounces] warm water
8 ounces cream cheese
1 cup [⅘ E.] biscuit mix
¼ teaspoon [⅕ E.] ground
   cardamom

3½ cups [2⅘ E.] sugar
3 cups [24 ounces] water
Vegetable oil for deep fat
   frying
1½ tablespoons [1¼ E.] rose water

1. Prepare *channa* as directed on page 19.
2. Knead *channa* with the heel of your hand until creamy. Add cream cheese, biscuit mix, and cardamom and mix well to make a soft smooth dough.
3. To prepare sugar syrup, boil sugar and water in a saucepan for 5 to 8 minutes. Reduce heat to low and keep syrup warm until ready to use.
4. Heat vegetable oil 3 to 4 inches deep in a deep fat fryer until it reaches 350°. Divide *channa* mixture into 30 to 40 equal portions. Take each portion and roll between palms until 2 inches long and the thickness of a pencil. Bring both ends together in a loop and pinch ends to join them. Drop loops, a few at a time, into hot vegetable oil. Fry, turning once, until evenly browned. Transfer to paper toweling to drain. Put loops in warm syrup while they are still hot. They will puff to double their original size. Simmer in syrup for 5 minutes and remove from heat. Serve hot or cold, sprinkled with rose water.

YIELD: 30 to 40 *channa gilipi*

PANTUA
(*Fried Cheese Balls in Syrup*)

3 quarts [120 ounces] milk
⅓ cup [3 ounces] white vinegar
1 cup [8 ounces] warm water
5 tablespoons [4 E.] biscuit mix
5 tablespoons [4 E.] sour cream
¼ teaspoon [⅕ E.] ground cardamom

5½ cups [2½ pounds] sugar
6½ cups [52 ounces] water
Vegetable oil for deep fat frying
1½ tablespoons [1¼ E.] rose water

1. Prepare *channa* as directed on page 19.

2. Rub warm *channa* with the heel of your hand until creamy. Add biscuit mix and sour cream and mix well. Mix in cardamom and knead until smooth. Divide *channa* into 50 equal-sized portions and form into balls.

3. To prepare sugar syrup, dissolve sugar in boiling water. Boil for 4 to 5 minutes over high heat, reduce heat to low, and keep warm until ready to use.

4. Heat vegetable oil 3 to 4 inches deep in a deep fat fryer to 350°. Watch oil temperature carefully since *pantua* will burn easily. Drop balls in hot oil, a few at a time, and fry until evenly browned. Slow frying is essential; it should take about 15 to 20 minutes. As *pantua* brown, transfer them to paper toweling to drain. Add them to warm sugar syrup while they are still hot and simmer for 10 minutes. *Pantua* will swell to double their original size. Remove from heat and soak *pantua* overnight in the syrup. Drain before serving. Sprinkle with rose water.

YIELD: 50 *pantua*

GULAB-JAMON
(*Puff Balls in Syrup*)

1½ cups [1⅕ E.] powdered milk
¾ cup [⅗ E.] biscuit mix
¼ teaspoon [⅕ E.] ground
　　cardamom
2½ tablespoons [2 E.] *ghee*
¼ teaspoon [⅕ E.] baking
　　powder

½ cup [⅖ E.] milk
3 cups [2⅖ E.] sugar
4 cups [32 ounces] water
Vegetable oil for deep fat
　　frying
1½ tablespoons [1¼ E.] rose water

1. Combine powdered milk, biscuit mix, and cardamom in a bowl, and mix well with your fingertips. Add *ghee* and mix well. Add baking powder to milk; then stir into dry mixture with a fork. The dough will be very soft and sticky.

2. To prepare sugar syrup, boil sugar and water for 5 minutes over high heat, reduce heat to low, and keep warm until ready to use.

3. Heat vegetable oil 3 to 4 inches deep until it reaches 335° to 340°. Take about one teaspoon of dough mixture and roll into balls the size of cherries. Drop balls into hot oil immediately after they have been formed. Fry about 15 to 20 minutes, or until evenly browned. Remove balls and drain on a paper towel. Put balls in warm syrup and simmer for 15 minutes. *Gulab-jamon* tastes better after soaking for 2 to 3 days in syrup.

YIELD: 20 *gulab-jamon*

BADAM KHIR
(*Almond Delight*)

1 quart [40 ounces] half-and-half
　　or 1½ quarts [60 ounces]
　　milk plus 2½ tablespoons
　　[2 E.] sweet butter
¾ cup [⅗ E.] sugar
　　Pinch of saffron threads soaked
　　in 1 tablespoon warm milk
½ cup [⅖ E.] ground almonds

¼ teaspoon [⅕ E.] ground
　　cardamom
1¼ teaspoons [1 E.] almond
　　extract
5 tablespoons [4 E.] slivered
　　almonds

Boil half-and-half in a heavy pan over medium high heat, stirring with a wooden spoon, about 15 minutes. Reduce heat to low and continue cooking 50 to 60 minutes, stirring occasionally. Add sugar and saffron mixture. Gradually add ground almonds one tablespoon at a time and mix well. Mix in cardamom, almond extract, and slivered almonds. Mixture will be like a thick heavy sauce. Pour into a bowl and chill before serving. Garnish, if desired, with silver leaf.

SERVES 6 to 8

PAYASAM
(*Sweet Creamed Rice*)

5 tablespoons [4 E.] *basmati* or long grain rice
½ cup [4 ounces] water
2½ cups [12 ounces] milk
1 quart [40 ounces] half-and-half
Dash of salt
1 cup [⅘ E.] sugar

2½ tablespoons [2 E.] raisins
¼ cup [⅕ E.] slivered almonds
¼ teaspoon [⅛ E.] ground cardamom
Few drops of rose essence or 1½ tablespoons [1¼ E.] rose water

Wash rice and soak in ½ cup water for 2 hours. Drain and boil in 2½ cups milk for 2 minutes. Cover and simmer about 15 minutes, or until rice is cooked. Add half-and-half and salt and continue cooking and stirring occasionally over medium-low heat until mixture has the consistency of thick cream. Add sugar and cook another 10 minutes. Stir in raisins, almonds, cardamom, and rose essence. Remove from heat and pour into individual crystal bowls, or one large serving bowl. Garnish, if desired, with silver leaf. Chill before serving.

SERVES 8 to 10

ALOO PITTHA
(*Sweet Potato Puffs in Syrup and Cream*)

2¼ cups [1⅘ E.] sugar
1¾ cups [14 ounces] water
1½ pounds sweet potatoes, peeled,
    boiled, or baked, and mashed
Pinch of salt
Pinch of baking powder
Pinch of cardamom
2 tablespoons [1⅗ E.] rice flour

2 tablespoons [1⅗ E.] all-
    purpose flour
Vegetable oil for deep fat
    frying
2 cups [16 ounces] half-and-half
2 tablespoons [1 ounce] *ghee*
¼ teaspoon [⅕ E.] ground
    cardamom
¼ cup [⅕ E.] ground almonds

1. To prepare sugar syrup, boil together 2 cups of sugar and the water for 10 minutes. Reduce heat to low and keep syrup warm until ready to use.

2. Combine mashed sweet potatoes, salt, baking powder, cardamom, rice flour, and all-purpose flour in a bowl and knead to make a soft dough. Divide dough into small balls the size of cherries. Heat vegetable oil 3 to 4 inches deep in a deep fat fryer to 350°. Drop balls in hot oil, a few at a time, and fry until evenly browned. If the first batch of balls breaks while frying, add a little more flour to the dough. Remove balls with a slotted spoon and drain on paper toweling. Place balls in warmed sugar syrup and allow to soak one hour.

3. Combine half-and-half, ¼ cup sugar, *ghee*, and cardamom in a saucepan. Cook over medium heat, stirring continuously, until mixture thickens to the consistency of evaporated milk. Stir in ground almonds and remove from heat.

4. Remove sweet potato balls from sugar syrup, and place in a serving bowl. Pour cream sauce over potato balls and garnish with chopped almonds. Serve warm or cold.

SERVES 10

PAYRA
(*Pistachio Sugar Cookies*)

¼ pound sweet butter
3 cups [2⅖ E.] powdered milk
⅞ cup [7 ounces] milk
½ cup [⅖ E.] sugar

¼ teaspoon [⅕ E.] ground
   cardamom
2½ tablespoons [2 E.] finely
   chopped pistachio nuts

1. Melt butter in a heavy pan over low heat. Remove pan from heat and set aside to cool. Add powdered milk and milk together and mix thoroughly with a wooden spoon. Return to medium heat, and cook, stirring continuously, about 40 to 50 minutes, or until mixture dries slightly and forms a dough. Mix in sugar and continue cooking another 10 to 15 minutes. Sprinkle with cardamom and mix well. Remove from heat.
2. Take about one tablespoon of warm milk mixture and form a round ball. Press ball with fingers or a fork to make a thin round. Sprinkle pistachio nuts on top of *payra* and press with a fork so nuts will adhere. *Payra* tastes better warm. They can be frozen: thaw to room temperature or place in an oven for a few minutes until warm.

YIELD: 30 *payra*

GILIPI
(*Puffed Spirals in Syrup*)

1 cup [⅘ E.] all-purpose flour
2 tablespoons [1⅗ E.] rice
   flour
2½ tablespoons [2 E.] plain yogurt
½ teaspoon [⅓ E.] dry yeast
¾ cup [6 ounces] warm water

Pinch of sugar
Yellow food coloring
2 cups [1⅗ E.] sugar
2 cups [16 ounces] water
Vegetable oil for deep fat
   frying

1. Combine all-purpose flour, rice flour, and yogurt in a bowl. Dissolve sugar and yeast in warm water and let stand for 10 minutes without disturbing. Add a few drops of food coloring to the yeast water, pour over flour, and beat together for several minutes. Cover and set aside in a warm place for 2 days in the summer and 3 in the winter. Batter must be well fermented both for crispness and flavor.
2. To make sugar syrup boil sugar, water, and a few drops of food

coloring about 15 minutes, or until the syrup is very sticky but not stiff. Turn heat to low and keep warm until ready to use.

3. Heat vegetable oil 2 to 3 inches deep in a deep fat fryer to about 375°. Beat the batter again. Place your finger over the opening of a small pastry bag or small-nozzled funnel and fill with the batter. Place your hand over the hot oil, remove your finger, and allow batter to run into the hot oil. Form double circles or figure eights, about the size of a doughnut. Allow *gilipis* to set and turn once. *Gilipis* will be attached while cooking, but separate easily when done. When crisp and golden in color, remove and drain. Place each *gilipi* in warm sugar syrup for a minute or two. The syrup will run through the pipes of the *gilipis*, which will still remain very crisp. Remove *gilipis* and serve hot.

NOTE: *Gilipis* can be made ahead of time. After frying and draining, put them in a covered plastic container and leave at room temperature. Just before serving, warm syrup, and place *gilipis* in the syrup for a minute or two. Remove *gilipis* from syrup and place in a single layer on a cookie sheet. Heat boiler to 400° and slip cookie sheet under the broiler for a few minutes, or until the syrup starts to sizzle. Serve at once.

YIELD: 20 to 25 *gilipis*

BUNDI
(*Rice Puffs in Syrup*)

In India there is a special kind of utensil used to prepare this kind of sweet. It is a circular steel or brass disc, 4 to 6 inches in diameter, with several fine perforations about ⅛ inch wide attached at the end of a long handle. But it is not hard to make a substitute of your own. Take a 9-inch aluminum foil pie plate and punch holes with a sharp pencil or very large nail about ½ inch apart over the bottom of the pie plate. The holes should be about the size of small green peas or small raisins. Or you may use a perforated strainer.

3 cups [2⅖ E.] sugar
3½ cups [2⅘ E.] water
　Red or yellow food coloring
1½ cups [1⅕ E.] *besan* (chick-pea flour) or 1 cup [⅘ E.] *besan* plus ½ cup [⅖ E.] rice flour

¼ teaspoon [⅕ E.] baking powder
1 cup [8 ounces] water
1 tablespoon [½ ounce] *ghee* or vegetable oil
Vegetable oil for deep fat frying

1. To prepare sugar syrup, boil sugar and water, with a few drops of food coloring, for about 10 to 15 minutes, or until it forms a thick syrup. Turn heat to low and keep syrup warm until ready to use.

2. Combine *besan* with baking powder in a bowl. Add water, a little at a time, and beat until all the water is used and batter becomes light and smooth. Mix in *ghee* and a few drops of food coloring.

3. Heat vegetable oil 3 to 4 inches deep in a deep fat fryer. When oil starts to smoke, reduce heat to medium. Hold strainer, or any other substitute utensil, over the pan, about 3 inches above the oil; pour batter over the strainer about ¼ cup at a time. Rub the batter through the holes with your fingers. As the batter falls in very fine drops into the hot oil, it sets into *bundi*. Fry for one minute, then stir and continue frying *bundi* over medium-high heat about 3 to 4 minutes, or until crisp. Drain on paper toweling.

4. Put fried *bundi* in warm sugar syrup. Stir with a fork until they are well coated. Simmer *bundi* for 2 minutes. The *bundi* will absorb syrup and will swell slightly. Remove from heat. Do not stir the *bundi*; they will be soft, light, and separated from each other. Cool and serve.

NOTE: Slight adjustments in quantity of water used for the batter may be required depending on the fineness of the flour.

SERVES 6 to 8

BUNDI LADOO
(*Almond and Raisin Puffs*)

3 cups [2⅖ E.] *besan* (chick-pea flour)	2½ tablespoons [2 E.] raisins
Pinch of salt	½ cup [⅖ E.] sliced almonds
Pinch of baking soda	2½ tablespoons [2 E.] melon seeds, unsalted and roasted (optional)
1¼ to 1⅓ cups [1 to 1⅕ E.] water	
Yellow food coloring	3 cups [2⅖ E.] sugar
Vegetable oil for deep fat frying	¾ cup [⅗ E.] water
2½ tablespoons [2 E.] *ghee*	½ teaspoon [⅓ E.] ground cardamom

, Combine *besan*, salt, and baking soda in a bowl. Add water, a little at a time, and beat until batter becomes light and smooth The batter should be a little thinner than pancake batter. Mix in a few drops of yellow food coloring.

2. Heat vegetable oil 3 to 4 inches deep in a deep fat fryer. When oil starts to smoke, reduce heat to medium. Hold a colander over the pan about 3 inches above the oil and pour the batter over the colander about ¼ cup [⅙ E.] at a time. Rub the batter through the holes with your fingers. As batter falls in very fine drops into the hot oil, it sets into *bundi*. Fry for one minute; then, stirring continuously, fry *bundi* about 2 more minutes over medium-high heat. Drain on paper toweling. Repeat until remaining batter is used up.

3. Heat *ghee* in a small pan. Cook raisins for one minute, or until they are swollen. Remove with a slotted spoon. Add almonds and melon seeds and cook another minute. Remove with a slotted spoon.

4. Boil sugar and water for about 2 minutes. Remove from heat and quickly stir in fried *bundi*, nuts, and raisins. Mix in cardamom and mash with the back of a spoon to break up some of the *bundi* to bind the mixture. With greased fingers quickly form into about 25 compact balls while mixture is still hot and sticky. Stir the *bundi* mixture from time to time while making the balls. Serve warm or cold.

YIELD: 25 *bundi ladoos*

AMIRTY
(*Crisp Spirals in Syrup*)

1 cup [⅘ E.] split *urad dal*, washed	Yellow food coloring
1⅓ cups [11 ounces] water	Vegetable oil for deep fat frying

1. Soak *dal* in 1⅓ cups water overnight. Place *dal* and soaking water in the container of a blender and blend until smooth and creamy. Cover and keep in a warm place for 24 hours to ferment. Add a few drops of food coloring and beat until light and fluffy.

2. Follow directions in *gilipi* recipe (page 203) for frying *amirty*, soaking them in sugar syrup, and serving.

YIELD: 10 to 12 *amirty*

GAJJAR BURFI
(*Carrot Fudge*)

3½ cups [28 ounces] half-and-half
2 to 2½ pounds carrots, trimmed, scraped, and coarsely chopped
⅓ pound sweet butter
¾ cup [⅗ E.] sugar
½ cup [⅖ E.] brown sugar
Orange food coloring
⅓ teaspoon [¼ E.] ground cardamom
½ cup [2 ounces] ground almonds
1½ tablespoons [1¼ E.] rose water
½ to ¾ cup [⅖ to ⅗ E.] chopped unsalted nuts, walnuts or almonds
Silver leaf (optional)

1. Put milk in an electric blender, add carrots, and grate coarsely. In a deep heavy pan, cook the carrot mixture over high heat, stirring constantly, for 10 to 15 minutes. Reduce heat to medium and cook for about one hour, stirring regularly, or until mixture is thick enough to coat a spoon heavily. Add butter and cook another 5 minutes. Gradually add sugar and stir to mix well. Mix in brown sugar, a few drops of food coloring, cardamom, ground almonds, and rose water.

2. Cook, stirring, another 10 to 15 minutes, or until the mixture is thick enough to draw away from the sides and bottom of the pan in a solid mass, adding a little butter if necessary. Remove from heat and mix in nuts. Spread mixture in a buttered baking pan and press silver leaf or more nuts on top. Cool and cut into squares to serve.

NOTE: One quart milk plus ½ pound sweet butter can be used instead of half-and-half and ⅓ pound butter.

SERVES 8

GAJJAR HALVA
(*Creamed Carrots*)

Gajjar Burfi
2 cups [1⅗ E.] powdered milk
5 tablespoons [4 E.] raisins
½ to ¾ cup [⅖ to ⅗ E.] chopped unsalted nuts, walnuts or almonds

Prepare carrot *burfi* as directed above through step 1. Add powdered milk, a tablespoonful at a time, and mix well with the carrot mixture. Stir in raisins and nuts and remove from heat. *Halva* will be softer than *burfi*. Mound the *halva* on a large heatproof platter and garnish with silver leaf. Serve warm.

SERVES 8.

MOHAN-THARR
(*Saffron Fudge*)

1 cup [⅘ E.] *besan* (chick-pea flour)
¾ cup [⅗ E.] *ghee*
2½ teaspoons [2 E.] milk
1 cup [⅘ E.] powdered milk
1½ cups [1⅕ E.] sugar
¾ cup [6 ounces] water
Pinch of saffron threads soaked in 1 tablespoon warm water

2½ tablespoons [2 E.] chopped pistachio nuts
2½ tablespoons [2 E.] chopped almonds
½ teaspoon [⅓ E.] ground cardamom

1. Combine *besan* and 2 tablespoons of the *ghee* in a bowl. Mix well with fingertips. Add milk and make a stiff dough. Leave about 1 hour at room temperature.

2. Heat the rest of the *ghee* in a small pan over medium heat. Fry *besan* dough, stirring all the time, about 10 minutes, or until light brown. Add powdered milk and cook over very low heat for one more minute, adding more *ghee* if necessary. Remove from heat.

3. Boil sugar, water, and saffron with its water in another pan for 10 to 15 minutes over high heat, or until syrup is very thick. Add fried *besan* mixture and stir very quickly. The syrup will evaporate, and the mixture will be like soft, sticky dough. Cook for about 2 minutes. Remove from heat. Add pistachio nuts, almonds, and cardamom; mix well. Pour onto a flat greased pan about ¾ inch thick Spread the mixture evenly. Sprinkle more chopped nuts on top if desired. Cool and cut into diamonds about 1¼ inch wide. Serve at room temperature.

YIELD: 20 *mohan-tharrs*

NAREAL BURFI
(*Coconut Fudge*)

¼ pound sweet butter
3 cups [2⅖ E.] powdered milk
About 1 cup [7 ounces] milk
½ cup [⅖ E.] sugar
¾ cup [⅗ E.] freshly grated
   coconut

¼ teaspoon [⅕ E.] ground
   cardamom
¼ cup [⅕ E.] chopped almonds
Silver leaf (optional)

Melt butter in a heavy pan over low heat. Remove from heat and set aside to cool. Add powdered milk and milk together and mix thoroughly with a wooden spoon. Return to medium heat and cook, stirring continuously, about 40 to 50 minutes, or until the mixture forms a dough. Mix in sugar and coconut and cook for another 5 to 10 minutes. Sprinkle with cardamom and stir in chopped almonds. Remove from heat and spread the mixture in a layer ½ inch thick on a greased baking sheet. Garnish with silver leaf. Cool and cut into diamond shapes with a heated sharp knife.

YIELD: 25 to 30 *burfi*

CHANA DAL HALVA
(*Sweet Creamed Lentils*)

1 pound *chana dal*, washed and
   soaked in 3 cups [24 ounces]
   water
5 to 6 cups [40 to 48 ounces]
   thin coconut milk
Pinch of saffron
Pinch of salt
1 quart [40 ounces] half-and-half
½ cup [⅖ E.] *ghee*

1 bay leaf
1 cup [⅘ E.] slivered almonds
2¼ cups [1 pound] sugar, or to
   taste
5 tablespoons [4 E.] raisins
¼ teaspoon [⅕ E.] ground
   cardamom
Silver leaf

1. Soak *dal* for one hour and drain. Bring coconut milk to a boil, add saffron, salt, and *dal* and boil, covered, until *dal* is tender and most of the liquid has been absorbed. Mash cooked *dal* or grind in a food mill.

2. Boil half-and-half over moderate heat about 20 to 30 minutes, stirring all the time to prevent sticking. Reduce heat to low and continue cooking, stirring often, about 2 to 3 hours, or until ⅔ of the milk evaporates.

3. Heat *ghee* in a large skillet and fry bay leaf and almonds for few seconds. Add ground *dal* and cook over low heat, stirring with a wooden spoon, about 8 to 10 minutes, or until golden. Stir in thickened half-and-half, sugar, raisins, and cardamom. Stirring continuously, cook about 15 to 20 minutes over medium heat, or until most of the liquid evaporates and *ghee* comes to the surface. Remove from heat and serve in a heated deep bowl. Garnish with silver leaf.

SERVES 10 to 12

KAYLA HALVA
(*Sweet Mashed Bananas*)

2½ tablespoons [2 E.] *ghee*
2 to 3 large ripe bananas, peeled and mashed
½ cup [⅖ E.] brown sugar
2½ tablespoons [2 E.] heavy cream

2½ tablespoons [2 E.] slivered almonds
2½ tablespoons [2 E.] raisins
⅛ teaspoon [1/10 E.] ground cardamom
1¼ teaspoons [1 E.] rose water

Heat *ghee* in a skillet over medium heat and fry mashed banana, stirring, for about 6 to 8 minutes. Add sugar and heavy cream, and cook about 10 minutes, or until the mixture is sticky. Stir in almonds, raisins, and cardamom, and cook for another 2 minutes. Mix in rose water and remove from heat. Serve warm in a deep bowl.

SERVES 2 to 3

GAUJA (No. 1)
(*Fried Pastry in Syrup*)

1 cup [⅘ E.] all-purpose flour
Pinch of baking soda
2 tablespoons [1 ounce] butter
½ teaspoon [⅓ E.] ground cardamom

½ cup plus 5 tablespoons [4 E.] water
Vegetable oil for deep fat frying
1 cup [⅘ E.] sugar

1. Combine flour, baking soda, butter, and ground cardamom in a bowl and mix well. Add 5 tablespoons water to make a stiff dough. Knead about 10 to 15 minutes. Form 15 to 20 equal-sized balls. Roll out balls on a lightly floured board to form very thin circles, approximately 3 inches in diameter. With a knife, make 4 to 5 parallel cuts in the pastry approximately ½ inch apart just to the edge but without cutting through the edges of the circle. Fold the pastry along the cut lines and pinch the ends to close.

2. Heat vegetable oil for deep fat frying to 375°. Fry *gaujas* until golden brown. Remove from oil and drain on paper toweling.

3. To prepare sugar syrup, combine sugar with ½ cup water and stir until sugar is dissolved. Bring to a boil and boil for about 15 minutes to make a medium syrup. Dip *gauja* in the prepared sugar syrup, remove, and dust with confectioners' sugar.

YIELD: 15 to 20 *gaujas*

GAUJA (No. 2)
(*Whole Wheat Pastry in Syrup*)

1 cup [⅘ E.] whole wheat flour
Pinch of baking powder
1 tablespoon [½ ounce] *ghee*
6 tablespoons [1½ ounces] ground almonds
⅛ teaspoon [1/10 E.] ground cardamom
½ cup [⅖ E.] sugar
½ cup [⅖ E.] milk
Vegetable oil for deep fat frying
½ cup [⅖ E.] confectioners' sugar

1. Combine whole wheat flour, baking powder, and *ghee* in a bowl and mix with fingers. Add almonds, cardamom, and sugar and mix well. Add milk to make a stiff dough and knead until soft and smooth. Roll dough into a large ⅙-inch-thick round. Cut dough into small (¼ inch) diamond shapes.

2. Heat vegetable oil 2 inches deep in a deep fat fryer to about 375° Fry *gaujas* until golden brown and crisp. Drain and sprinkle with confectioners' sugar. Serve warm or cold. Grated coconut may be used instead of ground almonds.

SERVES 4

CHANNA MALPUA
(*Crisp Cheese Pancakes in Syrup*)

1 quart [40 ounces] milk
3 tablespoons [1½ ounces] white vinegar
½ cup [4 ounces] water
1½ tablespoons [1¼ E.] all-purpose flour

Pinch of salt
½ cup [⅖ E.] cold milk
¼ cup [⅕ E.] *ghee*
1½ cups [1⅕ E.] sugar
2½ cups [20 ounces] water
1¼ teaspoons [1 E.] rose water

1. Prepare *channa* according to directions on page 19. Squeeze well to remove as much excess moisture as possible. Rub *channa* with the heel of your hand to make a smooth paste. Mix in flour and salt. Gradually add milk to make a pancakelike batter.

2. Heat *ghee* about one tablespoon at a time in a skillet over medium heat. Pour a small amount of batter into the pan to make a pancake about 3 inches in diameter. When the bottom of the pancake is brown and crisp (about 2 minutes), turn and fry about one more minute, adding more *ghee* if necessary.

3. To prepare sugar syrup, boil sugar and water for 15 minutes. Add rose water, reduce heat to low, and keep warm. Soak *channa malpua* for 3 to 4 hours in the sugar syrup. Serve pancakes drizzled with sugar syrup.

YIELD: 20 to 25 *channa malpua*

SUJI MALPUA
(*Crisp Saffron Pancakes in Syrup*)

1½ cups [1⅕ E.] all-purpose flour
1¾ to 2 cups [1⅖ to 1⅗] *suji* (farina)
3 cups [2⅖ E.] sugar
4 cups [32 ounces] buttermilk
Pinch of saffron threads soaked in 1 tablespoon warm milk
¼ teaspoon [⅕ E.] ground cardamom

½ teaspoon [⅓ E.] fennel seeds
Pinch of baking powder
½ cup [⅖ E.] *ghee*
1½ cups [1⅕ E.] sugar
2½ cups [20 ounces] water
1¼ teaspoons [1 E.] rose water

1. Combine all-purpose flour, 1½ cups *suji*, sugar, buttermilk, saffron mixture, cardamom, fennel seeds, and baking powder in a bowl and mix well. Let stand overnight, or 5 to 6 hours at least.

2. Add another ¼ to ½ cup *suji* and mix well. Heat one tablespoon *ghee* at a time in a skillet. Pour a small amount of batter in the pan to make a pancake about 3 inches in diameter. When bottom of the pancake is brown and crisp, turn and fry about one more minute, adding more *ghee* if necessary.

3. To prepare sugar syrup, boil sugar and water for 15 minutes. Add rose water, reduce heat to low, and keep warm. Soak *suji malpua* in sugar syrup for 4 to 5 hours. Serve warm or cold.

SERVES 5 to 6

PITTHA
(*Filled Indian Pancakes*)

Pancakes:

½ cup [⅖ E.] all-purpose flour
¼ cup [⅕ E.] *suji* (farina)
1 cup [8 ounces] water

1½ tablespoons [1¼ E.] sugar
Pinch of salt

1. Combine all-purpose flour, *suji*, water, sugar, and salt in a bowl, and beat until smooth and creamy. Let stand for 4 to 6 hours.

2. Heat frying pan and brush with melted butter or *ghee*. Pour in ¼ [⅕ E.] cup of the batter and tip the pan from side to side to spread it evenly into a flat pancake. Fry over medium-low heat until bubbles begin to form on the top; then, with a spatula, turn the pancake over and cook one more minute. Place 1 to 2 tablespoons of either of the following fillings inside of each pancake and roll; press a little with the back of your hand. This way the roll will be closed. Serve hot or cold.

YIELD: 10 to 15 *pittha*

Filling No. 1:

2½ cups [20 ounces] half-and-half
¼ cup [⅕ E.] sugar

⅛ teaspoon [⅒ E.] ground cardamom
1¼ teaspoons [1 E.] rose water

Boil half-and-half for 10 minutes over high heat, stirring all the time to avoid sticking. Reduce heat to very low and continue cooking for another 20 to 30 minutes, or until the milk thickens to a heavy sauce. Mix in sugar and cardamom and cook for another 2 to 3 minutes. Remove from heat and stir in rose water. Let stand overnight in refrigerator.

Filling No. 2:

2 tablespoons [1 ounce] *ghee*
1 cup [⅘ E.] freshly grated
  coconut
½ cup [4 ounces] milk
¼ cup [⅕ E.] sugar

¼ cup [⅕ E.] slivered almonds
2 tablespoons [1 ounce] seedless
  white raisins
1 cup [⅘ E.] powdered milk
⅛ teaspoon [¹⁄₁₀ E.] ground
  cardamom

Heat *ghee* in a pan, add coconut, and fry over low heat for one minute. Add milk, sugar, almonds, raisins, powdered milk, and cardamom, and cook, stirring all the time, about 5 minutes, or until the mixture is creamy. Remove from heat and set aside to cool.

MOONG HALVA
(*Sweet Yellow Lentils and Cream*)

1¼ cups [1 E.] *moong dal,* roasted
2 to 3 cups [16 to 24 ounces]
  water
5 tablespoons [4 E.] *ghee*
  Big pinch of saffron threads
  soaked in 1 tablespoon
  warm milk

1¼ cups [1 E.] sugar
1¾ to 2 cups [14 to 16 ounces]
  milk or coconut milk
2 tablespoons [1 ounce] raisins
5 tablespoons [4 E.] slivered
  almonds
¼ teaspoon [⅕ E.] ground
  cardamom

1. Wash *dal* and soak in water for 5 to 6 hours. Drain and wash again. Grind coarsely in a blender, adding 3 to 4 tablespoons water.

2. Heat *ghee* in a frying pan over medium heat, and fry ground *dal*, stirring all the time, until golden brown. Add saffron mixture, sugar, milk, raisins, and almonds and cook, stirring, over low heat until most of the liquid evaporates and *ghee* comes to the surface

Remove from heat and mix in cardamom. Garnish with silver leaf. Serve warm or cold.

SERVES 6 to 8

DAHI
(*Sweet Nutted Yogurt*)

⅔ cup [½ E.] sugar
2 cups [16 ounces] plain yogurt
2 16-ounce cans evaporated milk

2 cups [16 ounces] mango pulp (optional)
1½ tablespoons [1¼ E.] chopped pistachio nuts

---

1. Beat sugar and yogurt in a bowl with a fork until sugar dissolves. Add evaporated milk and mango pulp and stir to blend well.

2. Preheat oven to 200° to 225°. Pour the yogurt mixture into a large glass baking dish. Bake in the middle level of the preheated oven for about 2 hours, or until the mixture sets. Remove from oven and sprinkle nuts on top. Place the pan in the refrigerator to cool. Serve chilled yogurt with or without Indian sweets.

NOTE: Apricot purée may be used instead of mango pulp. Take 2 14- to 16-ounce cans of pitted apricots, drain, and blend in a blender until puréed.

SERVES 8 to 10

Glossary

Amirty: a yellow, crisp sweet, made from *urad dal*, deep fried, and soaked in sugar syrup

Badam: almond

Baingan: eggplant

Besan: chick-pea flour

Bharta: a vegetable preparation made by roasting and mashing vegetables

Bhendi: okra

Bhoonee: means essentially dry

Biryani: an elegant rice dish consisting of layers of cooked rice and cooked fish or meat baked together

Brinjal: eggplant

Bundi: a deep-fried ball about the size of a pea made from *besan* and rice flour

Burfi: squares or diamond-shaped sweet preparation, made from vegetables, flours, milk, sugar and nuts; very similar to fudge.

Cham-cham: a flattened yellow-colored sweetmeat, made from whole milk

Chana dal: split chick-pea lentil

Channa: Indian-style cottage cheese

Chappati: Indian bread, made from whole wheat flour

Chole: whole large chick-peas cooked Indian-style

Dahi: yogurt

Dahi-bora: lentil cake soaked in yogurt sauce

Dal: lentils

Degchi: Indian-style saucepan with no handle

Dhania: coriander

Dhoka: lentil cake, steamed or fried

Doo-piaza: doo means two and piaza means onion; it means the dish has lots of onions, and they have to be added in two different ways, both minced and sliced.

Dosa: South Indian pancake made from rice and lentils

Foogath: a vegetable dish cooked with coconut

Gauja: deep fried pastry dipped in heavy sugar syrup

Geela: a thin kitchuri

Ghoogni: whole dried peas made into curry

Ghee: clarified butter

Gilipi: deep fried circular twists, made from *besan* and rice flour and soaked in sugar syrup

Gulab-jamon: a brown round sweetmeat made from powdered milk

Halva: a sweet preparation rather like pudding, but essentially dry, made from vegetables, flour, egg, milk, sugar, *ghee*, and nuts

Idli: South Indian steamed rice cupcake

Jhinga: shrimp

Kalia: fish curry

Kamla-bhog: *kamla* means "orange"; a sweet which is orange-colored and orange-flavored

Kalonji: black cumin

Karahi: a traditional Indian cooking and frying pan

Karela: bitter-gourd or bitter-melon

Kayla: banana

Kheema: minced meat

Khir-kadambo: a stuffed sweetmeat made from *khir* (dried milk) and *channa* (Indian-style cottage cheese)

Khoa: solid milk made by evaporating fresh milk

Kitchuri: means "mixture"; a mixture of rice, lentils, vegetables, and spices rather like a casserole dish

Kofta: a 1-inch ball made from ground meat, fish, *channa*, or vegetable, and deep fried

Kuddoo: Indian white pumpkin; North American zucchini is the best substitute for it.

Kulfi: Indian-style ice cream

Ladoo: sweet ball made from different flours

Luchi: Bengali deep fried crisp bread, made from white flour

Malai: heavy cream

Malpua: little pancakes soaked in thick sugar syrup

Masala: spice

Methi: fenugreek

Moghlai: this term is Muslim; it means the dish is very rich and spicy
Moong: small light yellow lentil
Murgh: chicken
Naan: Indian-style roasted bread
Nimki: salted crispy pastry
Pakora: fritters
Pantua: a deep fried sweetmeat made from *channa*, and soaked in sugar syrup
Pappadum: very thin, crisp lentil bread
Payasam: a pudding preparation, made from rice, milk, and nuts
Poodina: mint
Poori: deep fried whole wheat bread
Pullao: rice preparation with saffron and nuts
Qorma: a thick rich spiced curry sauce
Rasam: South Indian, very thin hot spiced soup
Rasgulla: white cottage cheese balls cooked in sugar syrup
Rayta: seasoned yogurt with chopped vegetables
Rasomalai: *rasgulla* soaked in heavy cream
Rogan-Josh: North Indian lamb curry
Sambhar: South Indian lentil preparation
Sambhar spice: a combination of very hot spices with mustard oil
Samosa or *Singara*: salted pastry with meat or vegetable filling
Seekh Kabab: seekh means "iron rod" (skewer); a meat preparation threaded on an iron skewer
Shukto: a vegetable preparation made with different vegetables including *karela*
Shalgum: turnip
Shami Kabab: a small meat cutlet made from ground meat and ground lentils
Singara: see *Samosa*
Tamarind: sour fruit
Tandoori: Indian-style barbecue
Tava: Indian iron baking pan
Thali: dinner dish
Til: sesame seeds
Umchur: dried mango
Vadas: South Indian salted snacks
Vindaloo: a sour-type curry, made with tamarind juice, lemon juice or white vinegar
Yakni: stock

Index